BLACK HARVARD / BLACK YALE

Edited by

Jesse A. RHINES, Ph. D.

Cover photo: 1981, across the street from Sterling Library Vincent "Vinny" Peterson and I frame my mother. I, with glasses, still had to turn in my MA thesis and Vinny had just earned his BA at Yale.

Comments:
http://yalememoir.weebly.com/

http://www.yalealumnimagazine.com/issues/2011_09/editor.html

Library of Congress Control Number: 2011914248

Title ID: 3615992 createspace.com
ISBN-13:978-1463504410

Purchase:
https://www.createspace.com/3615992

Dedicated to:

- My mother, whom we 12 siblings call Mother, Mrs. Julia Marie Watson Rhines Steptoe Barbour, poet, federal government worker and teacher who performed her poems between 1968 and her death in 2006 at the Potter's House on Columbia Road, the Folger Shakespeare Library on Capitol Hill, and published Op Eds in the Washington Post starting in the late 1950s. I gave Dr. Elizabeth Alexander, Chair of Yale's African American Studies Department, a book length manuscript of her poems in hope it might find publication.

- Edward Alexander Bouchet, Yale's first African American graduate in 1874.

- Richard Greener, Harvard's first African American graduate in 1870.

Table of Contents

Preamble

"The 1960s saw the first significant presence of black men in Yale College. Forty years later, a disproportionate number have died. Did the racial barriers they faced all their lives play a part?" This article, "Before their Time," by Ron Howell, published in Yale Alumni Magazine, May/June 2011, prompted me to publish this document at this time. I publish this volume minimally edited because I have been unable to find a publisher since 1999 and don't know what kind of editing is needed. For example, I don't understand the difference between copy-, line- and content-editing. A publisher would know that and I am not a publisher. Rutgers University Press published my book, BLACK FILM/WHITE MONEY in 1996 and suggested that Ms. India Cooper be the editor. I paid her to turn that doctoral dissertation into a book manuscript for the academic market. That must have worked well enough since I earned royalties from that book as late as 2010. Agents and publishers are invited to inquire: donjesse48@gmail.com. I also have a complimentary memoir manuscript detailing my own 18-year passage through Yale University after earning nearly all failing grades in high school. Disabled and living in Los Angeles since 2003, I now focus on short story and novel writing.

1. PREFACE

I have been unable to get permission to reprint the experience of these persons but have included citation for their work in this preface written in 1999. Please update using your own research.

* Gwendolyn M. Parker, Radcliffe '72
* Gary Franks, Y'75
* Johathan Bramwell, Y'62

On August 25, 1999 the television series LAW AND ORDER took a position on the issue of affirmative action in elite American universities. LAW AND ORDER addresses current events covering timely media topics such as abortion, mass killings, political intrigue, and drug smuggling. The August 25th episode was broadcast approximately one week or so before the start of fall classes.

Affirmative action is a hotly debated topic as the millennium and a presidential election season approach. Ward Connerly, hero of California's attack on affirmative action, has taken his battle to Florida where he will attempt to force presidential candidate, George W. Bush to take a stance for or against the issue. Opposing it may risk Bush's non-white support, supporting it will risk his white support. LAW AND ORDER, rides the crest of a very controversial political iceberg.

Affirmative action is a response to white America's centuries long, violent physical, intellectual and emotional suppression of non-white peoples of

Africa and other parts of the world. It is an attempt to make amends and provide those peoples and their descendants opportunity to "catch up" with whites and eliminate white dominance. After 30-odd years, however, some say that the job has been accomplished and that affirmative action is harming whites in the same way that past white suppression harmed non-whites. In fact, some say that now some non-white groups receive unfair advantage relative to other non-white groups and whites. This new debate began a scant 15 years after affirmative action was originated.

Denish D'Souza is a prominent spokesperson against continuation of affirmative action in elite universities. D'Souza says that this is a difficult issue.

> It is not always obvious, in these disputes, whose side a reasonable person should take, or whether it is possible, in good conscience, to endorse any side at all. The middle ground seems to have disappeared as a consequence of ideological fracas and polarization; whether it can be restored is an open question.[1]

This article is based on a book of published and non-published memoirs I have collected from African American undergraduates at Harvard and Yale over the 20th century. It allows the testing of the lives of African American undergraduates against D'Souza's claims. Have these students seen D'Souza's "middle

---

[1] Denish D'Souza, ILLIBERAL EDUCATION, New York: The Free Press, 1991, p. 2.

ground," or is it still yet to come? What was the nature of the middle ground from the student's point of view? In fact, this is the central theme of the LAW AND ORDER episode referred to above. Has affirmative action gone so far wrong that it not only hurts whites, but damages the black students who, in some cases, are forced--sometimes kicking and screaming, according to D'Souza--to accept it?

D'Souza has specific grievances against affirmative action. The short, autobiographical statements in this volume place these grievances in historical perspective and will be juxtaposed against them to assess their significance for the lived conditions of African American students. From an analytical perspective it is important to read these essays as guideposts illuminating the current debate on how to redress the historic suppression of non-white peoples and to include them more fully as co-equal decision-partners in the American future.

D'Souza argues that affirmative action policies are harmful in three general indices: the political; the educational; and the social.

The Political

The political realm exists outside of the university. It is the battle for power between political parties and between racial groups--as opposed to individuals. The university is, by contrast, a refuge from national political contests. He therefore laments that today,

> "...universities hope that they can more conveniently regulate the

[2] D'Souza, p. 45.

> composition of their freshmen classes along politically acceptable lines."[2]

In D'Souza's view, university administrators fight personal, partisan battles using college resources--paramount among those resources is admission. Our essays present a view almost universally antithetical to the notion of political separation between the university and the outside worlds. In the essays, however, there is little mention of a middle ground with respect to admission. For example, both DuBois and Pickens spoke to the on-campus effect of racial politics on university life at the turn of the century. DuBois said that in 1888 he "went to Harvard as a Negro, not simply by birth, but recognizing myself as a member of a segregated caste whose situation I accepted."[3] In 1903, William Pickens used extra-campus politics to motivate his on campus performance "My ambition to win was stimulated by a desire to further the acquaintance of other peoples with my race."[4]

By the 1960s, Black students did not automatically expect political entanglements at college. As John Bramwell observed, "When I had entered Yale I thought, mistakenly as it turned out, that I had left racism behind. I felt that I was entering a world where the only thing that mattered was my capability in an academic setting." But first day on

---

[3] Werner Sollors, Caldwell Titcomb, and Thomas A. Underwood, eds., W. E. B. Du Bois, H'1890, "A Negro Student at Harvard at the End of the Nineteenth Century," Blacks at Harvard, New York:New York University Press, 1993, p. 72.

[4] William Pickens, Bursting Bonds, Bloomington:Indiana University Press, 1991, p. 39.

campus, during a welcoming party at President Griswold's house, whites sang an offensive song, "The last time I saw Susie, I ain't seen her since, she was jerkin' off a nigger through a barbed-wire fence."[5]

By the mid-1970s Black Power had nudged the Civil Rights movement somewhat aside. Charles Martin seemed mystified by on-campus objection of something feeling quite natural to him, "In other literature classes, I was always told that I read too politically...[But T]he political writings of Fanon made immediate sense to me and fit much of the confrontation of black and white societies." If, as D'Souza suggests, politics were banned from campus, would in-class readings be intended to aid students' encounter with real-world problems after college or teach them to ignore or side-step them? How, for example, would he have suggested Carlton Bush, Harvard '76, deal with this:

> Ah, distinctly I remember, that first year, a crisp September, walking outside the boundaries of the University in Harvard Square seeing a large photo dazibao positioning opposition to the Gulf Oil Company in the freedom fight for what would later become Angola. One poster had a large photo of smiling army men (Portuguese mercenaries in a happy platoon posing, smiling, smoking cigars in a tight group) The words above the photo read something like,

[5] Jonathan Bramwell, Courage in Crisis, New York: The Bobbs-Merrill Company, 1972, p. 49-50.

> "we have told you we oppose the Gulf Oil Company in their fight in Africa. This is the reason why..." And then I looked harder at the B&W photograph. The group was happy, smiling, and in the center of the group, one of the men is cheerily holding a freshly decapitated African man's head.[6]

In the 1980's students still saw politics as a significant part of university life. Susan Jenkins observed

> I saw the racism faced daily by African Americans as well as the individual and community strength we possessed. From an early private school education and other efforts of my parents, I was familiar with the "dominant" culture and from the rest of my life I was comfortable with my "minority" status. These are the worlds that collided when I arrived at Yale.[7]

Racial politics intrudes on student's lives. It would be naive for university administrators to function as if external politics--particularly racial politics--did not impact campus life. Despite hopes that it would be other wise, these students clearly see university as a site where political battles are fought on a daily basis.

---

[6] Original to this document.

[7] Original to this document.

Education

D'Souza's second battle ground, education, encompasses two areas. 1) comparative student academic success, and 2) creation of programs to study the history of different American, non-white-male groups. As to the former, D'Souza fears that

> "[A] student whose grades and qualifications are good enough to get him into Rutgers or Penn State finds himself at Williams or Bowdion, and the student who meets Williams' and Bowdoin's more demanding requirements finds himself at Yale or Berkeley."[8]

> "At graduation time, it turns out that only a fraction of the minority students enrolled four years earlier are still around, and even among them the academic record is mixed: a good number (most probably [my emphasis] not affirmative action beneficiaries) have performed well, but a majority conspicuously lag behind their colleagues..."[9]

Even Black matriculant, DuBois, admits to academic problems at the Ivy League.

---

[8] D'Souza, p. 231.

[9] D'Souza, p. 249.

> Senator Morgan of Alabama had just published a scathing attack on "niggers" in a leading magazine, when my first Harvard thesis was due. I let go at him with no holds barred. My long and blazing effort came back marked "E"--not passed!
>
> It was the first time in my scholastic career that I had encountered such a failure. I was aghast, but I was not a fool. I did not doubt but that my instructors were fair in judging my English technically even if they did not understand the Negro problem. I went to work at my English and by the end of that term had raised it to a "C."[10]

This student learned to adjust his political ire to meet the school's academic demands. His writings following college attest to DuBois' success at that charge since they are grammatically adequate yet reveal his political passion.

1975 graduate, Gary Franks, later elected a Congressional Representative from Connecticut, encountered trouble as well.

> One of my first courses quickly taught me how different college was going to be. I remember taking copious notes and listening to everything the teacher had to say in preparation for the first test. When we

[10] DuBois, p. 82.

> got our first blue book, my mouth watered. I looked at the exam and saw it was everything I had studied. I wrote the answers to the three questions, thinking, "Boy, this is easy." When I turned my blue book in, I was surprised to realize that 90 percent of the class was still working on the test. "I must have it all over these guys" I remember thinking to myself.
>
> As we waited to get our tests back the following week, I was absolutely positive I had gotten an A. When the teacher handed back the blue books, I walked slowly back to my seat, savoring the moment. I opened it slowly. There, in big red letters, the teacher had written: "I KNOW WHAT I SAID. WHAT DO YOU THINK?" My grade was a C.
>
> It was a valuable awakening. I realized that Yale did not simply want you to absorb ideas but to think about them and challenge them as well.[11]

Academic challenge the first years at school is expected. But the rationale for non completion of degrees espoused by D'Souza is challenged by these students as well. Bramwell observed that

> The average dropout rate at Ivy League colleges is on the order of one

[11] Gary Franks, Searching for the Promised Land, New York: HarperCollins Publishers, Inc., 1996, p. 23.

percent. By and large there are some exceptions--this is never for a financial reason. The schools will support any student who is performing. To some extent, the difference in dropout rate between (remember "highly qualified") black and (similarly highly qualified) white students is an indication of the nature and extent of nonacademic pressures that make it intolerable for a black student to continue there. I'm not talking about ghetto kids. I'm not talking about someone who has to drop out to support his family, but rather black kids who are capable. For kicks, write down how much greater their dropout rate was than that of their (equally qualified--I like that term) white classmates.

Forty! That's right, about 40 times as great. Of course, as rhetoric would have it, times have changed. Things have improved consistently over the years. Unfortunately for that argument, five years after our class, at Columbia the factor was 72. That's right, 72! Underprivileged students? From Choate, Andover (my brother and he was lucky, too) and Exeter; no, we have to look for some other reason than rats and roaches.

The universities, which make a big deal of "underqualified

admissions," don't seem to want to talk about "overqualified kickouts."[12]

"Skip" Gates, from a working-class family, dropped out of Exeter but at Yale,

> I stayed and I graduated, as a number of my friends did not, and I did so not as a matter of course but as a matter of will. I still remember that crucial first month, with daily sessions in the Linnonia and Brothers reading room, working out inorganic chemistry problems by the light of the low-wattage table lamps. I had convinced myself that at Yale I would be average; a C+ was what I was aiming for. Learning to speak out in class, always my forte before, now came slowly and painfully. But it was History 31 that made the difference, in Burrell Billingslea's discussion group. Never have I put so much work and expectation, fear and care, into the preparation of a five-page paper. Had the returned grade been a Pass, or just a High Pass, the tenor of my years at Yale would probably have been as gray as a New Haven winter. But there it was, in unforgettable bright red letters: "Honors. Nice Paper." Fifteen students--eight seniors, four juniors,

[12] Bramwell, p. 51.

> and a handful of others--and one Honors. [13]

D'Souza provides no evidence with which to disaggregate matriculants between what he calls "affirmative action admits" and other non-white, American admits. Students themselves don't usually know their own admission status. Can one tell from Robin Walker, Yale class of 1984:

> I wasn't exactly sure what that scholarship signified but I knew that it provided much needed money for tuition. I think I was the only minority recipient that year but I don't remember if I ever thought of my Sterling Scholarship as Affirmative Action. I did know that neither I nor my parents could have afforded to pay Yale's $22,000 annual tuition over four years. [14]

Without specific evidence it is impossible to determine the nature of the "good number" of students who have performed well alluded to by D'Souza. For example, was Robert Randall among that "good number?" On graduation from high school, he was "eligible for the Kennedy T. Friend scholarship to Yale, a scholarship established by a wealthy Yale Law School graduate". "Most

[13] Henry Louis Gates, Jr and Cornel West, The Future of the Race, New York: Alfred A. Knopf, Inc., 1996, p. 15-16.

[14] Original to this document.

probably" (D'Souza's term) is far too imprecise--and value-laden--a descriptor for informed policy debate.

Gates follows Bramwell in providing the most distressing reasons for failure among ivy leaguers.

> Some of the black students I knew at Yale dropped out, or pursued militancy to a point of no return, or went mad: these were still the early days of affirmative action, and this business of recruitment would be considerably refined in the years to come. Jerry was the first to die, stricken, as he was, in the middle of his junior year. Two rumors competed for his epitaph: "overdose," skeptics said; "hemorrhage," replied his friends. There was Tommy, gunned down by Gil Rochon--the tall Am. Stud. grad student from New Orleans who had freckles, a conical Afro, and a wife whom Tommy was sleeping with. There was Eddie Jackson, my roommate, who "broke down" not long after, in hot pursuit of his blackness; later he killed himself by plunging a butcher's knife into his heart. [15]

"Studies" Programs

D'Souza claims that there "are changes in the intellectual and moral infrastructure of the American university"[16] resultant of creation of programs and

[15] Gates, p. 48.

departments focused on American non-white-straight males and women. "Studies" programs are places where students can be assured of unchallenging curriculums and good grades regardless of performance. Students in and creators of such programs disagree. It would be hard to label Ernest L. Wilson III, H'70, a fourth generation Harvard student, an outsider except in terms of race. Yet he recalls,

> Harvard in those years admitted the occasional black student, but it did not admit the study of black life and culture as an important and legitimate element of the curriculum...Through the decade of the 1960s dozens of white and black students participated in challenges to fair Harvard's traditional sense of itself and they pressed to make Harvard more open to the scholarly examination of gender and race...Harvard denied--especially the validity and autonomy of Afro-American cultural life, and the importance of studying it...Now there is a niche in which interested black and white faculty and students can more easily find programs and materials on black life in America. They can also find an even more precious present than that which those of us in that time tried to leave behind-

[16] D'Souza, p. 2.

> -the institutional and intellectual legitimacy of studying black life without fear of being mocked or marginalized.[17]

Fifteen years later, Farah Griffin still found Harvard's approach to African American culture problematic.

> If [Black] hairshops were places where I established my equilibrium, Harvard was the place where it was again shattered. For me this was both a triumph and a tragedy. Harvard was a sea of contradictions. On the one hand, I sat in a lecture given by a noted historian who painted a portrait of the Old South, sentimental and full of little "playful pickaninnies" (those were his words); on the other hand, I came to know and love "my professor" Nathan Huggins, who taught me to begin taking myself seriously as an intellectual and to be committed to establishing African-American subject matter as material worthy of scholarly inquiry.
>
> In the journal entries I kept for my History and Literature sophomore tutorial I found myself engaged in a written debate with one of my tutors. In response to my frustration over the dearth of black authors on his syllabus, he wrote that he was forced by time to

[17] Ernest L. Wilson, Blacks at Harvard, p. 428.

> limit his selection to major American authors. "Henry James, my dear, is major because people like you have made him so," I thought. When I asked this same tutor if I could write my paper on Du Bois' The Souls of Black Folk, he said no because he had never read Du Bois. [18]

The Social

D'Souza is not, however, against affirmative action students themselves. In fact, he observes that Berkeley, for example,

> admits some of California's best black and Hispanic students, and many of them fail, in large part because of the pressures of a highly competitive environment. Would not these students be much better off at UC-Irvine or UC-Davis, where they might settle in more easily, compete against evenly matched peers, and graduate in vastly greater numbers and proportions? [19]

D'Souza policy prescriptions imply only these students' best interest. He provides no information, however, as to UC-Davis' or -Irvine's graduation rates. Affirmative Action students may do even

[18] Farah Griffin, Blacks at Harvard, p. 476.

[19] D'Souza, p. 40.

worse there as they may so excel above their "peers" that they become bored. In my own classes at Rutgers, freshmen who were refused admission to or were turned down by the Ivies are often troubled students or thirsting for a challenge. With the best of luck they become frustrated tutors, sometimes for upperclassmen. I do not know the rate at which such students fail to graduate.

The biggest problem affirmative action students cause on Ivy League campuses is, according to D'Souza, separatism.

> Separatist black and Hispanic groups become a haven from the anxieties that spring from sharp differences in academic preparation among various racial groups. Indeed separatism can serve as a form of group therapy, in which affirmative action beneficiaries persuade themselves that their difficulties on campus are predominantly, if not exclusively, the consequences of rampant bigotry. They view these bigots through lenses of heightened racial awareness, with suspicion bordering on hostility. [20]

Certainly this is not something new to non-white students at these schools. Dubois spoke about it in this way:

---

[20] D'Souza, p. 51.

Naturally, I could not afford a room in the college yard in the old and venerable buildings which housed most of the well-to-do students under the magnificent elms. Neither did I think of looking for lodgings among white families, where numbers of the ordinary students lived. I tried to find a colored home, and finally at 20 Flagg Street I came upon the neat home of a colored woman from Nova Scotia, a descendant of those black Jamaican Maroons whom Britain had deported after solemnly promising them peace if they would surrender. [21]

Following the attitudes which I had adopted in the South, I sought no friendships among my white fellow students, nor even acquaintanceships. Of course I wanted friends, but I could not seek them. My class was large--some three hundred students. I doubt if I knew a dozen of them. I did not seek them, and naturally they did not seek me. I made no attempt to contribute to the college periodicals since the editors were not interested in my major interests. But I did have a good singing voice and loved music, so I entered the competition for the Glee Club. I ought to have known that Harvard could not afford to have a

[21] Du Bois, p. 73.

> Negro on its Glee Club traveling about the country. Quite naturally I was rejected.[22]

Muriel Sutherland Snowden, Radcliff 1938, also noted that, like D'Souza, her college looked out for her happiness as a person of color.

> Despite everything that came afterwards, my most vivid memory of Radcliffe is of being denied access to a dormitory my freshman year. It continues to rankle to this day--despite the fact that Radcliffe was the only college to which I had applied; that I had graduated as Valedictorian from one of the best public high schools in the country at the time; that I had been admitted without examination under the then existing "highest seventh plan" without the need for scholarship assistance--[that] the Radcliffe administration focused on my race as the rationale for concern about whether or not I would be "happy" living in a dormitory.[23]

Charles Payne assumed that Yale of the 1950s had many room selection "hats" to pull from.

---

[22] Du Bois, p. 74.

[23] Muriel Snowden, "The Right to Participate," in Blacks at Harvard, Werner Sollors, p. 298.

> Yale had been designed in better times with only two students to a room, each with a bedroom and a common study. My letter informed me that I would have two roommates selected at random by names drawn from a hat.
>
> Somehow it didn't come as a surprise, however, that my two roommates were also young men of color. Dick was from Cincinnati (Wyoming, Ohio to be precise), tall, a mathematical whiz, and Jack, short, energetic and from New Haven. Jack wanted to live away from home and so was at least a mile and half away from home and felt good about it. After comparing letters, we decided that Yale didn't lie....it just had several hats. (It later transpired that the fourth Negro, as we were then called, was sufficiently fair to photograph white, and so was rooming with a freshman from Texas in the WW11 Quonset huts out near the Peabody Museum. Nathan was happy there and so were his roommates so that his freshman experience was truly unique.) [24]

Despite interaction with a broad range of people as freshman year opened, John Woodford, H'63, was suspicious of his roommate assignment.

---

[24] Original to this document.

Right from the beginning, awaiting the arrival of my unidentified roommate in Matthews Hall North in the Yard, I began meeting a range of classmates who, to a man were remarkable free spirits--friendly, energetic fellows--and neither then nor later did I encounter anything like the snob of stereotype. The company of almost any of my classmates delighted me right from the start and has continued to do so down the decades, singly or in numbers. Maybe it's because I had three sisters and no brother.

As it turned out, my roommate, Travis Williams of Durham, North Carolina, was one of the 16, if memory serves me, Afro-American men admitted that year. From starting off a bit edgy toward one another, as if the room assignment had deprived us of acquaintance with someone who might present a more novel--or culturally diverse, as they say now--outlook on life than a fellow Afro-American, we became about as close as brothers over the years. [25]

By the late 1960's, Yale had reformed enough to allow Ronald Matchett, '70, a fuller experience than that of Blacks before him.

---

[25] Original to this document.

Going to Yale really was like entering Camelot. Like Alice's wonderland, it was a whole new world for me. Into this setting, I was cast with three remarkable young people, my roommates. One, of Jewish ancestry, was out of the New York area, smart as he could be and he wanted to be a lawyer; he played a strange game called Squash. The only squash I had ever heard of one ate. And, I did not have much of an appetite for eating them either, much less playing a game bearing their name. Do you know that Yale had more squash courts than it had basketball courts? What a strange place indeed. As we came to say in those days, "different strokes for different folks." My other roommate, also of Jewish ancestry, was a Connecticut native who had grown up near Yale and he, like myself, was a psychology major with his heart set on medicine. The last of the lot, an All-American chap out of the best of mid-western Illinois tradition (right round Chicago area) had his mind made up to be a "rock and roll" star. He was already in character. He looked the part. Guess which of the three ended up sharing space with me? You got it. It was the rock and roll star. He was also a varsity swimmer and a great guy

> to boot. We got along famously. Actually, we all did.[26]

During this period, however, Negroes redefined themselves as Black People and began an internal self-assessment denied them for over 300 years in America. For many African Americans, close association with whites was rejected as a complicating factor in this reassessment, particularly since, on observation, the average white American did not seek or avoided close association with Black people. This situation persists today.

However, there was not monolithic acceptance of the separatist reassessment methodology. Some felt the need for it some did not. Problems developed when the former took this methodology as grail for all African Americans and, perhaps for the first time, were able to exert power and force over whites. For Gwendolyn M. Parker, Radcliffe '72, the situation was unnerving.

> One crowded lunchtime, I joined several of my black friends at a long table. Lani and Suzanne were there, as well as a number of boys who were emerging as leaders. I took a seat near the end of the table, listening to their serious conversations peppered with emphatic gestures, Suzanne's hair bobbing as it always did as she spoke. There were a few empty seats near me, but the other tables were full. A white

[26] Original to this document.

student approached my end of the table with a friend somewhere behind him.

"Are these seats taken?" he asked, and I nodded to him that they were empty. He sat down, and a few minutes later so did his friend. One of the boys at the other end began talking loudly.

"Do I see what I'm seeing?" he said. "Are there honkies sitting down at this table?"

A friend next to him took up his cue. "Yeah, I think I see some honkies sitting down there. In fact, I'm sure I see it. Some white butts filling those chairs."

Some people at the table began to laugh. It was a laugh that people have laughed since the beginning of time: the laugh of the ones with the upper hand. I stared at the two white students and tried to convey an apology with my eyes. I wanted to say that I was not laughing, that I was sorry, but the black boys at the other end of the table were staring as well, a look that was not lost on these boys. They both began to turn red in the face, then shuffled about in their seats, and then, finally apologizing, got up and left. When they did, uproarious laughter went up from part of the table. [27]

[27] Gwendolyn M. Parker, Trespassing, New York: Haughton Mifflin Company, 1997, pp. 114-115 .

The "Black table" remains a significant feature of Black life in the Ivies. But it goes beyond just that. Yale and other universities fund entire buildings designated for management by specific non-white groups. Denise Byrd, '88, said that this building, "The House," helped convince her to attend Yale.

> Having become a bit of a hippie in [Choate] boarding school, I often found my new self not fitting in when I arrived home to hang out with my "real friends". And, so, I longed for the day when I would not have to change my clothes to be around my pals. Later that night, standing in the House in the company of more Blacks than I had been around in years, something clicked. I felt at home--and properly dressed. [28]

Susan Jenkins had this to say:

> I put on that brave face until my parents left campus after getting me settled in [freshman year at Yale], and then I got scared. I didn't know anyone and wasn't sure what was expected of me. Luckily, as I had walked around campus with my family I ran into some others from the Yale minority recruitment weekend I attended the previous spring. We

[28] Original to this document.

exchanged phone and room numbers. That evening I called around to see what the plan for dinner was and from that point had a built in set of friends. We did what White/European American people always complain about: we (a group of 10 black students and one Chinese-American who had grown up in Detroit) went everywhere together. White/European American friends told me later that they felt we were so lucky to have built in friends. But it wasn't luck. We knew how hostile the majority group could be, and how unusual we were to our classmates. Plus, we all had things in common by being black-identified in America. Even though we were from different parts of the country we had common musical, television, cultural, and family lives. Many of us shared common values and to quote the advice from one parent was to say something we had all been told at one time or another. This set of friends guided me into college and gave me comfort. Over our first year we started to drift apart and develop separate interests and other friends, but as far as easing me into college life, they could not have been more valuable. [29]

[29] Original to this document.

Statements such as the following might almost make one suppose D'Souza empathized with Susan's plight.

> The impulse to retreat into exclusive enclaves is a familiar one for minority groups who have suffered a history of persecution; they feel there is strength and safety in numbers, and tend to develop group consciousness and collective orientation partly as a protective strategy.[30]

However, these organizations are not exclusive but merely predominantly uniracial as is the vast majority of EuroAmerican society. White people, neither male nor female, are forbidden entry. They just have to muster the guts to seek participation as did the non-whites who mustered the guts to apply to predominantly white schools. White predominance does not cease the entire time they are in school and will remain a fundamental part of their lives in the world of work.

One area in which racial exclusivity has been dented in recent years is campus fraternal organizations. While still overwhelmingly white and male, Yale's secret (now senior) societies have become modestly integrated. Bramwell described Yale's "tapping" ceremony thusly:

> When the witching hour arrived, as if in a Terry Thomas movie, a stalwart band shut the gates, bolted and chained them. "Loveliest of gates

[30] D'Souza, p. 234.

> at Yale town are fraught with chains, I wonder how"--a poem in bold Gothic script appeared at the locked trapdoors and windows. The refrain: "About the campus we shall go, to lock the gates to Fart and Blow."[31]

Ronald Matchett said:

> At the time, I do not think I truly realized and appreciated the achievement of being one of only 15 in the senior class at Yale to be "tapped" (personally selected) to join one of the two most prestigious societies at Yale--the Secret Society--Scroll and Key. However, as I was to learn, I was also only the second Black in the near two hundred year history of the society to be asked to join. This fact did not go unnoticed. For me this was a point of real sensitivity.[32]

Sensitivity or no, Ronald soon knew the real value of a Yale education.

> Being in Scroll and Key was like sitting around King Arthur's round table and being a knight of the realm. Scroll and Key was like a castle, and the table (in what I call the

[31] Bramwell, p. 54.

[32] Original to this document.

Great Room--the main room where we ate) was immense with a roundness that seemed like a perfect circle whose diameter approached 30 feet. This table steeped with so much tradition that in every nook and cranny lay a great tale to be told. This was the table where five Rockefellers had sat beginning with Godfrey in 1921, and James in '24; John in '28, Avery in '49, and James Jr. in '51. But even the Rockefellers could not out do the equally distinguished Auchinclosses. They put eleven around this table starting as early as 1879 with young Hugh Dudley Auchincloss. And Hugh Dudley begat Hugh (1901) who begat Hugh, Jr. (1938) who begat Hugh the III (1972). That's not even to count Charles Crooke Auchincloss (1903) brother of Hugh (1901) and Charles Russell Auchincloss (also 1903) whose younger brother John Howland Auchincloss would come to Scroll & Key in 1908, along with two other Auchinclosses, James Coates and Gordon. And they ain't done yet. We mustn't forget Reginald La Grange Auchincloss (1913) and Richard Saltonstall Auchincloss (1932). Following their Scroll and Key lineage was akin to a journey of biblical proportions, like tracing Abraham's seed. This was a family of great lawyers, physicians, military leaders, and statesmen, whose contribution to America and the world was substantial.

But the Rockefellers were not to be outdone. In this year, 1969 - 1970, Avery Rockefeller, Jr. who had sat at this table in 1949, now sat at the helm as President of the Kingley Trust Association (K.T.A.) which was in effect the Board of Directors of the Society. Not enough was it to be President of KTA, he was a Governor of the New York Stock Exchange as well, a position he had held since 1964. The Rockefellers and the Auchinclosses--and that's just two families. All had sat here. Now here we sat as well, around this table, in enormous chairs bearing our names, chairs more like thrones than seats, partaking of a feast befitting King Arthur's knights, but a feast for far more than the body. If my first impressions of Yale were like entering Camelot, those initial impressions were now being confirmed. Three years after my arrival, I had reached the inner sanctum, I was a knight at King's Arthur's table. I was set, some say "set for life." [emphasis in original] [33]

[33] Original to this document.

Matchett now set out to make his secret society both less secret and less exclusive.

> [O]ur class would begin the transformation of the Society as well, perhaps more than any group then or since then. It would be most immediately apparent the following year when more people of color would be asked to join our number. In my Collegium there were two people of color: yours truly as the only Black, and Ralph Rexach from Puerto Rico. The year that followed there were 4 blacks and 2 Hispanics; 6 people of color out of 15, about 40% of the Collegium minority? What a concept. [34]

Gary Franks related his first encounter with senior societies.

> Perhaps one of the most memorable moments of my college career came when I was asked to join one of Yale's senior honor societies. One day I turned a corner on campus and found sixteen members standing in front of me. They went through their ritual of asking me to become part of the organization.
>
> I said no. The sixteen members looked at me and one another as if I must be crazy. It was the most

[34] Original to this document.

> prestigious organization on campus--although I did not realize this until years later. Instead, I had a couple of good friends in another honor society, so I chose that instead. [35]

In recent years, uniracial predominance in some organizations has failed to prevent cross-cultural contact or friendship in the Ivy League. Ernest Wilson observed that at Harvard

> In the late 1960s bigoted nationalist students would taunt and insult other black students walking across the Yard with a white friend. I refused to be taunted, or a taunter. [36]

Charles Martin let music lead the way:

> In the marching band I watched the football games, though I stopped after freshman year, realizing at last--as I had not in high school--that the crowds came for the action on the field, not for the band. As I never liked football too much, I did not continue with the band. With the concert band I played in concerts around the campus and went on tour to England, Holland and Belgium. The high point for me was our bus trip through southern

[35] Franks, p. 28.

[36] Wilson, p. 432.

> England where we visited Stonehenge, which then was not fenced off. You could walk up to the stone monoliths and stand among them. [37]

You may laugh with Gary Franks, but you never learn the race of his roommate in the following snippet.

> My roommates for my freshman year were Rick Andre, from Chicago, Illinois, and Greg Beams, from Xenia, Ohio. One of our funniest moments occurred on the first day, when our parents all came to drop us off and meet one another. After we got acquainted, we went down to the dining room for lunch. A lady at the front desk was checking identification cards. As we walked up to her, Greg said, "Beams' and I said, "Franks." "Beans and franks? Hey, wait a minute, you two, come back here!" "Those are our names, Beams and Franks," we said, innocently. "We're roommates." People around us began to titter. She looked skeptically at our IDs. "Well, look at this--Beams and Franks. I thought you were playing a joke on me. And you two guys are roommates? Wouldn't you know it." [38]

---

[37] Original to this document.

[38] Franks, p. 22.

Similarly, Robin Walker, while emphasizing her roommates' wealth as they chided her with

> Robin, you're going to miss out on your 'Yale experience' if you have to work all of the time.[39]

Robin never mentioned their race. Class, not race, created the greatest difference between them. This, Robin reasoned, was something that they could over come.

A fitting end is found in Susan Jenkins' heart-felt description of her own transition into the Ivy League.

> Looking back at it now, I can see that while at Yale we dealt with our baggage. All of us in different ways, but we did what we had to do to gain from Yale and to contribute mightily. There were opportunities available that I don't think I would have gotten anywhere else. Personally, I was a member of the Fencing team, the Yale Hunger Action Project, active in the Yale women's center, did several independent study projects, worked in the Yale archives, and made friends with a wide variety of people. Among the other African Americans, I had a friend who went on to compete in the Pan-American games in fencing, another who did

[39] Original to this document.

research in Guyana on Fulbright scholarship, and another who went on to some political prominence in the republican party. These are not things everyone can do especially within the African American community. Being at Yale not only helped qualify us for these challenges it positioned us to have these kinds of opportunities.

While I was learning and broadening both my skill set and my mind, I was also changing some minds about African-American people. I met people from groups I had no familiarity with and whom, it was quite obvious, had had little to no contact with African-Americans. Through Yale, I made friends who were openly gay and bisexual, who were millionaires, who were from places like Haiti, Spain and Japan, who were from every region of the US, who had never had a television, who had attended some of the most prestigious prep schools in the country, and who had come from some of the worst neighborhoods imaginable. For me, Yale was a safe place to explore difference, to figure out who I was, to try on different hats, and to grow up. The student body was so diverse people brought their own norms and the requirement that first year students live on campus forced us learn to accommodate each other and, in some

> cases, appreciate dissimilar life styles. Even though I met many of my African American classmates as soon as I arrived and started hanging with them, I was forced (much to my benefit) to meet other people through my initial roommate assignment, extra-curricular activities, and classroom interactions. [40]

America would be a better place were Jenkins' experience the norm nation-wide. This is likely the nearest yet we've come to a middle ground.

###

[40] Original to this document.

2. W. E. B. Du Bois, H'1890[41]--A Negro Student at Harvard at the End of the Nineteenth Century[42]

Harvard University in 1888 was a great institution of learning. It was two hundred and [fifty-two] years old and on its governing board were Alexander Agassiz, Phillips Brooks, Henry Cabot Lodge, and Charles Francis Adams; and a John Quincy Adams, but not the ex-President. Charles William Eliot, a gentleman by training and a scholar by broad study and travel, was president. Among its teachers emeriti were Oliver Wendell Holmes and James Russell Lowell. Among the active teachers were Francis Child, Charles Eliot Norton, Justin Winsor, and John Trowbridge; Frank Taussig, Nathaniel Shaler, George Palmer, William James, Francis Peabody, Josiah Royce, Barrett Wendell, Edward Channing, and Albert Bushnell Hart. In 1890 arrived a young instructor, George Santayana.
Seldom, if ever, has any American university had such a galaxy of great men and fine teachers as Harvard in the decade between 1885 and 1895.

To make my own attitude toward the Harvard of that day clear, it must be remembered that I went to Harvard as a Negro, not simply by birth, but

---

[41] Reprint Blacks at Harvard, New York:New York University Press, 1993.

[42] W.E.B. Du Bois recorded a variant version of this memoir; the tape is in the Harvard Archives.

recognizing myself as a member of a segregated caste whose situation I accepted. But I was determined to work from within that caste to find my way out.

The Harvard of which most white students conceived I knew little. I had not even heard of Phi Beta Kappa, and of such important social organizations as the Hasty Pudding Club, I knew nothing. I was in Harvard for education and not for high marks, except as marks would insure my staying. I did not pick out "snap" courses. I was there to enlarge my grasp of the meaning of the universe. We had had, for instance, no chemical laboratory at Fisk; our mathematics courses were limited.

Above all I wanted to study philosophy! I wanted to get hold of the bases of knowledge, and explore foundations and beginnings. I chose, therefore, Palmer's course in ethics, but since Palmer was on sabbatical that year, William James replaced him, and I became a devoted follower of James at the time he was developing his pragmatic philosophy.

Fortunately I did not fall into the mistake of regarding Harvard as the beginning rather than the continuing of my college training. I did not find better teachers at Harvard, but teachers better known, who had had wider facilities for gaining knowledge and lived in a broader atmosphere for approaching truth.

I hoped to pursue philosophy as my life career, with teaching for support. With this program I studied at Harvard from the fall of 1888 to 1890, as an undergraduate. I took a varied course in chemistry, geology, social science, and philosophy. My salvation here was the type of teacher I met rather than the content of the courses.

William James guided me out of the sterilities of scholastic philosophy to realist pragmatism; from Peabody's social reform with a religious tinge I turned to Albert Bushnell Hart to study history with documentary research; and from Taussig, with his reactionary British economics of the Ricardo school, I approached what was later to become sociology. Meantime Karl Marx was mentioned, but only incidentally and as one whose doubtful theories had long since been refuted. Socialism was dismissed as unimportant, as a dream of philanthropy or as a will-o-wisp of hotheads. When I arrived at Harvard, the question of board and lodging was of first importance. Naturally, I could not afford a room in the college yard in the old and venerable buildings which housed most of the well-to-do students under the magnificent elms. Neither did I think of looking for lodgings among white families, where numbers of the ordinary students lived. I tried to find a colored home, and finally at 20 Flagg Street I came upon the neat home of a colored woman from Nova Scotia, a descendant of those black Jamaican Maroons whom Britain had deported after solemnly promising them peace if they would surrender. For a very reasonable sum I rented the second story front room and for four years this was my home. I wrote of this abode at the time: "My room is, for a college man's abode, very ordinary indeed. It is quite pleasantly situated- second floor, front, with a bay window and one other window...As you enter you will perceive the bed in the opposite comer, small and decorated with floral designs calculated to puzzle a botanist...On the left hand is a bureau with a mirror of doubtful accuracy. In front of the bay window is a stand with three shelves of books, and on the left of the bureau is an improvised bookcase made of unpainted boards and uprights, containing most of my library of which I am growing quite proud. Over the heat register, near the door, is a mantel with a plaster of Paris pug-dog and a calendar, and the usual array of odds and ends...On the wall are a few quite ordinary pictures. In this commonplace den I am quite content."

Following the attitudes which I had adopted in the South, I sought no friendships among my white fellow students, nor even acquaintanceships. Of course I wanted friends, but I could not seek them. My class was large--some three hundred students. I doubt if I knew a dozen of them. I did not seek them, and naturally they did not seek me.

I made no attempt to contribute to the college periodicals since the editors were not interested in my major interests. But I did have a good singing voice and loved music, so I entered the competition for the Glee Club. I ought to have known that Harvard could not afford to have a Negro on its Glee Club traveling about the country. Quite naturally I was rejected.

I was happy at Harvard, but for unusual reasons. One of these was my acceptance of racial segregation. Had I gone from Great Barrington High School directly to Harvard, I would have sought companionship with my white fellows and been disappointed and embittered by a discovery of social limitations to which I had not been used. But I came by way of Fisk and the South and there I had accepted color caste and embraced eagerly the companionship of those of my own color. This was of course no final solution. Eventually, in mass assault, led by culture, we Negroes were going to break down the boundaries of race; but at present we were banded together in a great crusade, and happily so. Indeed, I suspect that the prospect of ultimate full human intercourse, without reservations and annoying distinctions, made me all too willing to consort with my own and to disdain and forget as far as was possible that outer, whiter world.

In general, I asked nothing of Harvard but the tutelage of teachers and the freedom of the laboratory and library. I was quite voluntarily and willingly outside its social life. I sought only such contacts with white teachers as lay directly in the line of my work. I joined certain clubs, like the Philosophical Club; I was a member of the Foxcroft Dining Club because it was cheap. James and one or two other teachers had me at their homes at meal and reception. I escorted colored girls to various gatherings, and as pretty ones as I could find to the vesper exercises, and later to the class day and commencement social functions. Naturally we attracted attention and the Crimson noted my girl friends. Sometimes the shadow of insult fell, as when at one reception a white woman seemed determined to mistake me for a waiter.

In general, I was encased in a completely colored world, self-sufficient and provincial, and ignoring just as far as possible the white world which conditioned it. This was self-protective coloration, with perhaps an inferiority complex, but with belief in the ability and future of black folk.

My friends and companions were drawn mainly from the colored students of Harvard and neighboring institutions, and the colored folk of Boston and surrounding towns. With them I led a happy and inspiring life. There were among them many educated and well-to-do folk, many young people studying or planning to study, many charming young women. We met and ate, danced and argued, and planned a new world.

Towards whites I was not arrogant; I was simply not obsequious, and to a white Harvard student of my day a Negro student who did not seek recognition was trying to be more than a Negro. The same Harvard man had much the same attitude toward Jews and Irishmen.

I was, however, exceptional among Negroes at Harvard in my ideas on voluntary race segregation. They for the most part saw salvation only in integration at the earliest moment and on almost any terms in white culture; I was firm in my criticism of white folk and in my dream of a self-sufficient Negro culture even in America.

This cutting of myself off from my white fellows, or being cut off, did not mean unhappiness or resentment. I was in my early manhood, unusually full of high spirits and humor. I thoroughly enjoyed life. I was conscious of understanding and power, and conceited enough still to imagine, as in high school, that they who did not know me were the losers, not I. On the other hand, I do not think that my white classmates found me personally objectionable. I was clean, not well-dressed but decently clothed. Manners I regarded as more or less superfluous and deliberately cultivated a certain brusquerie. Personal adornment I regarded as pleasant but not important. I was in Harvard, but not of it, and realized all the irony of my singing "Fair Harvard." I sang it because I liked the music, and not from any pride in the Pilgrims.

With my colored friends I carried on lively social intercourse, but necessarily one which involved little expenditure of money. I called at their homes and ate at their tables. We danced at private parties. We went on excursions down the Bay. Once, with a group of colored students gathered from surrounding institutions, we gave Aristophanes' The Birds in a Boston colored church. The rendition was good, but not outstanding, not quite appreciated by the colored audience, but well worth doing. Even though it worked me near to death, I was proud of it.

Thus the group of professional men, students, white-collar workers, and upper servants, whose common bond was color of skin in themselves or in their fathers, together with a common history and current experience of discrimination, formed a unit that, like many tens of thousands of like units across the nation, had or were getting to have a common culture pattern which made them an interlocking mass, so that increasingly a colored person in Boston was more neighbor to a colored person in Chicago than to a white person across the street.

Mrs. Ruffin of Charles Street, Boston, and her daughter, Birdie, were often hostesses to this colored group. She was widow of the first colored judge appointed in Massachusetts, an aristocratic lady, with olive skin and high-piled masses of white hair. Once a Boston white lady said to Mrs. Ruffin ingratiatingly: "I have always been interested in your race." Mrs. Ruffin flared: "Which race?" She began a national organization of colored women and published the Courant, a type of small colored weekly paper which was then spreading over the nation. In this I published many of my Harvard daily themes.

Naturally in this close group there grew up among the young people friendships ending in marriages. I myself, outgrowing the youthful attractions of Fisk, began serious dreams of love and marriage. There were, however, still my study plans to hold me back and there were curious other reasons. For instance, it happened that two of the girls whom I particularly liked had what was to me then the insuperable handicap of looking like whites, while they had enough black ancestry to make them "Negroes" in America. I could not let the world even imagine that I had married a white wife. Yet these girls were intelligent and companionable. One went to Vassar College, which then refused entrance to Negroes. Years later when I went there to lecture I remember disagreeing violently with a teacher who thought the girl ought not to have "deceived" the college by graduating before it knew of her Negro descent! Another favorite of mine was Deenie Pindell. She was a fine, forthright woman, blonde, blue-eyed and fragile. In the end I had no chance to choose her, for she married Monroe Trotter.

Trotter was the son of a well-to-do colored father and entered Harvard in my first year in the Graduate School. He was thick-set, yellow, with close-cut dark hair. He was stubborn and strait-laced and an influential member of his class. He organized the first Total Abstinence Club in the Yard. I came to know him and joined the company when he and other colored students took in a trip to Amherst to see our friends Forbes and Lewis graduate in the class with Calvin Coolidge.

Lewis afterward entered Harvard Law School and became the celebrated center rush of the Harvard football team. He married the beautiful Bessie Baker, who had been with us on that Amherst trip. Forbes, a brilliant, cynical dark man, later joined with Trotter in publishing the Guardian, the first Negro paper to attack Booker T. Washington openly. Washington's friends retorted by sending Trotter to jail when he dared to heckle Washington in a public Boston meeting on his political views. I was not present nor privy to this occurrence, but the unfairness of the jail sentence led me eventually to form the Niagara movement, which later became the NAACP.

Thus I lived near to life, love, and tragedy; and when I met Maud Cuney, I became doubly interested. She was a tall, imperious brunette with gold-bronze skin, brilliant eyes, and coils of black hair, daughter of the Collector of Customs at Galveston, Texas. She had come to study music and was a skilled performer. When the New England Conservatory of Music tried to "jim-crow" her in the dormitory, we students rushed to her defense and we won. I fell deeply in love with her, and we were engaged.

Thus it is clear how in the general social intercourse on the campus I consciously missed nothing. Some white students made themselves known to me and a few, a very few, became life-long friends. Most of my classmates I knew neither by sight nor name. Among them many made their mark in life: Norman Hapgood, Robert Herrick, Herbert Croly, George Dorsey, Homer Folks, Augustus Hand, James Brown Scott, and others. I knew none of these intimately. For the most part I do not doubt that I was voted a somewhat selfish and self-centered "grind" with a chip on my shoulder and a sharp tongue.

Only once or twice did I come to the surface of college life. First I found by careful calculation that I needed the cash of one of the Boylston prizes in oratory to piece out my year's expenses. I got it through winning a second oratorical prize. The occasion was noteworthy by the fact that another black student, Clement Morgan, got first prize at the same contest.

With the increase at Harvard of students who had grown up outside New England, there arose at this time a certain resentment at the way New England students were dominating and conducting college affairs. The class marshal on commencement day was always a Saltonstall, a Cabot, a Lowell, or from some such New England family. The crew and most of the heads of other athletic teams were selected from similarly limited social groups. The class poet, class orator, and other commencement officials invariably were selected because of family and not for merit. It so happened that when the officials of the class of 1890 were being selected in early spring, a plot ripened. Personally, I knew nothing of it and was not greatly interested. But in Boston and in the Harvard Yard the result of the elections was of tremendous significance, for this conspiratorial clique selected Clement Morgan as class orator. New England and indeed the whole country reverberated.

Morgan was a black man. He had been working in a barber shop in St. Louis at the time when he ought to have been in school. With the encouragement and help of a colored teacher, whom he later married, he came to Boston and entered the Latin School. This meant that when he finally entered Harvard, he entered as freshman in the orthodox way and was well acquainted with his classmates. He was fairly well received, considering his color. He was a pleasant unassuming person and one of the best speakers of clearly enunciated English on the campus. In his junior year he had earned the first Boylston prize for oratory in the same contest where I won second prize. It was, then, logical for him to become class orator, and yet this was against all the traditions of America. There were editorials in the leading newspapers, and the South especially raged and sneered at the audience of "black washer-women" who would replace Boston society at the next Harvard commencement.

Morgan's success was contagious, and that year and the next, in several leading Northern colleges, colored students became the class orators. Ex-President Hayes, as I shall relate later, sneered at this fact. While, as I have said, I had nothing to do with the plot, and was not even present at the election which chose Morgan, I was greatly pleased at this breaking of the color line. Morgan and I became fast friends and spent a summer giving readings along the North Shore to defray our college costs.

Harvard of this day was a great opportunity for a young man and a young American Negro and I realized it. I formed habits of work rather different from those of most of the other students. I burned no midnight oil. I did my studying in the daytime and had my day parceled out almost to the minute. I spent a great deal of time in the library and did my assignments with thoroughness and with prevision of the kind of work I wanted to do later. From the beginning my relations with most of the teachers at Harvard were pleasant. They were on the whole glad to receive a serious student, to whom extracurricular activities were not of paramount importance, and one who in a general way knew what he wanted.

Harvard had in the social sciences no such leadership of thought and breadth of learning as in philosophy, literature, and physical science. She was then groping and is still groping toward a scientific treatment of human action. She was facing at the end of the century a tremendous economic era. In the United States, finance was succeeding in monopolizing transportation and raw materials like sugar, coal, and oil. The power of the trust and combine was so great that the Sherman Act was passed in 1890. On the other hand, the tariff, at the demand of manufacturers, continued to rise in height from the McKinley to the indefensible Wilson tariff, making that domination easier. The understanding between the Industrial North and the New South was being perfected and, beginning in 1890, a series of disfranchising laws was enacted by the Southern states that was destined in the next sixteen years to make voting by Southern Negroes practically impossible. A financial crisis shook the land in 1893, and popular discontent showed itself in the Populist movement and Coxey's Army. The whole question of the burden of taxation began to be discussed.

These things we discussed with some clearness and factual understanding at Harvard. The tendency was toward English free trade and against the American tariff policy. We reverenced Ricardo and wasted long hours on the "Wages-fund." I remember Taussig's course supporting dying Ricardean economics. Wages came from what employers had left for labor after they had subtracted their own reward. Suppose that this profit was too small to attract the employer, what would the poor worker do but starve! The trusts and monopolies were viewed frankly as dangerous enemies of democracies, but at the same time as inevitable methods of industry. We were strong for the gold standard and fearful of silver. On the other hand, the attitude of Harvard toward labor was on the whole contemptuous and condemnatory. Strikes like that of the anarchists in Chicago and the railway strikes of 1886, the terrible Homestead strike of 1892 and Coxey's Army of 1894, were pictured as ignorant lawlessness, lurching against conditions largely inevitable.

Karl Marx was mentioned only to point out how thoroughly his theses had been disproved; of the theory itself almost nothing was said. Henry George was given but tolerant notice. The anarchists of Spain, the Nihilists of Russia, the British miners--all these were viewed not as part of political and economic development but as a sporadic evil. This was natural. Harvard was the child of its era. The intellectual freedom and flowering of the late eighteenth and early nineteenth centuries were yielding to the deadening economic pressure which would make Harvard rich but reactionary. This defender of wealth and capital, already half ashamed of Sumner and Phillips, was willing finally to replace an Eliot with a manufacturer and a nervous war-monger. The social community that mobbed Garrison easily electrocuted Sacco and Vanzetti.

It was not until I was long out of college and had finished my first studies of economics and politics that I realized the fundamental influence man's efforts to earn a living had upon all his other efforts. The politics which we studied in college were conventional, especially when it came to describing and elucidating the current scene in Europe. The Queen's Jubilee in June, 1887, while I was still at Fisk, set the pattern of our thinking. The little old woman at Windsor became a magnificent symbol of Empire. Here was England with her flag draped around the world, ruling more black folk than white and leading the colored peoples of the earth to

Christian baptism, and, as we assumed, to civilization and eventual self-rule. In 1885, Stanley, the traveling American reporter, became a hero and symbol of white world leadership in Africa. The wild, fierce fight of the Mahdi and the driving of the English out of the Sudan for thirteen years did not reveal their inner truth to me. I heard only of the martyrdom of the drunken Bible-reader and freebooter, Chinese Gordon.

After the Congo Free State was established, the Berlin Conference of 1885 was reported to be an act of civilization against the slave trade and liquor. French, English, and Germans pushed on in Africa, but I did not question the interpretation which pictured this as the advance of civilization and the benevolent tutelage of barbarians. I read of the confirmation of the Triple Alliance in 1891. Later I saw the celebration of the renewed Triple Alliance on the Tempelhofer Feld, with the new, young Emperor Wilhelm II, who, fresh from his dismissal of Bismarck, led the splendid pageantry; and, finally, the year I left Germany, Nicholas II became Czar of all the Russias. In all this I had not yet linked the political development of Europe with the race problem in America.

I was repeatedly a guest in the home of William James; he was my friend and guide to clear thinking; as a member of the Philosophical Club I talked with Royce and Palmer; I remember vividly once standing beside Mrs. Royce at a small reception. We ceased conversation for a moment and both glanced across the room. Professor Royce was opposite talking excitedly. He was an extraordinary sight: a little body, indifferently clothed; a big, red-thatched head and blazing blue eyes. Mrs. Royce put my thoughts into words: "Funny-looking man, isn't he?" I nearly fainted! Yet I knew how she worshipped him.

I sat in an upper room and read Kant's Critique with Santayana; Shaler invited a Southerner, who objected to sitting beside me, to leave his class; he said he wasn't doing very well, anyway. I became one of Hart's favorite pupils and was afterwards guided by him through my graduate course and started on my work in Germany. Most of my courses of study went well. It was in English that I came nearest my Waterloo at Harvard. I had unwittingly arrived at Harvard in the midst of a violent controversy about poor English among students. A number of fastidious scholars like Barrett Wendell, the great pundit of Harvard English, had come to the campus about this time; moreover, New England itself was getting sensitive over Western slang and Southern drawls and general ignorance of grammar. Freshmen at this time could elect nearly all their courses except English; that was compulsory, with daily themes, theses, and tough examinations. But I was at the point in my intellectual development when the content rather than the form of my writing was to me of prime importance. Words and ideas surged in my mind and spilled out with disregard of exact accuracy in grammar, taste in word, or restraint in style. I knew the Negro problem and this was more important to me than literary form. I knew grammar fairly well, and I had a pretty wide vocabulary; but I was bitter, angry, and intemperate in my first thesis. Naturally my English instructors had no idea of, nor interest in, the way in which Southern attacks on the Negro were scratching me on the raw flesh. Tillman was raging like a beast in the Senate, and literary clubs, especially those of rich and well-dressed women, engaged his services eagerly and listened avidly. Senator Morgan of Alabama had just published a scathing attack on "niggers" in a leading magazine, when my first Harvard thesis was due. I let go at him with no holds barred. My long and blazing effort came back marked "E"--not passed!

It was the first time in my scholastic career that I had encountered such a failure. I was aghast, but I was not a fool. I did not doubt but that my instructors were fair in judging my English technically even if they did not understand the Negro problem. I went to work at my English and by the end of that term had raised it to a "C." I realized that while style is subordinate to content, and that no real literature can be composed simply of meticulous and fastidious phrases, nevertheless, solid content with literary style carries a message further than poor grammar and muddled syntax. I elected the best course on the campus for English composition--English 12.

I have before me a theme which I submitted on October 3, 1890, to Barrett Wendell. I wrote: "Spurred by my circumstances, I have always been given to systematically planning my future, not indeed without many mistakes and frequent alterations, but always with what I now conceive to have been a strangely early and deep appreciation of the fact that to live is a serious thing. I determined while in high school to go to college--partly because other men did, partly because I foresaw that such discipline would best fit me for life...I believe, foolishly perhaps, but sincerely, that I have something to say to the world, and I have taken English 12 in order to say it well." Barrett Wendell liked that last sentence. Out of fifty essays, he picked this out to read to the class.

Commencement was approaching, when, one day, I found myself at midnight on one of the swaggering streetcars that used to roll out from Boston on its way to Cambridge. It was in the spring of 1890, and quite accidentally I was sitting by a classmate who would graduate with me in June. As I dimly remember, he was a nice-looking young man; well-dressed, almost dapper, charming in manner. Probably he was rich or at least well-to-do, and doubtless belonged to an exclusive fraternity, although that did not interest me. Indeed I have even forgotten his name. But one thing I shall never forget and that was his rather regretful admission (which slipped out as we gossiped) that he had no idea as to what his life work would be, because, as he added, "There's nothing in which I am particularly interested!"

I was more than astonished--I was almost outraged to meet any human being of the mature age of twenty-one who did not have his life all planned before him, at least in general outline, and who was not supremely, if not desperately, interested in what he planned to do.

In June, 1890, I received my bachelor's degree from Harvard cum laude in philosophy. I was one of the five graduating students selected to speak at commencement. My subject was "Jefferson Davis." I chose it with the deliberate intent of facing Harvard and the nation with a discussion of slavery as illustrated in the person of the president of the Confederate States of America. Naturally, my effort made a sensation. I said, among other things: "I wish to consider not the man, but the type of civilization which his life represented: its foundation is the idea of the strong man--individualism coupled with the rule of might--and it is this idea that has made the logic of even modern history, the cool logic of the Club. I made of a naturally brave and generous man, Jefferson Davis, one who advanced civilization by murdering Indians; then a hero of a national disgrace, called by courtesy the Mexican War; and finally, as the crowning absurdity, the peculiar champion of people fighting to be free in order that another people should not be free. Whenever this idea has for a moment escaped from the individual realm, it has found an even more secure foothold in the policy and philosophy of the State. The strong man and his mighty right arm has become the strong nation with its armies. However, under whatever guise a Jefferson Davis may appear as man, as race, or as a nation, his life can only logically mean this: the advance of a part of the world at the expense of the whole; the overwhelming sense of the I, and the consequent forgetting of the Thou. It has thus happened that advance in civilization has always been handicapped by shortsighted national selfishness. The vital principle of division of labor has been stifled not only in industry, but also in civilization; so as to render it well-nigh impossible for a new race to introduce a new idea into the world except by means of the cudgel. To say that a nation is in the way of civilization is a contradiction in terms, and a system of human culture whose principle is the rise of one race on the ruins of another is a farce and a lie. Yet this is the type of civilization which Jefferson Davis represented: it represents a field for stalwart manhood and heroic character, and at the same time for moral obtuseness and refined brutality. These striking contradictions of character always arise when a people seemingly become convinced that the object of the world is not civilization, but Teutonic civilization."

A Harvard professor wrote to Kate Field's Washington, then a leading periodical: "Du Bois, the colored orator of the commencement stage, made a ten-strike. It is agreed upon by all the people I have seen that he was the star of the occasion. His paper was on 'Jefferson Davis,' and you would have been surprised to hear a colored man deal with him so generously. Such phrases as a 'great man,' a 'keen thinker,' a 'strong leader,' and others akin occurred in the address. One of the trustees of the University told me yesterday that the paper was considered masterly in every way. Du Bois is from Great Barrington, Massachusetts, and doubtless has some white blood in his veins. He, too, has been in my classes the past year. If he did not head the class, he came pretty near the head, for he is an excellent scholar in every way, and altogether the best black man that has come to Cambridge."

Bishop Potter of New York wrote in the Boston Herald: "When at the last commencement of Harvard University, I saw a young colored man appear...and heard his brilliant and eloquent address, I said to myself. 'Here is what an historic race can do if they have a clear field, a high purpose, and a resolute will.'"

Already I had now received more education than most young white men, having been almost continuously in school from the age of six to twenty-two. But I did not yet feel prepared. I felt that to cope with the new and extraordinary situations then developing in the United States and the world I needed to go further and that as a matter of fact I had just well begun my training in knowledge of social conditions.

I reveled in the keen analysis of William James, Josiah Royce, and young George Santayana. But it was James with his pragmatism and Albert Bushnell Hart with his research method who turned me back from the lovely but sterile land of philosophic speculation to the social sciences as the field for gathering and interpreting that body of fact which would apply to my program for the Negro. As an under I had begun with a bibliography of Nat Turner and ended with a history of the suppression of the African slave trade to America; neither would need be done again, at least in my day. Thus in my quest for basic knowledge with which to help guide the American Negro, I came to the study of sociology, by way of philosophy and history rather than by physics and biology. After hesitating between history and economics, I chose history. On the other hand, psychology, hovering then on the threshold of experiment under Miinsterberg, soon took a new orientation which I could understand from the beginning.

Already I had made up my mind that what I needed was further training in Europe. The German universities were at the top of their reputation. Any American scholar who wanted preferment went to Germany for study. The faculties of Johns Hopkins and the new University of Chicago were beginning to be filled with German Ph.D.'s, and even Harvard, where Kuno Francke had long taught, had imported Münsterberg. British universities did not recognize American degrees and French universities made no special effort to encourage American graduates. I wanted then to study in Germany. I was determined that any failure on my part to become a recognized American scholar must not be based on lack of modern training.

I was confident. So far I had met no failure. I willed and lo! I was walking beneath the elms of Harvard--the name of allurement, the college of my youngest, wildest visions! I needed money; scholarships and prizes fell into my lap--not all I wanted or strove for, but all I needed to keep me in school. Commencement came, and standing before governor, president, and grave, gowned men, I told them certain truths, waving my arms and breathing fast! They applauded with what may have seemed to many as uncalled-for fervor, but I walked home on pink clouds of glory! I asked for a fellowship and got it. I announced my plan of studying in Germany, but Harvard had no more fellowships for me. A friend, however, told me of the Slater Fund and that the Board was looking for colored men worth educating.

No thought of modest hesitation occurred to me. I rushed at the chance. It was one of those tricks of fortune which always seem partly due to chance. In 1882, the Slater Fund for the education of Negroes had been established and the board in 1890 was headed by exPresident R. B. Hayes. Ex-President Hayes went down to Johns Hopkins University, which admitted no Negro students, and told a "darkey" joke in a frank talk about the plans of the fund. The Boston Herald of November 2, 1890, quoted him as saying: "If there is any young colored man in the South whom we find to have a talent for art or literature or any special aptitude for study, we are willing to give him money from the education funds to send him to Europe or give him advanced education." He added that so far they had been able to find only "orators." This seemed to me a nasty fling at my black classmate, Morgan, who had been Harvard class orator a few months earlier.

The Hayes statement was brought to my attention at a card party one evening; it not only made me good and angry but inspired me to write ex-President Hayes and ask for a scholarship. I received a pleasant reply saying that the newspaper quotation was incorrect; that his board had some such program in the past but had no present plans for such scholarships. I responded referring him to my teachers and to others who knew me, and intimating that his change of plan did not seem to me fair nor honest. He wrote again in apologetic mood and said that he was sorry the plan had been given up, that he recognized that I was a candidate who might otherwise have been given attention. I then sat down and wrote Mr. Hayes this letter:

May 25, 1891

Your favor of the 2nd. is at hand. I thank you for your kind wishes. You will pardon me if I add a few words of explanation as to my application. The outcome of the matter is as I expected it would be. The announcement that any agency of the American people was willing to give a Negro a thoroughly liberal education and that it had been looking in vain for men to educate was to say the least rather startling. When the newspaper clipping was handed me in a company of friends, my first impulse was to make in some public way a categorical statement denying that such an offer had ever been made known to colored students. I saw this would be injudicious and fruitless, and I therefore determined on the plan of applying myself. I did so and have been refused along with a "number of cases" beside mine.

As to my case, I personally care little. I am perfectly capable of fighting alone for an education if the trustees do not see fit to help me. On the other hand the injury you have--unwittingly I trust--done the race I represent, and [am] not ashamed of, is almost irreparable. You went before a number of keenly observant men who looked upon you as an authority on the matter, and told them in substance that the Negroes of the United States either couldn't or wouldn't embrace a most liberal opportunity for advancement. That statement went all over the country. When now finally you receive three or four applications for the fulfillment of that offer, the offer is suddenly withdrawn, while the impression still remains.

If the offer was an experiment, you ought to have had at least one case before withdrawing it; if you have given aid before (and I mean here toward liberal education--not toward training plowmen) then your statement at Johns Hopkins was partial. From the above facts I think you owe an apology to the Negro people. We are ready to furnish competent men for every European scholarship furnished us off paper. But we can't educate ourselves on nothing and we can't have the moral courage to try, if in the midst of our work our friends turn public sentiment against us by making statements which injure us and which they cannot stand by.

That you have been looking for men to liberally educate in the past may be so, but it is certainly strange so few have heard [of] it. It was never mentioned during my three years stay at Fisk

University. President [J.C.] Price of Livingstone [then a leading Negro spokesman] has told me that he never heard of it, and students from various other Southern schools have expressed great surprise at the offer. The fact is that when I was wanting to come to Harvard, while yet in the South, I wrote to Dr. Haygood [Atticus G. Haygood, a leader of Southern white liberals], for a loan merely, and he never even answered my letter. I find men willing to help me thro' cheap theological schools, I find men willing to help me use my hands before I have got my brains in working order, I have an abundance of good wishes on hand, but I never found a man willing to help me get a Harvard Ph.D.

Hayes was stirred. He promised to take up the matter the next year with the board. Thereupon, the next year I proceeded to write the board: "At the close of the last academic year at Harvard, I received the degree of Master of Arts, and was reappointed to my fellowship for the year 1891-92. I have spent most of the year in the preparation of my doctor's thesis on the suppression of the Slave Trade in America. I prepared a preliminary paper on this subject and read it before the American Historical Association at its annual meeting at Washington during the Christmas holidays. . . .Property to finish my education, careful training in a European university for at least a year is in my mind and the minds of my professors, absolutely indispensable." I thereupon asked respectfully "aid to study at least a year abroad under the direction of the graduate department of Harvard or other reputable auspices" and if this was not practicable, "that the board loan me a sufficient sum for this purpose." I did not of course believe that this would get me an appointment, but I did think that possibly through the influence of people who thus came to know about my work, I might somehow borrow or beg enough to get to Europe.

I rained recommendations upon Mr. Hayes. The Slater Fund Board surrendered, and I was given a fellowship of seven hundred and fifty dollars to study a year abroad, with the promise that it might possibly be renewed for a second year. To salve their souls, however, this grant was made half as gift and half as repayable loan with five percent interest. I remember rushing down to New York and talking with ex-President Hayes in the old Astor House, and emerging walking on air. I saw an especially delectable shirt in a shop window. I went in and asked about it. It cost three dollars, which was about four times as much as I had ever paid for a shirt in my life; but I bought it.

Massachusetts Review (1960)

3. William Pickens, Y'1904[43]--Yale-The Henry James Ten Eyck Oratorical Contest[44]

My first year at Yale was full of experiences for which former school struggles had in a measure prepared me. After the Christmas examinations, when students are graded for the first term's work, I was classed in Grade A, which according to the policy of the Self-Help Bureau exempted me from payment of tuition, and I stayed in Grade A, never paying another dollar of tuition during my years at Yale. Board I could earn, and other expenses I could manage. A room in White Hall was secured by the kindness of Dean Wright, into whose Latin class I had luckily fallen. After Christmas my Yale studentship was no longer an experiment, and I set out with confidence on the run toward June. Early in the year there appeared on the bulletin ten subjects for the "Ten Eyck Prize" in oratory. Among them was the simple word, "Hayti." The oration is first written and passed in under an assumed name; there were over three hundred men in my class and about thirty-five passed in papers. Of these the judges chose ten to enter the first speaking contest. At this first speaking five are dropped and five advanced to the final contest. The five who are dropped receive the five third prizes. Of

[43] Reprint from William Pickens, Bursting Bonds, Bloomington: Indiana University Press, 1991.

[44] Delete this empty note

the five who are advanced the successful one will receive the first prize and the four will receive the four second prizes.

I decided to win the first prize. It is a bold thing to acknowledge, but such was my decision. I kept my work at the Young Men's Christian Association until I should see my name among the ten. Once among the ten I felt as sure to win the first prize as I had ever felt that I would master the difficulties of a lesson.

About three weeks before the time for the final contest, which was to take place about the first of April, the "ten" were published and my name appeared with the subject Hayti.

My subsequent plans and decisions seem as audacious to me now as they must to the reader of this narrative. I told my Young Men's Christian Association friends that my name was among the Ten Eyck "ten," and that the first prize would settle my bills for the rest of the year, and that I should win if I gave up extra work and devoted myself to the last three weeks of the contest. "If you do not win," they said, kindly, "you may return." I wrote Doctor Andrews of Talladega College that I was among the ten and that I would be among the "five" at the close of that week. After the preliminary contest I wrote him that I was one of the five and that I would win the first prize two weeks later unless the gods should interfere. I learned later that Doctor Andrews read these missives in public as fast as he received them in the South, and they must have seemed utter audacity to all but him. On April 1 in College Street Hall I was awarded the first prize by the five judges.

My ambition to win was stimulated by a desire to further the acquaintance of other peoples with my race. I had noticed that when I did my class work among the best, more curiosity was awakened than when a Jew or a Japanese ranked among the best. The surprise with which I was taken struck me as due to a lack of expectation in my fellows, and I would succeed in order to cause others to expect more of the American Negro.

The Negro students were less than one-half of one per cent. of the three thousand men at Yale. The Negro might not be expected to win often. But judging from the press and personal comment that followed, it would seem that the whole world was a little too much surprised.

But not all that was said and done was prompted by curious surprise rather than positive appreciation. The next morning I found in the Yale post office a check for fifty dollars with appreciation from the Yale Glee, Banjo and Mandolin Clubs Association. For weeks there came daily twenty-five or more appreciative letters. Mrs. Corinne Roosevelt Robinson, sister of the President, had never quite forgotten me since my little summer campaign speech in 1900, and she sent Godspeed and a personal check. One of the most highly appreciated letters came from ex-Pres. Grover Cleveland. A good lady of Newport gave me my first and only diamond pin. There came through the mails from New York City three fifty-dollar gold certificates in an anonymous letter signed by "An Unknown Well-wisher." It contained half a dozen words, the briefest and the fullest missive ever sent me. I remembered the text that begins "Unto him that hath."[45]

---

[45] See Luke *:18.

So many good and sensible letters were bound to be offset by some others of more or less eccentric ideas and suggestions. Some organization in Kentucky, which seemed from their literature to have had some designs on Hayti for some time, wrote me a proposal that they would seize the island by some sort of filibustering expedition from the United States if I would accept the presidency. Shades of Dessalines and Toussaint L'Ouverture![46] I had no desire to add to the volcanic little government's already too numerous chief executives.

The appreciation of my classmates was generous. When my name was seen among the ten, there was a mixture of amused and sympathetic interest. The proportion of amusement was overdone only by one Jew who was an unsuccessful aspirant for the honor and who referred to me among the boys as "the black Demosthenes."[47] I told him it would have been more Jew like for him to say black David, or black Jacob. When I entered the five, I was taken more seriously. And when I won the final contest there was a burst of generous and manly enthusiasm.

I never like to describe human ugliness for its own sake, but there was one fellow who is worth describing because he is such a good illustration of a

---

[46] Francois Dominique Toussaint L'Ouverture (c. 1744-1803) led a successful slave revolt in Haiti and after conquering Santo Domingo in 1801 became ruler of the entire island. After Toussaint was treacherously deposed by a French expedition in 1802, one of his generals, Jean-Jacques Dessalines (c. 1758-1806), led a campaign that threw out the French invaders. On January 1, 1804, Dessalines proclaimed Haitian independence and was chosen governor for life.

[47] Demosthenes (383-322B.c.) was an Athenian statesman generally regarded as the greatest of the ancient Greek orators.

type--not a Yale type, but a type of man. Among the best and seemingly sincerest of my Yale friends were some boys from the South, especially from the freedom-loving hills of the border states. But there was one fellow from the state school of my own state. We entered Yale together and he, knowing me to be a Southern Negro fighting for my very existence, was at first very, very patronizing. He would "hello" me a block away, inquire with a half amused, half good-natured smile "how I was making it?" and make every effort of bland superiority. I uniformly and politely accepted all his good advances, never seeking them. Soon my classmates began to talk on the campus about my work. He became less friendly--I had to be nearer to him than the distance of a block to get a "hello." After the Christmas "exams" the boys had tales to tell; how I walked out from nearly every examination when most of them were not half through. Then he hardly spoke when he met me face to face; I tried hard to be uniform and unconscious of change. Next day after the oratorical contest I met him squarely on the street, and as I was about to give the friendly greeting he pulled down his hat over his eyes and passed as one passes a lamp-post.

People naturally ask how I fared during my next year, my senior year, at Yale. A month before my graduation I was invited to address the State Congregational Association of Illinois, and when a minister of that body asked me that question I told the story of a Negro woman in the South who believed in "voodooism." Her husband was fussy and disagreeable, so she went to the "conjure doctor" to get a remedy for the old man's distemper. The conjurer gave her a bottle of clear liquid, and directed that when the "fuss" started in the house she must take a mouthful of it herself, and added his particular direction that it must not be swallowed under a quarter of an hour after being taken into the mouth. She followed directions and the vicarious treatment completely cured the old man. Returning to the doctor in astonishment she asked what the remedy could be, and he replied: "Cold water-but it kept your tongue still!"

But there is nothing more generous and noble than the heart of a boy, and young men are but "boys grown tall." During my senior year they acknowledged my right to a part of their world. They never quite got away from the surprise that "you do your lessons as well as anybody!" While crossing the campus at examination times I was often stopped by a crowd of fellows who had just finished some examination. They would hand me the list of questions, and as I answered them they would say, "I made it," or "I failed," according as their answers had agreed or disagreed with mine. "Pickens, you ought to be a lawyer!" shouted one fellow after I had gone through such a list of questions from our five-hour law course. I could hardly have registered to vote in that fellow's state.

At graduation time I was ranked in the "Philosophical Oration" group of the class who are credited with "honors in all studies." I had been with the class two years, just the time required to merit a Phi Beta Kappa Key if one's scholarship warrants it. So much was printed and said about my admission to this society that a clear statement might correct some error. It was said that my admission was opposed. Well, a great university is much like the outside world; it holds many different spirits. No one should be surprised at differences of opinion in a university.

In our senior year a resolution was introduced in the Phi Beta Kappa Society that no one be admitted to membership that year except such as began as Freshmen. I entered Yale as a Junior; but there is no way of determining that this was a "grandfather clause"[48] inspired by my presence. A few fellows tried mischievously to impress me that the legislation was in my honor, but I consistently and persistently refused to acknowledge it--and somehow the resolution proved ineffective and I was awarded a key. The Phi Beta Kappa Society is based on scholarship, and Yale is a very democratic community.

After-word

After Yale, what? A famous lecture bureau of New York City laid before me a tempting contract to be carted around over Europe and America for three years as a sort of lecture-curiosity. I had been invited to speak before various dignified gatherings, at Newport, Hartford and at the annual banquet of the Citizens' Trades Association of Cambridge, Mass. But after seeking and finding good advice in the secretary of Yale University, the secretary of the American Missionary Association and Paul Laurence Dunbar who had tried the curiosity-show business, I decided that show-lecturing would be of doubtful influence on my future--although it would have given me an opportunity to accomplish one of the desires of every college man, a visit to the Old World.

[48] An ironic reference to laws enacted between 1895 and 1910 in a number of southern states restricting the right to vote to those descended from persons who had the right to vote as of January 1, 1867. The so-called grandfather clause was declared unconstitutional by the U.S. Supreme Court in 1915.

The work of education seemed to offer a greater field of usefulness to a Negro than any other profession. My own school struggles emphasized this thought. Back to the South was my inclination. That section is big with the destiny of the American Negro, and therefore with the future of the Negro race in the whole world. After considering the timely offers of various educational authorities, including those of Tuskegee and the American Missionary Association, I decided to begin work in the American Missionary Association College at Talladega, Ala., where I have been teacher of languages since leaving Yale in 1904. My experience of the usefulness of this institution, as well as gratitude for the greatest of benefits, made this decision logical and good.

On my way from New England to Talladega a visit to the World's Exposition in St. Louis brought me by Little Rock, Ark., and the scenes and memories of public-school days, the "skiff-ferry" and the "stave factory--and the colored citizens and a few white friends gave me the biggest and most pleasant reception of all my life.

In the last six years it has been impossible for me to supply all the demands upon my energies as a lecturer or speaker at institutions and gatherings. I have visited nearly all of the important Negro schools of the South, and it has given me a good look into the condition and needs of my people. In 1906 I took up Esperanto, and after a correspondence with Esperantists all over the world, I was awarded a diploma by the British Esperanto Association. In 1908 Fisk University honored me with the degree of Master of Arts.

In 1905 I met the most helpful and the most enduring good fortune of all my life, the traditional and the real "best woman in the world." Miss Minnie Cooper McAlpine, who like myself was a product of the American Missionary Association work, had graduated at Tougaloo University in Mississippi and taught for three years in the American Missionary Association school at Meridian. Since this meeting there have come in succession three of the brightest and best joys that high heaven lends to earth, William, Jr., Hattie Ida and Ruby Annie,

These latter years have a history of their own--which can be better written, perhaps, when they are seen through a perspective of years. Had I written of my boyhood experiences right on the heels of their passage, I could not have presented them in their truer light and proportion. The distance of years lends not merely enchantment but sobriety to the view.

To advance your life is but to push forward the front of your battle to find the same inspiriting struggle still. Oh, the blessing of a boyhood that trains to endurance and struggle! To do the best one can, wherever placed, is a summary of all the rules of success. When I was in the public school of Argenta, Ark., I one day missed a word in the spelling class, the only word I missed during the five years, and a word that I could easily have spelled. The teacher took quick advantage of the careless trick of my brain and passed the word on to my neighbor without giving me the usual second trial, saying as he did so that a boy who had never missed a word had no right ever to miss a word. He wished, no doubt, to punish carelessness. That one missed word was more talked of among my fellows than all the hundreds of words I had spelled, and I was taught the lesson that the man who succeeds is never conceded the right to fail.

I have learned that righteousness and popularity are not always yokefellows, and sometimes run a contrary course. From early boyhood I was laughed at among my fellows for the contemptible weakness of totally abstaining from strong drink and tobacco, while in my manhood the best of my fellows commend the abstention as a virtue. I have learned the uplifting lesson that the real heart of humanity appreciates manhood above things; as a copperless struggler I was often accorded a place above the possessor of gold. I have been impressed, not that every single thought and deed in the world is good, but that the resultant line of humanity's movement is in the direction of righteousness, and that human life and the world are on the whole good things.

4. Muriel Sutherland Snowden, H'1938[49] --Right to Participate

Muriel Sutherland Snowden was born in Orange, New Jersey, on 14 July 1916, one of three children of a dentist. She grew up in nearby Glen Ridge and was class valedictorian at its high school. She received her A.B. from Radcliffe in 1938 with a concentration in Romance Languages, but soon decided that her future lay in social work. From 1938 to 1943 she worked for a New Jersey welfare board, and then won a fellowship for graduate study in community organization and race relations at the New York School of Social Work. After a return to Cambridge in 1948 as executive director of the city's Civic Unity Committee, she and her husband Otto in 1949 conceived, founded, and directed Freedom House, Inc., a nationally renowned civic center in the heart of Boston's black community, for 35 years until their retirement in 1984 to become private consultants.

Despite indefatigably throwing herself into an endless series of tasks promoting urban renewal and social betterment, Muriel Snowden made time to serve on countless committees and boards (she was the first black and only woman on the board of directors of the Shawmut Bank) and to teach community organization at Simmons College for more than a dozen years.

---

[49] Reprint from Blacks at Harvard, New York:New York University Press, 1993 and Radcliffe Quarterly, 1988.

In 1972 she became the all-time top vote-getter for director of the Associated Harvard Alumni, and in 1977 was the first black woman elected to the Board of Overseers. She received many honors, including the College Alumnae Achievement Award from Radcliffe (1964), and honorary degrees from the University of Massachusetts at Amherst (1968) and from Boston College (1984). In 1987 she was the recipient of a $375,000 no-strings-attached "genius" grant from the MacArthur Foundation. She succumbed to cancer at her Boston home on 30 September 1988.

Right to Participate

Despite everything that came afterwards, my most vivid memory of Radcliffe is of being denied access to a dormitory my freshman year. It continues to rankle to this day--despite the fact that Radcliffe was the only college to which I had applied; that I had graduated as Valedictorian from one of the best public high schools in the country at the time; that I had been admitted without examination under the then existing "highest seventh plan" without the need for scholarship assistance--[that] the Radcliffe administration focused on my race as the rationale for concern about whether or not I would be "happy" living in a dormitory.

For my mother, however, determined that I should not miss out on the essence of college life, this was definitely a non-issue. For her, the "quality" of my social life was our problem and not theirs; so after being forced to live out my freshman year as a "day hop" commuting from Belmont, I was finally assigned a room in Whitman Hall.

Thus, (I believe) as only the second Black woman in the history of the college up until that time who had been "allowed" to live in a dormitory, my life took on a somewhat different coloration from that of other Black students who commuted the entire four years.

I remember those three years in Whitman as warm and happy ones, where I shared with my dormitory mates the buzzing excitement of the date one of them had with Joseph Kennedy, Jr.; the intense dinner discussions about whether one should accept religious dogma without question; gossipy sessions about sex, love, and marriage; the agony of studying all night for exams; the secret champagne celebrations on the stairs after lights outs; and the anxiety of getting back to the dorm by sign-in time.

Although I was to learn later that my presence sparked special meetings about what would be the procedures should I decide to sign up for the dorm dances, who would exchange dances with me and my date, etc., there was very little open evidence of prejudice, hostility, or discrimination. Life was easier for me as the result of growing up in an all-white community, attending all-white schools, being carefully nurtured in self-esteem and self-confidence by a close-knit family, and being shielded from the inevitable racial incidents that no Black family, no matter who they are, wholly escapes in this society.

In reality, I came to Radcliffe carefully wrapped in the cocoon of an "oreo," the nickname for those of us considered to be "black on the outside;

white on the inside"--a living, breathing reflection of what whites thought Black people ought to be like.

However, even I had another life outside the dormitory. The Black Greek organizations at the time actively sought out the newcomers at the start of each year and provided us with the opportunity to meet students from other colleges around the New England area through the Interfraternal Council "mixers" (shades of today's students' Black Freshman Orientation?). Also, since I had been "properly" introduced to Boston's Black community by the couple with whom I had lived my freshman year, "racial isolation" did not become a problem.

Radcliffe did for me what college is supposed to do. It gave me time to grow up and to start finding out for myself who and what I was. From an educational point of view, though, I do not have that sense of challenging intellectual stimulation about which so many graduates rhapsodize. The excitement about "sitting at the feet of the masters" and finding direction through the guidance and encouragement of professors and tutors eluded me completely. As a matter of fact, I cannot now even recall the name of my tutor, an elderly gentleman who obviously could not have cared less about me or I about him.

Essentially, I found my way through the educational maze alone, choosing courses, deciding on a major (the wrong one), and ending up with an AB in Romance languages and literature rather than in sociology and social relations, where I really belonged. When I think about those days, the only names that come to mind are Pitirim Sorokin and Robert Merton, the eminent sociologists, who struck a responsive chord in my soul and jogged me out of my middle-class complacency, and the legendary [George Lyman] Kittredge under whom I did not study.

As much as I chafed at my liberal arts education as not being a "salable product," it has indeed provided me with the discipline and inner resources that have enriched my personal life so immeasurably. I continue to believe that Radcliffe should exist as Radcliffe in order to give women the space they require even if they are now something called "Harvard women."

Above all, I have Harvard and Radcliffe to thank for the degree that not only opened the door to my first job, but also has commanded the respect and attention I have needed over the years to promote the causes in which I so deeply believe.

There are undeniable pluses, but I have hopes that the day will come when I and other Black alumni/ae will be able to sing the Radcliffe and Harvard alma maters with a lump in the throat and nostalgic reverence for what "our" college meant to us. That will also be the day when the statistics will not show Black students opting for other educational institutions with a more sensitive and welcoming climate and where they will not have to pay the "oreo" price for acceptance.

To paraphrase the late Whitney Young, executive director of the National Urban League:

Look at us, we are here. We have our pride. We have our roots. We have our culture and rich heritage. We insist, we demand your recognition and your respect and our right to participate in those decisions which affect our lives and those of our children. Radcliffe Quarterly (1986)

5. Robert J. Randall, Y'1943--Affirmative Action And Me

I was born in Pittsburgh in 1922, one of seven children of Attorney and Mrs. Clyde Randall. I graduated from Westinghouse High School in 1939 at the head of my class and won a scholarship to Yale, where I majored in mathematics. On graduating, I enlisted, after several racially based rebuffs, in Army Air Corps, and served as part of the ground support staff at Tuskegee Air Field, where the famous Tuskegee Airmen were trained. My career as an actuary began right after the war, in 1946, when I was hired as an actuarial trainee by the Mutual Life Insurance Company of New York, their first African-American employee ever. Mutual Life is the first and oldest mutual life insurance company in the United States. Later, in 1953, I became the first black employee and officer of TLAA-CREF, the largest private retirement system in the world, and still later, in 1970, the first black officer of Equitable Life. I retired in December, 1990, after a second three-year stint at TLAA-CREF. Throughout this journey through life, I have been hampered in one way or another by racial discrimination and segregation, and have struggled against these twin evils. Affirmative action, which came along in the later stages of my career, was a great step forward, benefiting me and many others, including many white women. The changes for the good have been enormous. Many large employers who had no black employees now have many black employees and executives, but there are still many barriers to advancement and proper treatment, and meaningful efforts to remove them should go forward.

Pittsburgh public schools in the 1930's were partially integrated. Blacks attended the same schools and classes as whites but there were no black teachers or administrators and black students were not allowed to take part in most extra-curricular programs, such as proms and the Hi-Y. When I graduated in 1939, I ranked first not just in my class at Westinghouse but also in the county-wide Civic Club test, thereby winning a scholarship to Carnegie Tech. But I was also eligible for the Kennedy T. Friend scholarship to Yale, a scholarship established by a wealthy Yale Law School graduate and open only to sons of members of the Allegheny County Bar. My father submitted my name, and I was interviewed by a committee of three, the presidents of the Allegheny County Bar Association and the Pittsburgh Yale Alumni and a representative of the Friend family. The committee promptly rejected me, on some grounds I've forgotten, but changed their minds when they got a very strong letter from my father threatening a public dispute. Before being admitted as a Yale undergraduate, I first had to take the College Board exam, an exam used at that time only by the Ivy League schools. Yale at that time was a very racist institution, with quotas on the number of Jewish and Negro students to be admitted. I received a letter from the chairman of the Board of Admissions, telling me that I had passed the exam and was therefore admitted bur urging me in very strong language not to come to Yale as I would be lonely and unhappy. I considered this a racist act and ignored his advice. The last black undergraduate admitted before me was Edward Goins, (son of Reverend Goins, pastor of the Dixwell Avenue Congregational Church who graduated in 1924. Thus for a period of twenty years, no black undergraduates were admitted to Yale. Prior to that, there had been black students in very small numbers for many years. In my junior year, a second black student, Billy Cousins, was admitted to Yale College. At the time of my admission, an outstanding black student, Tony Villa, graduated from Hillhouse High School in New Haven at the top of his class. He was not awarded one of the Hillhouse scholarships granted every year by Yale. Tony went to Howard and became a successful engineer. I am convinced that I was admitted only because I had already been awarded the Friend scholarship, sponsored by the Pittsburgh Yale Alumni and the Allegheny County Bar Association.

I was not lonely and unhappy at Yale. I enjoyed my classes, taught by distinguished scholars full of challenging ideas. My fellow students largely ignored me. But the black community of New Haven and the dozen black graduate and professional students (six of whom were in the Divinity School) welcomed me most warmly, adopting me as a sort of mascot. Through these social connections I met the young lady who has now been my wife for more than fifty years, Doris Farrar of Bridgeport. One of the graduate students, Hubert Ross, a student of sociology and anthropology, became my mentor and closest friend. Not only did he invite me regularly to Sunday dinner at his cousins' home on Admiral Street, but he also introduced me to

African-American culture, in particular the music of Bessie Smith, Louis Armstrong, and Billie Holiday. But most important was the friendship and help proffered by a remarkable black couple. Burt and Ella Scantlebury. They were the stewards (managers of the kitchen, dining room. bar, etc.) of Chi Psi Fraternity and Scroll and Key Senior Secret Society. It was Burt's practice to seek out black students at Yale to see if they needed jobs to help meet their expenses. I desperately needed help, since my scholarship covered tuition and room only, and my father, struggling to recover from the Great Depression, was not able to help me at all. So I washed dishes and ate my meals in the Chi Psi kitchen. Now there was a racist aspect to this. Yale had a student job program, known as the bursary job program, which took over in the sophomore year and was intended to provide jobs to needy students that would enable them to eat in the College dining halls with their classmates. I applied for one of these jobs and, for the first three weeks of my sophomore year, worked in the stacks of Sterling Memorial Library and ate in the Davenport College dining hall with my fellow students. But Mr. Emerson Tuttle, the Master of Davenport College, noted my presence there and took it upon himself to cancel my library job and to contact Mr. Scantlebury to see if he would rehire me. He told Mr. Scantlebury that I had quit my Chi Psi job because I considered myself superior to Mr. Scantlebury and his other employees. I did not consider myself superior to Mr. Scantlebury but I will always consider myself superior to Mr. Tuttle. The result was that I was not allowed to eat in the college dining halls with the other students for one three week period.

World War II began, and I went from Yale into the Army, ending up at Tuskegee Army Air Field, where the famous Tuskegee Airmen were trained and where I served as a maintenance engineering officer. But first racial barriers had forced two detours. The Navy in 1942 had no ROTC program, so at that point they decided to start such a program, designating it the V-1 program. I attempted to enlist in that program--this would have allowed me to stay in school till graduation in 1943 and to enter the Navy as an officer. After much hypocritical hemming and hawing, the enlisting officer bluntly told me that no Negroes were being accepted. At that time a small group of Yale students had been attempting to promote a postcard campaign demanding a "Second Front", an Allied invasion of France to help relieve the Soviet Army then being overwhelmed by the Nazis. The Yale Daily News strongly denounced the postcard campaign as constituting improper civilian interference in military decisions. So I wrote a one paragraph letter to the Daily News, proposing a proper postcard campaign to protest the racist action of the Navy. Suddenly I became a center of attention. Over the next several weeks the Yale Daily News published twenty articles and letters commenting pro and con, and one campus organization, Dwight Hall, the Christian Association, wrote to the Navy asking it to justify its action. Seth Taft, a News editor and a grandson of President Taft, wrote an article praising the South for reducing the lynching rate in which he said--"ask the man on the street or the seaman in the Navy if he would serve under a negro superior. No, we may as well admit." The Navy Bureau of Personnel responded to Dwight Hall with a statement that said in part---The Navy has for some time refused to accept Negroes for appointment as commissioned officers. This policy was instituted in the interest of harmony and efficiency aboard ship after many years of experience. This policy is in no way a reflection on the Negro, either individually or collectively. It is simply a matter of practicality." After weeks of letters and columns, no postcards were mailed and no change was made in the Navy's decision. Some years later, President Clinton proposed some modest changes in the unfair treatment of homosexuals in the military, but he was blocked by Senator Nunn and others. I wrote to Senator Nunn, pointing out that some of his language echoed word for word the 1942 statement of the Navy Bureau of Personnel. He answered with a letter containing additional echoes.

Rebuffed by the Navy, I turned to the Army Air Corps. A recruiting unit visited the campus, and I enlisted for training as a navigator. My class graduated in December, 1942, and I enrolled in graduate school while waiting to be called to active duty. The call came, directing me to report to Boston for assignment to training as a navigator. But in Boston it turned out there had been a mistake--the recruiting unit which visited Yale had failed to report that I was a Negro, and there were just no facilities for training Negroes as navigators. I was sent home to await further orders.

Several weeks later, I was called out of my class at Yale to meet an Air Corps colonel who had come down from Boston to settle my case. He told me that the only flying training available to Negroes was at Tuskegee Air Field as fighter pilots and that I was over the height limit for fighter pilots--accordingly, I was being offered two alternatives: basic training as an enlisted man or Air Corps OCS training as a maintenance engineering officer. The colonel insisted there was no aspect of racial discrimination in this treatment since the problem came from my height. He claimed to believe this. We went thru what I later called a "Silly Circle" discussion about four times before I finally agreed to accept the second option.

The Air Corps OCS really consisted of two schools, three months of basic training at the Boca Raton Club and Resort in Florida and five months of technical training in aircraft maintenance, coincidentally back at Yale in New Haven. To a limited degree, OCS was one of the few integrated areas in the entire armed services. But sadly, incident after incident of racial discrimination warped my experience there. I shall recount a few.

I arrived at Boca Raton in February, 1943, one of six black cadets who constituted the "second wave" of black cadets there. The first two black cadets had arrived some months earlier, and, when the first one reported, the commanding officer, Major Weiss, told him there must have been some mistake and ordered Cadet Lewis not to participate in any training but to remain confined in his room awaiting reassignment. A few days later, Lewis was summoned to the Major's office where Major Weiss told him that his orders had indeed been correct and he was free to begin training, but, he was warned, as the only black cadet there, he would have to be most careful to follow all rules, obey all commands, and not cause any trouble. Whereupon Lewis informed the Major that he was not the only black cadet, that a second one had arrived that morning. The Major was horrified and jumped up from his chair shouting, "My God-they're coming in droves!" A more serious incident occurred the first week-end that we were permitted time off post, and four of us went to a bar in the black section of West Palm Beach, where we met some girls. As we were sitting drinking and laughing at a window table, we noticed a small crowd gathering in the square on which the bar faced. The objects of attention were three men, one black and the other two white, all dressed in civilian clothes. Suddenly a white policemen arrived, the crowd grew larger, and the three white men began beating the black man with billy clubs. They beat him and beat him. A woman came out of the crowd, knelt before the white men, and screamed, "please don't kill my husband!" We were told that the man was beaten to death. Neither we nor the all-black crowd had done anything to stop the beating. The three white men left, leaving the body crumpled on the ground.

At Boca Raton, the training had mostly to do with military drilling and discipline, with a few sessions of target practice with rifles on the firing range. At Yale, the training had to do with repairing aircraft bodies and engines. As one who had never attempted automobile repairs as a teen-ager, I was not at all sure that this rush course would really qualify me to supervise the repair and maintenance of complex aircraft. Nevertheless, graduation day approached rapidly, and I had to be ready to deal with my first assignment as a maintenance engineering officer. It was then that the most serious instance of racist discrimination occurred at Yale.

It just happened at that time that the Air Force was introducing a new heavy bomber into active duty, the B-29, later to become famous for carrying the two atom bombs used to destroy Hiroshima and Nagasaki and several hundred thousand Japanese civilians. This plane was unique in that the maintenance engineering officer was part of the flight crew, instead of staying behind at the base supervising the mechanics in relative safety. The Yale OCS was the only source of officers who could be trained for this assignment and, in order to complete the B-29 crews, each class was canvassed for volunteers for B-29 training. To the extent that the number volunteering fell short, additional graduates were assigned. Our class contained six Negro cadets, three of whom, Mosley, Merriweather, and I volunteered for B-29 training. Our applications were rejected, even though the number of volunteers fell short, and additional graduates had to be drafted for this training. It was then that I was told by one of my white fellow cadets, an Irishman named O'Bannon, that one of the usual motives for volunteering for maintenance engineering training was to avoid combat.

Instead of training on the newest combat plane, we Negro officers were instead assigned to two months training at Dothan Field, Alabama, on P-40 airplanes, and then to permanent assignment as engineering officers at Tuskegee Army Air Field, where the first black pilots in the Air Force were being trained. The P-40 had been used by General Claire Chennault's famous Flying Tigers in fighting against the Japanese in China before World War II started in Europe. It was the oldest combat plane then in use and was the plane in use at Tuskegee. Disappointed but obedient, we journeyed from New Haven to Dothan Field, Alabama, using the sleeping car tickets furnished us by the Air Corps. When we reached Washington, D.C., we were forcibly moved into the segregated and overcrowded Jim Crow cars reserved for all Negroes, with or without sleeping car tickets. The cars lacked adequate toilets. Finally we reached Dothan Field, But we did not receive any P-40 training. We were ushered into a cell-like room, and, after more than an hour of confinement, we were informed that the commanding officer had countermanded our orders, that there were no facilities for training Negro officers at Dothan Field, and that we were to report for permanent duty at Tuskegee after a one-week leave to visit our families. We asked to be allowed to use the toilet but were told that there were no toilet facilities for Negro officers at Dothan Field. Back to the Jim Crow railroad cars.

Tuskegee Army Air Field (often referred to as TAAFU, a take-off on the term, SNAFU-meaning situation normal-all fouled up) was a trip, a strange and unique experience. There were two conflicting views of TAAFU, one held probably by the majority of the staff, including the brave young men being trained there as the only black pilots in the US air forces, and the other by a few rebellious spirits like Mosely and me. The majority view was that TAAFU was a grand and noble experiment, designed to prove that Negro pilots, given proper training, could perform as well as anyone, and that the participants in the experiment owed it to themselves and to future generations to do all in their power to help it succeed. My view was that it was just another clever device of the white man to maintain his vicious policies of segregation and oppression. There were facts supporting both views. TAAFU had been established in response to years of pleading, demanding, and begging by various Negro organizations, including the NAACP, and supportive individuals like William Hastie and Eleanor Roosevelt. A small and timid step towards ending the racial discrimination that pervaded the military as well as most other areas of American life, it was a giant step when then compared to any and all other comparable efforts. In later life, I have been continually amazed by the fact that so many of the outstanding present-day black leaders had been part of the Tuskegee experiment, men like Coleman Young, the long-time mayor of Detroit, and George Brown, former lieutenant governor of Colorado who helped pressure the commercial airlines into hiring Negro pilots. Some of the realities of Tuskegee supported my view. The commanding officer, Colonel Noel Parrish, was white as were all of his principal assistants with two exceptions, the chaplain and the trial judge advocate, the legal officer responsible for defending soldiers accused of crimes. All the white personnel were supported in luxurious off-base private housing, while all black personnel were required to live in on base crude barracks. The white officers, with one exception, were either in charge of major areas of base operations, with black assistants, or flying instructors. The one exception was Lt. Miller, the assistant Post Exchange officer, whose boss was black. There were seven white enlisted men, and they constituted the payroll unit. Every payday, all the black officers and enlisted men had to queue up to receive their pay envelopes from these seven men.

TAAFU was also used as a dumping ground, a place where competent Negro personnel whose skills the military was unwilling to use, were sent to be stored away. I arrived eager and anxious to perform my duties as a maintenance engineering officer, only to find that there were no duties to perform. Captain Clarence 'Big Sparky' Jones was the chief engineering officer in charge of the squadron which maintained all the planes used in "basic training", about a third of the planes at the base. But he already had three assistants and did not need another. My principal assignment was to stay out of his way. As a result, I learned to play tennis, jogged around the airfield, and took correspondence courses in Modern Algebra from the University of Chicago. The most grotesque example of dumping was the infamous case of the "Rebellion of the Thirty Quartermaster Officers." These thirty officers had been part of a large quartermaster outfit of Negro troops being trained for overseas service. When the outfit was finally ready to be shipped to duty in Europe, all the black officers who had worked with the troops throughout their training were replaced by white officers. These thirty replaced black officers were assigned to Tuskegee, where there were no duties for them to perform. Colonel Parrish, presumably with good intentions, decided to set up thirty units, one enlisted man and one quartermaster officer each, and send them out to plant trees throughout the base. The quartermaster officers refused to do this, and were thus liable for court-martial. Many months later, they were all sent overseas to France, for proper quartermaster duty.

Finally, the Air Corps changed its regulations so that I and other ground support officers became eligible for pilot training--this included removal of the height restrictions. I and my old buddies Mosley and Woody were among the six officers who applied, and we joined about eighteen eighteen year-olds to form the class of 46H. I logged 45 hours in the PT-13 and soloed but was not able to fly skillfully enough to avoid "washing out" and so I returned to ground duty as Post Night Light and Weight and Balance officer. Then came V-E Day and V-J Day, at which point I resigned my commission, citing the grievances outlined above. I went thru the normal processes, being discharged in February, 1946, and months later received a letter accepting my resignation, with no comments at all on my criticisms. After discharge, I returned to New York City, where my mother was then living, and resumed my graduate studies in mathematics, this time at Columbia, not Yale. More importantly, in March I got married, to Doris Farrar of Bridgeport. We have been married for 51 years and are very proud of our three children, Robbie, Julie, and Peter, and our two granddaughters, Elizabeth and Cristina.

6. Charles Payne, Y'1952—Retribution

At 18 and away from Charleston, West Virginia to live alone for the first time, I came to Yale in 1948. I was a member of the first freshman class which was composed of non-veterans. Some of my self-confidence and sophistication had been rudely challenged in New York when, dressed in my new gray suit, tie and accoutrements from Frankenbergers Men's Department in Charleston, I was offered the chance to buy a choice diamond ring after only about 45 steps into Grand Central Station. After declining, I walked on somewhat amazed and chagrined by the ability of a New York hustler to pick me out of the crowd of exiting passengers. In any case, I was not amazed at Grand Central Station having been to New York with my Mother three years earlier. I looked at the Hoffritz collection of cigarette lighters, gifts, cutlery and Swiss Army knives, glanced at magazines and found the New Haven Railway and hence off to Yale without losing my suitcase, ticket, letters or spending-money. The trip to the University was accomplished by taxi and the sight of the "Old Campus" arising out of the Green like a medieval castle was impressive.

I was assured, when I asked the Campus Cop that the gates were never closed and that there was no curfew at 10:00 or 11:00 p.m. as there had been at West Virginia State College. He seemed somewhat bemused by my query but I was impressed. After following directions, I got the key to my assigned freshman room in Welch Hall, then found the building and after three flights of stairs, found the room. Yale had been designed in better times with only two students to a room, each with a bedroom and a common study. My letter informed me that I would have two roommates selected at random by names drawn from a hat.

Somehow it didn't come as a surprise, however, that my two roommates were also young men of color. Dick was from Cincinnati (Wyoming, Ohio to be precise), tall, a mathematical whiz, and Jack, short, energetic and from New Haven. Jack wanted to live away from home and so was at least a mile and half away from home and felt good about it. After comparing letters, we decided that Yale didn't lie....it just had several hats. (It later transpired that the fourth Negro, as we were then called, was sufficiently fair to photograph white, and so was rooming with a freshman from Texas in the WW11 Quonset huts out near the Peabody Museum. Nathan was happy there and so were his roommates so that his freshman experience was truly unique.

My parents arrived by car that afternoon, having driven from Charleston. They packed stuff I couldn't carry and gave me the thrill of traveling to school on my own. My Mother had packed Bates curtains and bedspread, sheets and other bedclothes, together with my radio, winter clothing, a few favorite books, my camera and other essential items together with two blankets. Mother was both wise and frugal and had summoned forth an olive drab blanket and one of more coarse wool with olive drub interwoven edging which, she said, had been in the family since World War I. Apparently the blankets had been kept in the fitted suitcases from the trunk of my Dad's old Packard touring car. My Mother had spirited away the suitcases and trunk when the car was sold after WWII. The blankets certainly looked as if they had been locked away, but while both smelled musty, the old woolen one certainly looked warm. It would be covered by the new bedspread which, I was reminded would match the curtains, so there was no further discussion. The blanket stayed and was appreciated later.

Freshman year now seems like a big pudding with events lying at or just below the surface like raisins. I had played football in high school and so went out for the Yale freshman team. No one at Yale knew anything about Negro high school football in West Virginia. Levi Jackson had been the varsity captain the year before, so this new black athlete got a really fair trial. Unfortunately at 6'3" and 176lbs. with full equipment in August, I was neither an offensive nor a defensive end. The fact that I could punt and pass and was the scrub team quarterback in high school gave me an unusual combination of useless skills which remained unused after the results of the first math quizzes were received. My father had not sent me to Yale to be an athlete.

Of more lasting importance was the discovery of station WJZ, New York one autumn afternoon and listening to a then 17-year-old Stan Getz play his first recorded solo at the end of the Coda to "Summer Sequence", a Ralph Bums extended jazz composition performed by the Woody Herman orchestra. The discovery of Charlie Parker, Dizzy Gillespie, Machito, Lester Young, Thelonious Monk, Charlie Ventura and his Bop for the People and the whole world of modern jazz and bebop soon followed introduced by the late night voice of Symphony Sid Toren from Birdland and Bop City. I have grown up, grown gray and have been saddened as one-by-one these inventive musicians have died. I have also grown in introspection, appreciation and delight at the legacy which they have left to influence Rock and Roll, Rap and Hip-Hop, Reggae, Ska, and now World Music. Without having heard Sarah Vaughan, Harry Belafonte's recording of "Lean on Me" as a jazz vocalist and George Shearing's "The Fourth Deuce", I wouldn't have been able to study until 2 or 3 a.m. in the most challenging academic environment I had ever faced. It turned out that many of the white students had already seen the freshman courses at Yale through their preparatory schools but it was all new to me.

One lovely discovery was that I had family in New Haven. The Powell family lived there at that time and my Aunt "Princess" resided in the Hanna Gray Home on Dixwell Avenue. I do not know whether or not the home still functions but it was a place of quiet, escape and wonderment to walk down to visit Aunt Princess who must have been in her seventies. On far too few Sunday afternoons I could sit and talk with her and marvel at her clarity of thought and expression and her beauty. There was never a question as to why she was called "Princess".

I never understood the "heeling" system for participation in the Radio Station, WYBC, the Yale Daily News, the Lit and other activities and, as far as I know, it was never formally explained to anyone who didn't have a need to know. There wasn't enough time to do any of these things and stay abreast of the pre-med course requirements so that freshman year was work broken only by a "Dear John" letter from my high school girl friend who found it necessary to marry a young man from West Virginia State

College; learning the amount of beer I could imbibe; an occasional date with a New Haven high school girl; Italian neorealism post-war films like Bitter Rice and the Bicycle Thief and Christmas Vacation. To my regret, it seemed that the Ivy League began its Christmas vacation just as the more traditional schools, which did not have two week reading periods before exams, ended theirs. I got to see three or four friends boarding the trains back to school as I arrived on the Chesapeake and Ohio and that was that.

Summer passed none too rapidly. Because I was the first male honor student in my high school class, I took considerable kidding when my struggle to maintain a Dean's List average was mentioned. It seems that my female high school honor peers were leading the classes at their respective schools while I appeared to be a playboy way up there in New England. I do remember getting the reputation as being eccentric, if not totally mad, because I was collecting butterflies for Dr. Remington in the Zoology Department. The ecological distribution of lepidoptera in West Virginia, not to mention much of the area South of the Holland tunnel was not readily available to the Yale zoologists. Spending two mornings a week in a meadow on the W.Va. State College campus with butterfly net, notebook and cyanide jar was a real stimulus to acquiring a rich vocabulary of humor. None of us students who collected were credited in the brief paper on the species variation of Coleas philodice as deduced from the phenotypic pattern of their spots, but I took some pride in seeing it published.

Pierson College beckoned in the autumn and, to save train fare, my Mother allowed me to drive her prized 1946 Chevrolet sedan to New Haven via the

West Side Drive through New York to the Merritt Parkway and into Connecticut. Mother and I carted my stuff up to one of the two rooms in the third floor of Pierson which we four Negro students had decided to share as roommates. Pierson, with a reputation as being very "white shoe" and with "Slave Quarters" seemed to be taking a risk in reducing its real estate values but we actually enjoyed the ambience. Unfortunately, one of our two rooms was on the opposite side of the hall from the other so we turned one into a living room and the other room housed two bunk beds. Yale had just begun allowing student telephones as I recall, and we enjoyed that luxury and the shared bill.

Mother and I then went down Dixwell Avenue to see Aunt Princess and, because I was told that she had once worked for Yale during the 1920's and 1930's, we invited her down to see that one of her family had, at last, achieved admission to Yale. The University had provided maid service for its young gentlemen, as I understand it, well into the 1930's. Apparently these ladies tidied up, made beds, removed trash, cleaned and otherwise served the students. Such had been the lot of Aunt Princess and, for a maid to see a young member of the family enrolled as an Eli was a signal occasion.

To see an expression of panic and despair on the face of your seventy-odd year old beautiful aunt is a harrowing experience. Visions of fainting, heart attacks, strokes, rapidly course through your mind and both my Mother and I were quite concerned. Mother and Aunt Princess sat down on my unmade bed with the bedding piled at one end including the sheets and the folded blankets and had a whispered discussion which was so obviously private that I did not dare intervene. Mother seemed reassuring and supportive and after some minutes the previous atmosphere of pride and smiles and even a subdued laugh was achieved. The rest of the day was extraordinarily pleasant. I was allowed to show off my accomplishments and my second year was off to a running start

Just before Mother left to return to Charleston via New York for shopping, I asked her about the incident which had so shocked Aunt Princess. Family progress was underlined when Mother, quite seriously, told me that Aunt Princess was afraid that the Yale authorities would seek her out when they saw the coarse woolen, WWI surplus blanket on my bed. It seems that she had purloined it years before when she left Yale's employment, and now it had returned! Retribution was sure to follow.

I have told this true story to my own tribe, most recently my youngest son, the last of seven children, during his August vacation with me while swimming at Caesar's Creek lake park. We shared a coarse woolen blanket with olive drab trim which will remain in our possession until at least the 21st Century.

7. John Woodford, H'1963--My Years at Harvard

Biography:

John Woodford, Harvard Class of 1963, was born Sept. 24, 1941, in Chicago. The son of Dr. Hackley E. and Mary Steele Woodford, he received BA (magna cum laude) and MA ('67) degrees in English Language and Literature. He began his journalistic career with the Johnson Publishing Co. on Jet and Ebony magazines in Chicago in 1964. After finding the law distasteful during a semester stint at Yale Law School in 1967, he returned to journalism on the staff of the New Haven Register before rejoining Ebony in 1968. He moved later that year to Muhammad Speaks newspaper and served as editor-in-chief from 1969-72. He joined the Chicago Sun-Times (1972-74) and the New York Times (copy editor on the National Desk, (1974-77), then moved to the editorial staff of the Ford Motor Co. publication Ford Times (1977-80). In 1981, he became executive editor of medical center publications for the University of Michigan in Ann Arbor, and from 1985 to the present he has been executive editor of Michigan Today, the largest-circulated (300,000) alumni publication in the world. He is also a contributor to the journal The Black Scholar. Woodford and his wife and former classmate Elizabeth (Duffy) Woodford (Radcliffe '63) have three children, Duffy, Maize, and Will, and one granddaughter, Caroline.

Arriving at Harvard in 1959 from the small (pop. 12,000) town of Benton Harbor, Michigan, provide me with a big cultural boost but no shock. I never felt in awe of the place; my great uncle James Waring was in the class of 1913, my grandfather lived in Roxbury, and my mother grew up in Cochituate, Massachusetts, so there was little chance of that. But I did feel I'd entered a grand new world bustling with plenty more people and ideas than I'd been used to, not to mention the traffic.

Right from the beginning, awaiting the arrival of my unidentified roommate in Matthews Hall North in the Yard, I began meeting a range of classmates who, to a man were remarkable free spirits-friendly, energetic fellows--and neither then nor later did I encounter anything like the snob of stereotype. The company of almost any of my classmates delighted me right from the start and has continued to do so down the decades, singly or in numbers. Maybe it's because I had three sisters and no brother.

As it turned out, my roommate, Travis Williams of Durham, North Carolina, was one of the 16, if memory serves me, Afro-American men admitted that year. From starting off a bit edgy toward one another, as if the room assignment had deprived us of acquaintance with someone who might present a more novel--or culturally diverse, as they say now--outlook on life than a fellow Afro-American, we became about as close as brothers over the years. His death from stroke in 1968 is a loss I've felt almost every day. Throughout Harvard's history up until 1959, in the very few years in which Blacks were enrolled at all, there had been only about three of us maximum in an admitted class. This was certainly the case for the three undergraduate classes above us when we arrived. Some donor, we heard, had given Harvard big bucks to admit a good handful of fellows from the South and send them to a rigorous preparatory session at Andover that summer to make up for the suspected inadequacy of their high schools. Some of them had just as good preparation (and in a few cases better) as that received by some of us from the North. Harvard also admitted more Black men from the North that year, too. Perhaps the increase reflected the influence of Sputnik and the intensification of the civil rights movement.

Right from the beginning, we met in rooms and sometimes ate in a big but in no way exclusive group in the Freshman Union. We laughed about being part of some sort of sociological experiment while simultaneously being turned into "normal" Harvard men. I don't think any of us was so naïve as to be surprised by various peculiarities of our status. We knew what kind of society we lived in. To my knowledge, very few of us had any difficulties different from those experienced by young men of other backgrounds.

A few of us did find it disappointing, however, to find ourselves the subjects of a fellow freshman's class project. What kind of faculty member would OK such a project? We were singled out as objects of the sociological/anthropological research of one of our classmates, Ronald Blau, for a survey paper called "Shadows in the Yard." Perhaps Daniel Moynihan was behind it, I'm not sure. I think the course came out of the Department of Social Relations, and that was Moynihan's bailiwick at the time. Ronnie interviewed us as representative natives, as it were, with Ronnie in the role of anthropologist.

The title alone told us a lot about the sensibilities of the people we were among. We regaled Ronnie (who three years later became one of my series of roommates) with accounts of our experiences, feelings, plans, ideas. Sometimes we answered his questions sincerely, often we didn't, preferring to play the role of mischievous natives like the ones who have bamboozled Margaret Mead and other anthropologists. And we enjoyed dubbing some of our bull sessions as a gathering of shadows, or greeting one another, "Hey, Shadow," or riffing off the joke about the Black applicant for a radio job: "Who knows what evil lurks in the hearts of men?" he began in a perfect announcer baritone. But when he slipped and said, "The shadow do!" he lost his job.

In retrospect, I see that Blau's project placed us within a relationship and subjected us to a process that reflects our country's perennial open season for those targeting the identity of young Black males and Black Americans in general. Much of the current nonsense about special Black genetic characteristics--masked as a concern for our health--that segments us out of the general population is part of this ideological warfare designed to desensitize us, offer some of us money to supply "expertise," and dehumanize us in the eyes of the majority. This conferring of special status sets up an economically troublesome population for genocidal policies of one kind or another, whether via the reservation, the ghetto, the gas chamber, prison, welfare or what have you. Different strokes for different folks.

I remember how Ronnie seemed incredulous when I firmly stated, in response to a survey question, that I would not wish to switch identities to become white if that were possible. The question carried the weight of centuries of racism. How could we want to be what we were? How could we state, as I and most of the other fellows did, that we got pride, stimulation, moral insight and pleasure out of our identities? Wasn't--this question, this project implied--our identity in essence a stigma, a disability, a blotch? Our youths today need to learn to recognize the subtle forms of onslaught on their sense of identity and how to stand up to them and resist them and counter them. We got this from it: "O-ho, so that's their game here at Harvard. It's good we could peep it right off the bat." And having peeped it, we could move on, we had our bearings. Today's Black college youth are being encouraged to whine and to complain and to call in some sort of external authority figure to rescue them when they encounter bigotry. They aren't tough enough. Yet they cloak themselves in the phony and escapist toughness of rap, hip-hop and gangster clothing, and adopt silly and superficial cultural forms like special spellings gangsta', brotha', sistah and on and on. Somehow they are inculcated into demeaning themselves and their people.

W.E.B. DuBois's famed disquisition on the "twoness" of African-American lives and consciousness always draws a great deal of breast-beating attention, as if this is an affliction, and one unique to Blacks at that. In fact, twoness offers many rich and enjoyable experiences, delicious ironies, opportunities for private humor. Twoness is neither essentially tragic, nor is this sense of a dualistic identity and mode of living limited to our people. My judgment is that most of humanity lives this way. The most influential circumstances of my first year, and therefore perhaps my Harvard career in general, resulted not from ethnic identity but from my admission to the Riesman Freshman Seminars. The sociologist David Riesman convinced Harvard to try an innovative experiment by forming small groups of Harvard and Radcliffe students who would meet together in sections of eight or ten twice a week and once a month in a big gathering. We'd get credit for two courses--one of them being the required Gen Ed (General Education) writing course--and our work would be ungraded. I think there were perhaps four groups. Dorothy Lee, the Greek-American anthropologist, led mine. Paul and Susan Rudolph, Edward (Pat) Patullo, and Kenneth Keniston led other sections. I began to meet a number of classmates in a seminar format that let us get to know each other quite well. And I began to see one classmate in the monthly gatherings whom I very much wanted to get to know--a young woman whose every feature and facet filled me with awe. This was Elizabeth Penelope Subeva Charlotte Duffy of Akron, Ohio, who spoke about as little at the general meetings as I did. She stood at the edge and listened to our more voluble seminar classmates, and I stood at a vantage point that let me gaze at her.

Under the seminar format we'd all read whatever our section leader or fellow students had selected as a basis for discussion and reflection. Our group's subject usually related to issues of growing up in a cohort while developing individually, too. Supposedly we would do a lot of writing, too, hence liberation from the Gen Ed assignment. Each month all 30 or so of us would hear a famous figure tell his life story and then answer questions. And I do mean "his," for it strikes me now that none of these symbols of personal growth and achievement was female. The guests included Edward Land of Polaroid fame, Erik

Erikson, Erich Fromm, Dizzy Gillespie, James Robinson (founder of Operation Crossroads Africa), Arthur Maslow, and others.

Academically, however, I was just treading water. I'd said upon entering that I planned to study law, and I took Government 1 and Humanities 6. For most of the year, I understood very little of what was said in the former, a New Criticism-oriented lit course, and paid little attention to the lectures, reading or discussion in the latter. I had had little preparation for the kind of classroom discussion or analytical papers expected of us. And I felt, in the government course, that the various famous lecturers (Henry Kissinger among them) were spoonfeeding us a world view and a set of assumptions about democracy that seemed unsettlingly phony to me. I didn't know enough to know why I felt dissatisfied and perplexed. The prep school grads and grads from top New York City public and private schools were way ahead of me and most others from ordinary high schools on both the talking and writing fronts, and I enjoyed seeing and hearing them do their stuff without any feeling that their prowess reflected poorly on me. My grades on my Hum 6 papers were awful, with excoriating marginalia from the graduate section man, Stephen Orgel. We met individually now and then with our section men, and one day Orgel went over my paper and tried to keep a pained look from overwhelming his features as I offered my interpretation of what I meant to say about the assigned poem. Hum 6, headed by Reuben Brower, required a close reading of poems, meaning real knowledge of literary devices and an ability to tackle a work from the inside. We'd had nothing like that in high school.

Word got out that some of us Riesman Seminarians should probably not have escaped the required writing course, so the seminar brought in a special writing tutor, Babette (I believe) Spiegel, to help us. Several of us received notice that Spiegel expected to see us. I could not think of my writing with the dispassion and interest expected of me even to benefit even from remediation, however, so I skipped out after the first session or so. I was at sea but feeling no distress. That's because on the social front I was operating on all cylinders. I spent my waking hours visiting various rooms not only in Matthews North but around the Yard till 3-5 in the morning, which meant I arose at about 11 am. I headed our dorm sports teams and was responsible for making sure we fielded our squads in touch football, basketball and volleyball. Those responsibilities I carried out pretty well, except for costing us the volleyball championship by oversleeping.

Hanging out, I learned a lot about music and literature and, especially, art from my future best man the artist Michael Cain and his roommate Jim Weiss; about political theory from quintessential New York radical genius Fred Gardner, Frank Bardacke, Jon Weiner and my roommate Travis Williams; about life in the segregated South from Travis, Robert Gibbs and Charles Frazier; about music and literature from Fritz Eager. An Afro-American graduate student in economics named Amon Horne, who was somewhat mysterious in that he had a varying American, West Indian and East European accent, befriended Travis and me freshman year. Horne said he had received some schooling in Prague or Moscow, and he often lectured us with his Marxist-Leninist interpretation of domestic and international affairs. His knowledge and insights impressed us, and we delighted in his masterly debating skills, which he used to demolish more conventionally thinking white visitors to our room. I understood little of the theoretical aspects of his discourse at the time; he made his greatest impression on me when he told us about the heroic leader of the Monroe, North Carolina NAACP Robert Williams (no relation to Travis), who was then leading an armed defense of Black people against Klan marauders. The mass media reported next to nothing on this event. A couple of years later, Horne brought us copies of the then-exiled Williams's autobiography Negroes With Guns. The fact that our supposed enemies, the Communist countries, offered Williams sanctuary gave Travis and me a deeper insight into the complexities of the Cold War. The ability to expose U.S. racism on a world stage dominated by two vying superpowers gave African Americans precious political leverage back then--the careers of Williams, DuBois, Robeson, MLK and others show as much--and the downfall of the Soviet Union has given the American elite tactical space in which to turn its back today on the systemic prejudice and oppression that blast the life chances of so many Black people in our country. Travis and I strongly approved Robert Williams's analysis and actions, and the book was an eye-opener to the tradition of militant and radical responses to American racism. (About ten years later, I was among the first American journalists to interview Robert Williams upon his return from exile, but that's another story)

I studied piano throughout my youth, but no one discussed music seriously back home. Here, people did. My first of many listenings to Mingus's Pithecanthropus Erectus and Schubert's Death and the

Maiden in Fritz's room are indelible pleasures. I also recall that when I mispronounced "poignant," in commenting on a piece of music (I'd never heard anyone say it before and put in a hard 'g'), Fritz, a great poet and wit who wielded a sometimes maliciously sharp tongue, quickly used the word correctly in speaking to someone else in the room, rather than directly mortifying me for my ignorance. Fritz died of diabetes shock in 1969, a year after Travis, and that was an equal loss for me.

Fritz memorialized me in our 1963 Class Poem for my iconoclastic, anarchic nature, especially as I displayed it in snapping in two the wooden fence poles throughout the Yard with a forearm blow. Another episode chacteristic of my multilevel encounter with Harvard was my series of run-ins with a freshman proctor (proctors were graduate or professional school students who resided in freshman dorms). This law student didn't like the rebellious way I barely tied and loosely wore the mandatory necktie in the dining hall. Some preppies wore their ties loosely, too, but he singled me out in the Union one day and ordered me to adjust my tie. I said I would after everyone else with a loose tie tightened his. He formally ordered me to come to his room so we could discuss my "attitude." There, he said that one goal Harvard had in accepting more young men like me was to turn us into gentlemen. I burst out laughing and replied that I hadn't accepted admission to become a gentleman and that I probably had a much different definition of what constituted a gentleman than did the Harvard types who didn't care where their money came from.

Especially fascinating for me that first year was to hear the intense political discussion of classmates whose friends had been or perhaps still were Communists. This was right after the McCarthy repression, an era still influential enough to convince some classmates that they should not sign any ban-the-bomb or other petitions. Several said their parents had explicitly told them as they left home, "Don't sign any petitions!" The World Federalists and some other groups hooked me up at registration. They featured tremendous upperclassmen--orators who knew what was going on in the world. I agreed to take nuclear weapons freeze petitions around. This led me later to join the group picketing Woolworth's in Harvard Square that winter or spring in support of the sit-ins in the South. I think the late activist attorney W. Heywood Burns, who was a year ahead of me, was the only other Afro-American student who picketed regularly. I went every Saturday. Jewish guys and gals predominated in these activities. They were sincere, imaginative, brave, hard-working, fun, well-read, and dynamite arguers. One of them, Tony Roberts, I believe, suggested that Travis and I don Minuteman clothing and join him to protest against segregation at Concord cemetery on Patriot's Day. We struck an American Revolutionary pose and our photo appeared full-page in Life magazine.

I had participated in no activism back home. Kids of all backgrounds got along well in my southwestern Michigan community. Industrial and agricultural jobs were plentiful then. What's more, I was too well off to perceive the racist economic and social forces at work in that politically reactionary community until I left high school. But in late spring of 1959, a Virginia amusement park refused to let me enter with two white classmates from high school during spring break. That made me more sensitive to and primed me for battle against Jim Crow racism when I got to college that fall even though I had experienced little of it growing up, other than noticing the segregated facilities on our infrequent trips to the South. At college, I began to feel ever more strongly that in addition to being a mavericky individualist I was also part of a people with a rich and challenging history and culture, a people who needed to step up the battle for freedom, justice and equality and not take s**t from anybody.

In any event, my freshman year assumed a pattern: I learned a great deal from a variety of classmates, paid little attention to class work, skipped most lectures in government, and tried to figure out how I would meet the aforementioned Elizabeth Duffy. Social life for us Black men was out of the campus norm. When Harvard had only a handful of us in any given class, a woman in Boston whom we dubbed "the Great Black Mama" arranged little chaste parties at her house, to which she invited local college girls presumed to be of suitable status for match-making. There were too many of us, too much testosterone, for the local young socialite Jack-and-Jill types to absorb, even if only metaphorically. And as far as Black women classmates went, there was just one. In all of Radcliffe, there may have been three Black women at that time. At the mixers at Radcliffe, Wellesley, and other area colleges, we danced with those Euro-American girls who seemed to give off vibes that they were not racists. Sometimes we misinterpreted vibes and got a polite, "I'd rather not." The search for female companionship intensified as the weeks went by. We did a lot of walking around Boston University, Simmons, and other schools, dropping in on parties with "our folks." Most of us rejected the Black fraternity-sorority scene, though. My father wanted me to be an Alpha like him, so I went to a couple of initiation meetings. At the second one, we went individually into a dark room where "Brothers" holding candles asked us questions. I found the procedures too silly to continue any further and have never changed my opinion. The taboo-busting awakening of the 1960s had not yet begun, so there were few let-it-all-hang-out neighborhood parties. Those times were, praise be, right around the corner. Working individually and in concert, those of us who were sufficiently hormonally charged, or who had a social network deriving from their Big City status, found dates or at least pressed a hot and continual search for them. Our seminar went to Bunny Hollow, New Hampshire, for spring break, the weekend of Shakespeare's birthday, around April 22nd. Someone had volunteered us to spruce up a camp for underprivileged kids from the New York City area. I took a date from the University of Maine, the daughter of a Black Air Force colonel who had been buddies with my dad at Tuskegee in World War II, and whose family and ours kept in touch. But my eyes couldn't stray long from Eliza Duffy as we chopped down trees, cleared brush, nailed cabins, roasted food outdoors. After everyone else had retired--a few of them pairing up romantically--I made a bet with Eliza and our mutual friend Joan Strasser that they would fall asleep before I did. This permitted me an exclusive and infatuating evening in Eliza's company. After spring break was over, I told Travis I had confirmed the fact that I had fallen in love at first sight. He advised me to be bold.

First, I joined a little group from our seminar that biked to Walden Pond, swam there and biked back. I was among a few who drank quite a bit of rum at the pond, and on the return, Eliza and I broke ahead of the group and biked closely enough to talk all the way back, right through those racist Boston suburbs, I being as smitten as a person can be and she not suspecting it. Near the end of our first year, having begun to converse with her whenever possible at the seminar, I invited Eliza to join me, Mike Hattwick and another Cliffie in climbing the outside of Memorial Church to the belfry, and then to continue the climb to the pinnacle from inside that venerable structure's tower. The other girl chickened out, but Eliza, Mike and I did it. As the year closed, I asked her if I might write her some letters in the summer to describe my experiences as a barbecue deliveryman in Chicago.

My pursuit of Eliza, contesting for her attention with three or four other suitors, consumed my sophomore year. I had decided to take all pre-med courses at one time--physics, chemistry and biology--despite my lack of interest in any of those fields or in medicine. My father is a physician, so I thought I should give it a crack, then get a law degree and practice forensic medicine. I wasn't interested in law much either, however. Eliza was my lab partner in biology. I soon stopped attending physics lectures or labs, and chemistry became a blur after we entered mathematically demanding areas. I didn't care. I was at Radcliffe every day, or invited her to Leverett House, where I roomed with three swimmers, Al Engelberg, Gordy Lund and John Arnold, and a lawyer-to-be, Jack Nordby. I knew if I roomed with Travis again I would do no studying. Besides, he had begun to drink too much after being a teetotaler from youth. I visited him regularly at Dunster House, nonetheless.

Kennedy-Nixon Election Day remains a strong memory. The previous spring of freshman year, Fidel Castro had come to campus to seek support from the United States, and campus Democrats had held a national mock political convention in which the organized student supporters of Hubert Humphrey, John F. Kennedy, G. Mennen Williams (our delegation's favorite son), and others showed up. Great young orators from the political clubs showed their skills, and leftwing Democrats (the Humphreyites) pretty much prevailed over moderates to the Kennedy group's keen chagrin, because they had poured in lots of money and political operators to avoid defeat in his home state and at his alma mater at that. On November election day, I joined Eliza and other former Seminar members at the apartment of Peter and Sharon Labovitz. Pete was among the first '63ers to marry, and Sharon was the daughter of ABC TV newsman Frank McGee. We drank a lot, and I reeled into Cabot Hall, Eliza's dorm, despite the rule barring men after hours. I still recall the distressed look of the dorm mother as she shooed me and a comrade out. Most of the girls, all bedecked in flowing nightgowns, were amused. Only three or so shrieked briefly. "We just want to see the vote returns," I protested. "Don't worry about how you look. I have three sisters." A senior girl, the future New York politico Elizabeth Holtzman, politely ushered us out.

In sophomore year we were supposed to select our major and write an essay in the second semester to show our stuff. After one semester, I figured I'd better bail out with my bad grades and my energies channeled in nonacademic directions. Many fellows took leaves of absence to explore some extracurricular interest, sight-see, or pull themselves together. You simply told an adminstrator you were going off in the boonies or somewhere overseas to acquire discipline, maturity and worldly knowledge. That's what I said I planned to do. But I may have been the first person to spend his leave in Cambridge. This permitted me to see Eliza at any time she was available, read on my own, audit classes, carouse, and enjoy free rooming and almost free board by sacking out in dorms and sneaking into the dining halls. For spending money, I took a little part-time job with Michael Cain, putting gummed sheets over the windows of a 19th century factory. We hitchhiked to New York City, where well-heeled Bohemian types he knew gave us our first marijuana. All I can remember is sitting under a table giggling and later identifying very closely with a piece of gum I spit out an 8th floor window.

I decided that I would major in English literature when I resumed my studies, the area that had always furnished delight since boyhood. Why not spend your college days learning about what you love? To hell with professionaldom and practicality. That April, President Kennedy mounted the criminal Bay of Pigs invasion, convincing most Harvard men on leave that they'd better head back to school pronto or risk being drafted into World War III. At the end of the year, I said farewell to Eliza after we'd enjoyed visits to museums and parks thanks to Miles Jaffe's loan of a motor scooter. When I got home, my father diagnosed me with the mononucleosis that sapped me for much of the summer. I figure if you contract mono on a leave of absence, you've had an exceptionally productive experience. The mono gave me plenty of time to read. Two books proved unusually affecting, I.A. Richards's The Meaning of Meaning and Henry James's The Portrait of a Lady. Somehow, poring over and parsing these two knotty texts sharpened my mind. If I or anyone else knew how such a transformation occurs, we'd be the leading gurus of educational development. My reading constituted some sort of mental calisthenics that got my mind in academic ship-shape.

The rumors of war that I've mentioned meant that when I returned as a second-semester sophomore in the fall of 1961, so many other fellows cancelled or cut short their leaves that Harvard lacked dormitory space for us. They put the overflow in a barracks, but classmate Mike Hattwick and I decided that that was unacceptable housing. Prof. Dorothy Lee, our Riesman Seminar mentor, let us room in the third floor of Howard Mumford Jones's house, which she was house-sitting. It was on Francis Avenue, Cambridge's most prestigious street; our neighbors were top faculty like John Kenneth Galbraith. Mike and I and a few others were among the first Harvard men to successfully petition for the right to live off campus--out of the house system that was meant to mold us into Harvard men. Once off, we never returned, and I lived in a series of apartments ever afterward. (Twice in the remaining three years my roommates and I had to take landlords through anti-discrimination procedures once they discovered that Afro-Americans were among the lessees. This proved to be good training for the real world; my wife and I had to wage a similar legal battle in New Haven in 1967.) That fall I enrolled in Einar Haugen's course on Henrik Ibsen and Albert Lord's "Singer of Tales," about the oral epic. Haugen, a Swede, I believe, was a visiting professor from the University of Minnesota, about 55 years old then, which made him an old gentleman to us in those days. He was gracious, supportive, and encouraging, and invited our class to his home to feast with him and his wife a couple of times. He told me my papers on Ibsen were excellent. I did well in Lord's course, too, and he too was kind and supportive. I was also taking a course in intellectual history with H. Stuart Hughes. Though I'm interested in politics, the reading was hardly magnetic, though his lectures were fine and Eliza also took the course.

That year, I received another intellectual jolt I can recall to this day in my individual tutorial with David Littlejohn, the brilliant head section man of Walter Jackson Bate's great course on literary criticism and now an incisive arts critic for the Wall Street Journal. Littlejohn assigned me Rousseau on the social contract, and asked me in tutorial what was the most obvious hole in Rousseau's theory. I suggested several possibilities, but plainly had not hit the intended mark. And then Littlejohn asked me, "What does this contract say? Who drew it up? Who signed it?" As I reflected on this soon afterward, and in all the years since, I felt I'd received a mind-opening gift, a magical instrument of analysis. A bulls**t detector, as it were. Because Rousseau's grand notion was a concoction, and to accept such abstractions--constructs, as they are called in today's critical jargon--as if they are "really real" is to disarm yourself in the face of Rousseau or any other propagandist.

My courses confirmed my decision to major in English language and literature, and that spring began a run of English courses that, over the next three years, saw me cover all of English literature from Anglo Saxon through the early 1900s quite thoroughly (except Chaucer, which I took in grad school, when I got my MA at Harvard). A favorite study game I enjoyed was to have Eliza or a friend read from any poem in any anthology, and I would guess the poet. I got quite good at that. During these Harvard days, I never detected the hint of condescension or bigotry from any professor or section man, and my radar is as fine-tuned as the next Afro-American's on such points. In fact, never in my entire Cambridge experience did I experience a racist action or demeaning remark from a classmate. Many had different views on the nature and sources of racism and what to do about it, but that's another matter. Friends don't have to coincide in ideas, tastes and ideology. The school was still keeping the lid on women in those days, and I think female students encountered much more squelching, disrespect, and bias than we Black men did.

Once I hit academic stride, with my relationship with Eliza stabilizing and our having the freedom to be with each other at class and meals for most of the day, I thrived. At the end of the 1962 academic year, or maybe that spring vacation, Eliza and I hitchhiked from Cambridge to Ithaca, New York, where she was born, and caught a bus from there to her parent's home in Akron. A classmate who saw us on the highway thought some Klan-type would probably kill me or both of us, but even though we did foolishly accept a brief turnpike ride with some drunken and dangerous hoodlums, we made it, and I met her parents. Her father was an English professor from an Irish-American family from Dubuque, Iowa, and her mother was a Bulgarian her father met in Sofia when he was a member of the U.S. legation in the late '30s, right before World War II.

My Harvard days had plainly turned into everything a college student anywhere could have hoped for, with the love of literature and intellectual stimulation joining socializing with a variety of firm friends, and the meeting of one's beloved wife-to-be. I joined the literary magazine, The Harvard Advocate, and was book editor though I did hardly any work. Earlier, I joined a group that put out a short-lived literary journal called The War Baby Review.

I was also a charter member of the Harvard Association of African and African-American Students, one of the first campus groups of its kind. I discovered that I was a "race man" in the 1920s-30s sense of a person keenly interested in defense and advance of his ethnic group, but I was also a strongly anti-racist man, including the kind of chauvinist nationalism in my own group, which I saw was psychologically and spiritually composed of the same elements as racism. In other words, I see in a number of Blacks the same narrow-minded group-mindedness that White racists evince, the difference being that such Blacks are not in a position to act on these tendencies.

When Malcolm X came to campus in the fall of 1963 or early 1964, I remembered how thrilling it had been to watch him, when I was home summers in Benton Harbor, take on all sorts of White scholars and pundits on the Irv Kupcinet talk show on Chicago TV. Malcolm's informed, bold, witty and incisive rebuttals stirred young men and women like me. But he studded his Harvard lecture with all sorts of crackpot Black-racist nonsense and condemned Whites as persons no Black person could trust or befriend. I saw quite a number of Afro-American Harvard students, staff and faculty beam, nod, and laugh at Malcolm's every reverse-racist jest.

Even though I would later write one of the first laudatory reviews of his autobiography for Negro Digest when I was at Johnson Publishing Company, I found certain of Malcolm's statements and the fawning reception they received from most of the Blacks there disgusting and disturbing. Years later, the longtime Dean of Harvard Students Archie Epps even published Malcolm's Harvard speeches with no critique of Malcolm's false historical concepts, anti-Semitism and reverse bigotry. I still regret that I did not denounce certain of Malcolm X statements right then and there, as I was tempted to do. I detest hypocrisy and nationalism of that sort, and almost all nationalism is of that sort: the kente cloth nationalism of today, the pork chop nationalism of those days. I can sympathize with occasionally but never share the nationalism of any individual or nationality unless they are physically, literally, fighting for their lives against a nationalistic oppressor. And even this justified nationalism quickly turns sour if its carriers chance to triumph. I could point to several instances of this phenomenon today.

My Harvard teachers all stand out to me: my tutors David Littlejohn and Barry Hayne; superb graduate student instructors like Anthony Heilbut and Rachel Jakoff; William Alfred who granted me independent study during my extra semester (I stayed for four and a half years since I returned from my leave after only one semester off) and whom I still owe a paper; great lecturers and scholars Douglas Bush, Herschel Baker, Bartlett Jere Whiting, Harry Levin, Walter Jackson Bate, Daniel Seltzer, Monroe Engel, the poet Robert Lowell, and even, in my last semester, the great I. A. Richards, himself. I wrote an idiosyncratic thesis on Henry James's What Maisie Knew and graduated with high honors.

By the close of my undergraduate days, I had had a great group of roommates as well. In addition to Williams, Engelberg, Nordby, Lund, Hattwick, Cain and Blau whom I've already mentioned, they were Richard Silberg, Lionel Deckle McLain, Peter Kelley, Gary Robertson and Leonard Gottlieb (Boston U.).

After graduation I joined a group of fellow recent graduates, graduate students and a few professors and went to Tougaloo College in Mississippi to teach summer school. I was the only Black Harvardian in the group. I didn't want to work in SNCC because I simply don't have whatever it takes to face armed attackers with no matching weapons of my own. It was the summer of the murders in 1964 and full of too many impressions and adventures to record here. That fall I was off to the University of Chicago to take a crack at grad school sociology in the Committee of Social Science or something like that. I hated it. Why I selected this field I don't know. I thought it might be broadening and also that I might discover a field that led to social action and change. I was at sixes and sevens again because after graduating in 1963, Eliza had gone to Germany during my 1963-64 senior year to get her MA in German languages and literature. Her parents hoped that the separation would end a relationship that they feared would lead to their daughter's facing painful life experiences as a result of American racism. One day in late fall of 1964, Eliza called and said, "Let's get married." We did so about as quickly as we could, in January 1965, and lived briefly in Chicago's Hyde Park. After being drafted and narrowly managing to avoid entry into the armed service (which meant narrowly missing becoming a Canadian citizen, because that's where I was headed if I didn't get a 1-Y deferment), I returned to Harvard for two years of graduate school in English that fall. The war and civil rights struggles were kicking up, and I'd already had the pleasure of working in journalism, having joined Jet and Ebony after quitting the University of Chicago after a month of the dullest reading and lectures I've ever encountered.

Deciding an English professorship would offer me little excitement, I went to Yale Law School in the fall of 1967, and we had our first child, Duffy. Hated the reading, hated the law, and returned to journalism, first in New Haven, then back to Chicago. In 1968, I joined the staff of the Black Muslim newspaper, Muhammad Speaks, and became editor-in-chief for three years beginning in 1972. It may seem an odd choice, perhaps symptomatic of the divided self I spoke of at the outset of this piece. Actually, it was a matter of covering what I wanted to cover and giving utterance to radical opinions at full throat. I was free, and I had more than 400,000 weekly readers. The experience also, I think, give my views on nationalism some credibility. They are based on close-hand experience. I became more politically involved, went to many pro-socialist, anti-war and progressive Black events in those years, traveled to Mongolia, editorially supported the Vietnamese in their defense against the United States as well as other Third World anti-imperialist movements, and made connections that later helped me visit Afghanistan, Czechoslovakia, the Soviet Union, East Germany and Cuba.

Later, I worked for the Chicago Sun Times and New York Times, for Ford Motor Company publications, and now edit a University of Michigan alumni publication with the nation's largest circulation for a publication of its kind. I try to keep my hand in Black affairs by occasionally writing for the Black Scholar, a journal where our daughter Maize works as assistant editor. Our third child, Will, is a mechanical engineer. And the eldest, Duffy, is, of all things, a Marine helicopter pilot. They say what goes around comes around, but I'll be darned if I know what it was that went around.

8. Yale Memories: A Look Back, By yolanda joe, Yale Class of 1984,Trumbull College.

To the Tune of "I Wish" by Stevie Wonder

Looking back on when I was a little girl enrolled at Yale.....
Then my only worry was for finals what I'd pass or fail.....
Even though we sometimes did not get good good grades
we were happy with the effort that we made!
Sneaking out of Harkness, hang out with my Buddies
at The House....
Greeted at the Bur-sar with, Girl, thought I told you not
to charge that stuff!
Trying your best to bring the water to your eyes
thinking it might stop them from taking your lunch card!

I wish those days would come back once more
why did those days ev-er have to go...
I wish those days would come back once more
why did those days ev-er have to go...
we loved them so... Do-do-dupe-dupe-do-dupe-do-do...

Professor says Im sorry, can't accept ah-nother Deans excuse...
Just one more, Ill give you nothing but the best I can
really do....
Mama tells you baby, go to Sunday school...
Sermons at Black Church are what get you through...
Smoking pipes and waving hankys on the march thru Phelps hall....
Parents goin crazy especially when your name is called..
You grad-u-ate and learn that, college was alright...
But while you were doing it, the diploma seemed out of sight!

I wish those days would come back once more
why did those days ev-er have to go...
I wish those days would come back once more
why did those days ev-er have to go...
we loved them so... Do-do-dupe-dupe-do-dupe-do-do...

9. Ernest L. Wilson, III, H'1970[50]-- The Reform of Tradition, the Tradition of Reform

Ernest James Wilson III was born on 3 May 1948 in Washington, D.C., where he attended the Capitol Page School. At Harvard he was business manager of the Harvard Jounal of Negro Affairs, and edited its special issue on "The Black Press." A concentrator in government, he received his A.B. in 1970. Pursuing graduate studies in Berkeley at the University of California, he earned his M.A. in 1973 and Ph.D. in political science in 1978. For a time he served as legislative assistant to Congressman Charles Diggs Jr., and in 1974 was the first-prize winner in the first Du Bois Essay Awards established by Black Scholar magazine. A specialist in the oil market, he has traveled and lectured in Europe, Africa and Latin America, and been an energy consultant for the World Bank and the U.S. Departments of State and Interior. From 1977 to 1981 he was on the faculty of the University of Pennsylvania.

Since then he has been a professor of political science at the University of Michigan, where he also became Director of the Center for Research on Economic Development in the fall of 1988.

The Reform of Tradition, the Tradition of Reform

---

[50] Reprint from Blacks at Harvard, New York:New York University Press, 1993.

Two influences, outside of the family, did the most to form my character. The first was the educational and religious enthusiasm at Howard University, Washington, D.C., where my father was professor of Latin, and where I lived on the campus from birth until I entered Harvard. The second great influence was the atmosphere of tolerance, justice, and truth at Harvard. Endeavoring not to swerve under the stress from the principles thus engendered, sometimes to the detriment of material and official advancement, has been the greatest satisfaction of my life.

This quotation from my grand-uncle, Harvard class of 1897, expresses at least two interesting elements relevant to this essay. First, it acknowledges the formative role that Harvard College can play in an individual's life. This is a traditional refrain in the writing of black and white college graduates--Harvard shaped their lives.

Seventy years later, the black student experience at Harvard College put a twist on this refrain. For in the mid to late 1960s we changed Harvard as Harvard changed us. In our own selective acceptance and rejection of the traditional Harvard experience, my fellow students and I challenged Harvard in unprecedented ways, and in the process we changed the scholarly structure of the University.

Some of us were also guided by the second element of Eugene Gregory's class report--his firm grounding in autonomous Afro- American values and the supports provided by an indigenous black institution--Howard University. These values of cultural autonomy and worth also informed our own time at Harvard College.

In my freshman year there was no Department of Afro-American Studies, no Du Bois Institute, no cultural center for black students. Racial issues were not high on the priority of the University administration. The subject of Afro-America was not widely treated in the traditional disciplines and departments. My freshman year there were few black students in leadership positions in major campus-wide organizations. In other words black campus life was not unlike what it had been in the 1930s when Ralph Bunche was a student, or for that matter, when W.E.B. Du Bois was a student in the late 19th century. When Du Bois and others wrote of their lives at Harvard they usually described themselves as black refugees to fair Harvard. They came; they studied what the University offered; they left. Harvard in those years admitted the occasional black student, but it did not admit the study of black life and culture as an important and legitimate element of the curriculum. This was the Harvard I found in 1966. By the end of the 1960s, these conditions were to change.

I have elsewhere described the political and institutional history of Afro-American studies at Harvard [Harvard Magazine, Sept.-Oct. 1981]. Here, I want to indulge the personal side of that history and to indicate some of the personal motivations and values that led at least one undergraduate into student activism. In my own case these values include an assumption of the validity of Afro-American life and culture, and that their study was a high calling. With this came another family-instilled value--a strong belief that excellence in scholarship could, and should, be combined with intellectual activism. Third, I benefitted in my student days from a long familiarity with university life.

Through the decade of the 1960s dozens of white and black students participated in challenges to fair Harvard's traditional sense of itself and they pressed to make Harvard more open to the scholarly examination of gender and race. Many found common purpose to press for educational reform. They came from a variety of places and from different backgrounds. They were motivated by a variety of personal and political reasons.

In my freshman year (1966), I often sensed more than a whiff of condescension toward black students. Some whites acted as if we were a black tabula rasa ready to be filled with New England education and high culture. Others caricatured us as the carriers of the culture of James Brown; any interest in the written word, or in Beethoven, was somehow disappointing and inauthentic. Then in 1967 and 1968 the black rebellions in the cities and the upsurge in nationalism and activism among black students created conditions ripe for a black student movement at Harvard, as at other colleges and universities.

What we accepted and what we rejected during this highly politicized period reflected the personal history that each of us brought to the institution. Many black students eventually seized on similar political values, usually reformist and nationalist; all took different roads to get there. My own experience at Harvard certainly reflected my personal--and family--history. Some of the values and interests that I brought from home Harvard positively reinforced--intellectual curiosity, delight in a spirited and partisan argument, a breadth of experiences, social and political engagement. Some skills and outlooks I learned for the first time. However, other personal values Harvard denied--especially the validity and autonomy of Afro-American cultural life, and the importance of studying it. Nonetheless, I strengthened my commitment to these values as I struggled to give them a reality and meaning within the University. Indeed, struggling against the rejection of values that I took to be self-evident became an important part of my Cambridge education.

I grew up on the campus of Howard University in Washington, D.C., born in Freedman's Hospital, living in campus housing. Each day I walked through the center of the campus, past the clustered classroom buildings named for Frederick Douglass and Sojourner Truth, and under the imposing if familiar presence of Founder's Library, to attend Lucretia Mott School, the segregated elementary school just catercornered from Freedman's on Fourth Street. My young world was well contained on the campus, and Howard University was home. I had a proprietary feel for the place, and as a child I felt it was (almost literally) my own and my home. My father worked in the new red brick administration building overlooking Benjamin Banneker School just across Georgia Avenue. My maternal great-grandfather was in Howard's first graduating class of five students and later taught there; my maternal grandfather taught Latin and English, and co-founded the Howard University Players, the first drama society. In the 1940s my father studied at Howard with E. Franklin Frazier, Alain Locke ['08], [William] Leo Hansberry [A.M. '32] and Rayford Logan [Ph.D. '36]. And into the 1960s, siblings and assorted cousins passed through its gates. University life for me was immediate and personal.

In that community, and around our warm and constantly crowded kitchen table, came professors and poets and students and friends (for example, poet-professor Sterling Brown [A-M. '23], my grandfather's student and friend, and my father's teacher and friend). Discussions were debates and all were engaged, enthusiastic and loud. My father led discussions that ranged from Negro spirituals to Nietzsche, and an important constant was the everpresent threat and fact of racial inequality in a racist society. That external threat, and the values of my extended family, meant that learning and scholarship were from the earliest days tied to social relevance. Howard University had a mission--to better the race through medicine, through law, through philosophy. It was to demonstrate too that black people could excel. Relevance did not mean any less excellence. On the contrary. Our best scholars devoted themselves to superior social and natural science, and to moral uplift.

If I felt proprietary about Howard University, and if it nourished in me a strongly critical sense of committed learning, I felt somewhat the same way about Harvard University. Not in an immediate sense, but as a place I was familiar with but hadn't yet visited. My maternal grandfather, T. Montgomery Gregory, was a member of the Harvard class of 1910, a friend of John Reed and Walter Lippmann, to whom he introduced me in 1966. He was active on the debating team and a lifelong loyal son of Harvard. His son [Thomas Montgomery Gregory, Jr.] was a member of the class of '44, and his older brother, Eugene, was in the class of 1897.

It was assumed that after high school I would follow one part of the family tradition and become the fourth member of the family to go to Harvard. I would take with me a tradition of critical thinking, a predisposition to teach, a familiarity with university life, and an abiding belief in the importance of studying Afro-American life. All of this helped me, I now believe, in helping to bring Afro-American studies to Harvard.

As an underclassman at Harvard, I felt a mixture of sheer delight and naive surprise. The former was promoted by the enormous wealth of things to do and learn in Cambridge--lectures, recitals, and plays, people to talk to and to listen to. The surprise (and several years later, as race relations deteriorated nationally, outrage) flowed from the invisibility of the things I took for granted at home--the disciplined and serious and sustained study of black culture, politics, and life.

Part of that struggle between 1966 and 1970 involved me and other undergraduates as negotiators with a not inconsiderable array of faculty, administrators, overseers and alumni. Those of us on the negotiating team (most notably Robert Hall ['69], now professor of history at University of Maryland, who also grew up on a college campus and had experiences similar to my own; Francesta Farmer ['71], President of Crossroads Africa; business executive Craig Watson ['72]; and Harlan Dalton ['69], on the Yale Law School faculty) drew up lists of those from whom we expected opposition, and support, and we visited each in turn to lobby and to discuss the merits of bringing Afro-American Studies to Harvard.

In retrospect, we had a lot of gall even to attempt such changes; we were just wet-behind-the-ears undergraduates. Part of the hubris came from our feeling that, at last, history was going our way. We knew that we were riding the crest of a wave. With Nina Simone singing that all of us were "young, gifted and black," we felt our newly assertive blackness was not just an extra burden, as it was for many of our predecessors, but also at times a decided social benefit. And after all, cities were literally burning over the question of black equality; and the real heroes of the black revolt, courageous black students in the Deep South, were engaged in far less genteel and more dangerous battles at Ol' Miss and Texas Southern. For us, pressing for Afro-American Studies in Cambridge seemed the least we could do. And the excitement of creating something new, scholarly and socially relevant was exhilarating.

Part of my own self-confidence came from my earlier experiences as a page in the U.S. Supreme Court between 1963 and my graduation from high school in 1966. During those three and a half years, I met senators and congressmen on a regular basis, lunched with Chief Justice Warren, met President Johnson and Vice President Humphrey, and got to know many in the Washington diplomatic community. Fortunately, some of these contacts were substantive and not merely ceremonial, and I gradually assumed that talking to one's elders, including putatively distinguished ones, was not in the least unusual.

Washington and the Page School were good preparation in other ways. While enjoying a successful high-school career in a student body that, like Capitol Hill as a whole in those days, was entirely dominated by southern whites, I was able to sustain my close friendships with friends in my northwest Washington neighborhood. Nor did being a page prevent me from joining the "Free DC" movement led by activist Marion Barry, or other progressive causes. I also developed life-long friends in Washington's diplomatic community. I relished the rich multicultural life of the city, and I was determined to continue that life in Cambridge. Thus, while I was very active in and head of several campus black-student organizations and publications, I also joined the Harvard Lampoon, wrote for the Crimson, ate at the Signet, was elected a Class Marshal and joined one of Harvard's final clubs [the Fly], well-known locally for its splendid spring garden parties.

All of this seems very neat and tidy in retrospect, and I suppose I view it as such today. But re-reading my diaries and journals from that period I can also see it in a different light. I recall feeling the demands and pulls from different directions by different communities. In the late 1960s bigoted nationalist students would taunt and insult other black students walking across the Yard with a white friend. I refused to be taunted, or a taunter. Nonetheless, the pressures to conform to narrow and preconceived notions of racial or social categories were intense. I and others resisted as best we could. Harvard did not teach me these particular "balancing" skills, but it certainly sharpened them. Harvard reinforced my love of politics and of the intellectual life, and, however imperfectly, showed me that the intellectual life and the life of commitment can, with effort and imagination, be combined.

I left Harvard with the usual complement of new intellectual skills and classroom learning. I also learned valuable lessons about institutional change. Black students in this topsy-turvy time did succeed in expanding the realm of the possible and opening new possibilities for choice in the College and the University. We helped to legitimate and expand the study of Afro-American life at the University.

In retrospect, I also left Cambridge somewhat naive about the resilience of big institutions and their ability to follow their own worn paths, and the manifold ways that institutions resist and thwart change. Inertia, racism, and unhealthy elitism proved harder to change than we as undergraduates realized. Forcing choices into seemingly choiceless conditions still does not guarantee that the choices made will be the most desirable ones. The imperfect and odd choices that all parties made in the early days of the Afro-American Studies Program and the Du Bois Institute at Harvard, including some that students made, are cases in point.

The Harvard I left in 1970 (and revisited in 1980 as a Fellow at the Kennedy School of Government) is different from the one I found in 1966. Now there is a niche in which interested black and white faculty and students can more easily find programs and materials on black life in America. They can also find an even more precious present than that which those of us in that time tried to leave behind--the institutional and intellectual legitimacy of studying black life without fear of being mocked or marginalized. That struggle is not yet completely won at Harvard or at other universities. It is, however, an important beginning that we bequeath to students and scholars who follow us. I am confident they will continue the tradition.

10. Ronald Matchett/ Muhammad Abdullah, Y'1970

As my Aunt Margie and Uncle Harry took me up interstate highway 95 along the Atlantic Ocean, an ocean that was not as pretty as what I had seen of the Pacific, I recall what occurred to me when I first laid eyes on New Haven and Yale. "New Haven was definitely no New York." At that point, the best that could be said about New Haven is that it was near New York (a fact often cited in Yale Admissions literature). Skyline? If you blinked, you could miss the New Haven skyline. And I think I must have blinked. Because the next thing I knew we were approaching the entrance to Yale University: Phelps Gate.

I don't know who in the hell Phelps was, but this was his Gate. It served as the threshold to the section of Yale where all the freshman lived: the O-l-d campus. Now that should have been my first clue. What did Dante say upon entering his inferno? "Abandon All Hope Ye Who Enter Here!" Phelps gate was intimidating! Beyond this gate was Yale. At least, so I thought. It was really only a part of Yale. As vast as the area beyond Phelps gate appeared, it was only a small portion of Yale; Yale was bigger still. "Should I turn back now?" The thought crept into my mind. It was too late now. My Aunt Margie was with me. If she, with her little self, could conquer the greatest city on the face of the earth, New York City, then I, with my big self, had better conquer the greatest university in the world (Harvard, Cambridge and Oxford notwithstanding). After all, I had been exposed to that Tuskegee air too. It was conquering time, and now was as good a time as any. I pressed on, but not as they do in Star Trek: "boldly where no man has gone before." Now that I think of it, this was before Star Trek. Can you imagine that today when we have had so many offspring or generations of Star Trek (Star Trek, Star Trek the Next Generation, Star Trek Deep Space Nine, Star Trek Voyager, and that's not counting the Trek movies). Well in 1966, standing before Phelps Gate was a challenge of "universal proportions" for me, and I was going boldly where no "Matchett" had ever gone before.

Phelps Gate opened onto the city of New Haven and its center Green. As I was to learn, in the early days of the American English Colonies and the young democracy of which New Haven, Connecticut was a part, it was the custom throughout the New England States for local citizens to practice governing themselves upon greens in the midst of the towns in which they lived. I was now looking upon such a green. It was the original center of town where citizens of the early colonies would gather to vote, to discuss, and to govern. Not coincidentally, that Yale would first locate itself adjacent to this governing center, is a fact whose meaning I did not then fully appreciate. It seems that Yale had been interested in governing from the beginning.

As I approached the building where I'd live, Vanderbilt hall, I noticed that it was a lot like Phelps Gate: impressive. Legend has it that the Vanderbilts did in fact build Vanderbilt Hall. In the Vanderbilt will it states that when a descendent of the Vanderbilts comes to Yale, he would be allowed to live in the Vanderbilt suite that sits above the Vanderbilt Hall archway. As fate would have it, a young Vanderbilt came to Yale in 1969, and even though this was the year that Vanderbilt Hall became a residence for Yale women only, he wanted his suite. Supposedly, Yale refused, and in the suit that followed, the young Vanderbilt won and got his way. He and his three roommates lived in the midst of the Women of Yale, one of which is now the "ex wife" of the young Vanderbilt. I wonder who got the best of who. Another Yale legend. I suspect there is story behind every building at Yale.

On our walk to Vanderbilt, I passed Connecticut Hall in front of which stood a statute of young Nathan Hale, Yale Class of 1773. Said Hale: "I only regret that I have but one life to give (lose) for my country." Rumor has it that this statute was not in fact the actual likeness of Nathan Hale. He was killed so young that they had no photographs of him. So after the Revolutionary War, they gathered the entire class at Yale, and selected the "Yalie who looked the most patriotic" to be the likeness from which the Nathan Hale statute would be made. It is another one of those Yale legends I would learn. But, since Nathan Hale is synonymous with patriotism, I believe the legend to be true. This was indeed history, and I was to be living in the midst of it.

I don't know what I was expecting to see. I thought Yale, with all its money, would be this super-fabulous place with great new facilities and state of art in everything. After all, like most people, when we are growing up we associate money with having the ability to go out and buy anything you want, go where you please and do what you please. The more money, the more good "new" stuff you could buy, new like the wonderful smell of the interior of a brand new car; that's "what I'm talkin' bout." Hey, it cost enough to go there. Man, the tuition alone was $3,000 per year. By the time you add in room and board, you could spend $5,000 per year to go. At the time, that was one of the highest price tags for college education in all of America.

With great anticipation, I opened the door to my room in Vanderbilt Hall. I looked around at this vast room. But, the thought that rushed to the surface of my mind screamed: "This is old! I mean rusty dusty Old. You hear me, Old." You could see the dust in the air. You could cut it with a knife. If I had had my sinus condition back then, I would have long ago run out into the courtyard gasping for air. My chin must have hit the floor. I was extremely disappointed. I did not want my Aunt Margie to leave me in this place. "Can I get a nice new hotel room until we get this room stuff right?" That was what was going through my mind. Seeing and visiting the historical is one thing, but living in it, is quite another.

This place was ancient and truly did not resemble what I was expecting or hoping to see. It was dark and there was little or no furniture in the place. I walked around in this rather massive living room, that contained a large fireplace, the hardwood floors, a mahogany mantelpiece, and custom molding. There were two windows in the living room that looked out from our first floor room unto the court yard of Vanderbilt. Off of the living room, there were two bed rooms. Each bedroom contained two twin-size beds (looked like army issue, military type stuff. You know, the kind of stuff even the Spartans would have considered a little tough). Nearby there was adequate study space. I would rarely study here, my domain would become a comfortable chair in front of the fireplace in the L&B room in Yale's main Sterling Library, or 15 stories up in the dusty stacks of Sterling (the real Ivy Tower) where real thinking was done and preserved. Before leaving Yale, I would take up smoking a pipe (which generally contained tobacco). The L&B room had a lot to do with that. It seemed the appropriate thing to do. O o h?the aroma of a pipe with cherry tobacco. Can you smell it? Mixed with the smell of a good fire, and you are talking about some studying; ya hear me! You talking about curling up with a good book. At Yale, you are talking about a lot of good books. I would spend a lot time reading Hegel and the other great philosophers in this room.

Going to Yale really was like entering Camelot. Into this setting, I was cast with three remarkable young people, my roommates. One, of Jewish ancestry, was out of the New York area, smart as he could be and he wanted to be a lawyer; he played a strange game called Squash. The only squash I had ever heard of one ate. And, I did not have much of an appetite for eating them either, much less playing a game bearing their name. Do you know that Yale had more squash courts than it had basketball courts? What a strange place indeed. As we came to say in those days, "different strokes for different folks." My other roommate, also of Jewish ancestry, was a Connecticut native who had grown up near Yale and he, like myself, was a psychology major with his heart set on medicine. The last of the lot, an All-American chap out of the best of mid-western Illinois tradition (right round Chicago area) had his mind made up to be a "rock and roll" star. He was already in character. He looked the part. Guess which of the three ended up sharing space with me? You got it. It was the rock and roll star. He was also a varsity swimmer and a great guy to boot. We got along famously. Actually, we all did.

South Dakota had conditioned me so well that it had not initially occurred to me that I had yet to see much less meet another Negro in my class. Not surprising, for when I came to Yale in the fall of 1966, there had only been about 14 Negroes in all of Yale College. Keep in mind, that Yale College consisted of 4,000 males, 1,000 per class. All being trained to lead the country and the world. And to be a Negro at Yale, when the total number was about 14, was to be the "creme de la creme." Unfortunately, they acted like it. As natural consequences, the Negroes at Yale were despised in the New Haven Negro community (which while surrounding Yale, New Haven Negroes only entered Yale to do labor, mostly of the manual and domestic variety). From a New Haven Community perspective, Yale Negroes were the modern equivalent of slavery's "House Niggars." In 1966, the Yale Campus Police knew who all the Yale Niggars, excuse me, the Yale Negroes were. If you were not one of them, you got stopped before you could enter the Yale campus. You were a 'persona non grata' (not welcomed).

On arrival, full of expectations - yes, and fear, and uncertainty, students knew one thing, - that Yale was going to be tough, and we were going to work like hell to stay in. Well, we did work like hell. Some until midterms. Some until January. Some all year. There were even some of us who worked like hell for four straight years. But most of us decided in January that a Yale education was not confined to the classroom. We were going to learn from our environment." (B. Reid Detchon, one of the Yale Banner Class Histories, p. 5).

I needn't tell you that I was in the "most of us in January who had decided to learn from the environment, not just the classroom" group. When I first got to Yale, I worked on my studies like the Booker T. Washington I had heard about as a boy. He cleaned a room so many times that had been placed in his charge, that if you went over it with a clean toothbrush you wouldn't find any dirt. I worked 8 hours a day. By the midterms, I was barely passing in some areas. It was reminiscent of how I had fared when I first hit Axtell Junior in Sioux Falls, South Dakota after experiencing Chambliss Children's House in Tuskegee Institute, Alabama. Who was Chambliss anyway? At any rate, more Ds. My Dean and the student counselors (we all had them freshman year) came up to me, and they underscored how impressed they were with my work ethic. I had made a good "first impression." I got that implicit "you are a credit to your race" feeling. They knew I could do it, I just needed to close the gap and learn what was important to focus on.

I was trying to learn everything. Any good college student knows, you can't learn everything. But, in 1966, nobody had told me the deal. I had a near photographic memory, but even that was not enough at Yale. You had to be able to think and reason, and do so with depth and speed. I was in for a lot of surprises. I truly had some gaps to close.

Close the gap is right. In my high school chemistry class, for example, we spent several weeks on the Periodic table of natural elements. We focused on learning how to identify the symbols for each, their valence points, and how they combined to form natural substances like water, or in the language of the chart: H20. But in my Yale chemistry course, man we covered that stuff in a day or so. You had to learn that stuff on your own. Knowledge of that type was assumed, the teacher wanted to focus on the application of and reasoning with such knowledge. Like Einstein, our teacher wanted us to use our minds to think, not just as a warehouse for facts. Actually, that is not completely true. He wanted us to warehouse the facts and reason with them as well. To make matters worse, the chemistry building and chemistry labs were way up a hill at the edge of the campus. We not only had to walk a mile to get to class going up hill most of the way, often in snow and seemingly fighting 'the Hawk' (Mr. WIND) with every step, but we had to still take the pain of facing that unforgiving chemistry course as well.

At Yale, the idea of pacing and self-discipline was key. Help was always near and readily available, but no one really policed you. So, after getting those Ds at midterm, I quickly surmised what was necessary to pass and to do well. Once I had that under control, I got better grades, doing half the work, and I got busy doing extracurricular activities like a fish taking to water.

A Yalie who was now serving as the Dean of Undergraduate Admissions, R. Inslee Clark, was a principal architect of major changes at Yale. He was called Inky, and many in our class considered our class, the Class of 1970, as Inky's kids. His words of retrospective reflection in March of 1970, would put in perspective who he was and what he sought to accomplish beginning with our class.

"My most crucial concern was diversifying the student body. I felt that when I was at Yale the student body was not diversified enough nor intellectually strong enough to make Yale the national and international resource it ought to be. We all felt at least in retrospect - a certain inbreeding, parochialism, and clubbiness. There were too many people whose thinking processes were all too similar. Thus most of the additions to the admissions office program during my tenure have aimed at providing this diversity. It's an expensive policy but a necessary one to eliminate the somewhat unsavory image Yale has had of a rich man's sanctuary."
He certainly succeeded, and no where more profoundly than with the coming of people of color. Those before us were Negroes, we were the first Blacks to enter Yale. We were the first wave.

In our class, 33 of us arrived in the Fall of 1966. We were larger in number than the 14 Negroes then on campus. We were vastly different. They were organized into a group called the "Negro Literary Society." We changed that and gave birth to "The Black Student Alliance at Yale," more popularly known as BSAY. Our first chair being that colorful revolutionary brother from New York's Bronx High School of Science, the late Glen DeChabert; "my brother." I say that with great affection. He was a large part of who we were and who we became. In fairness, I must acknowledge that some of my best friends, many who I came to admire and respect, were among those 14 already at Yale. They did not resist our efforts to change Yale, they sought to shape the fashion in which that change was to occur. Paul Jones, Don Oglivy, Doc Marshall, Allard Austin the III (he drove a bad MGB GT), the late Bill Brown,

Calvin Hill, the late Armstead Robinson, and of course, Allan Woods were good men who helped us change Yale. But sadly, of the 33 three of us who entered in the fall of 1966, four years later, less than half would graduate.

In large measure, the failure to graduate on time had more to do with the fact that we, along with Yale, were all entering unfamiliar territory, uncharted waters. We were charting a different course and breaking new ground. Like the nation, we were all trying to find our way, and as such, there were casualties; some personal, some institutional. We were all undergoing a transformation in which we would play an active part.

Yet it was more than that for us; we did not have the "accumulation of advantage" that generation upon generation of Ivy Leaguers had enjoyed. Many of us were first time Ivy Leaguers. Some, first time college period. We were from public schools and inner cities, and some of us from remote areas like South Dakota. We were not from the traditional watering holes where Yale had routinely cast its net. We were not a part of the feeder schools like Andover and Hotchkiss that had long supplied Yale with its new recruits. And, we were at Yale at time when the country was undergoing its most radical change, and Yale was to play an integral part in that change.

At Yale, music, for example, was to take a most interesting twist. It began with the mixers. Mixers ought to be against the law. See at Yale the mixers were designed for men and women to mix. Remember, Yale was still an all male school. All the Ivy League schools like Harvard, Princeton, Brown, Columbia and Dartmouth were still a bastion "for men only." The Ivy League equivalent for women, the caliber schools where the best, the brightest, and the most connected women attended, were called the Sister Schools. Schools like Radcliffe, Smith, Wellesley, Mount Holyoke, Vassar, Barnard and the Connecticut College for Women. On the weekends, busloads of women from the sister schools would descend upon the Yale campus to participate in dances "euphemistically" called mixers. The dining halls would be cleared of tables and the room would become like an elegant ballroom, at least in the beginning. By the time I would graduate from Yale, these elegant ball rooms would be more like discos. Anyway, there was a Yale practice, a tradition if you will, that I am sure the women hated. When the bus would arrive. Yale men would line up from the door of the bus all the way to the door of the dance. The women would exit the buses and find themselves walking, parading might be a more apt description, through this tunnel of men, much like a football team entering the field of competition running through the line or tunnel of cheerleaders and band members numbering two hundred strong. (i.e. a lot of folks). Can you see it? Women walking as much as a half mile being oogled by Yale men who were checking them out. We thought our sisters should not have to go through such indignity.

When the buses came to campus, we would meet the bus and as soon as a sister got off, we would pull her to the side. We would meet all the buses throughout the campus in this way. We would let them know that the party in the dining hall was "lame." The music wasn't right, at least not yet. We would change that too. But in the beginning, the music was the Beatles, the Dave Clark Five, the Doors, mainly English groups now that I think about it. Nice to listen to, but not party music. The exception was the Rolling Stones. Looking at Mick Jagger's big lips some of us thought he might be passing. "Hey man, Mick is a brother. I don't know who he think he's fooling." The Stones were hip to our music. They knew how to party, so they made those mixers tolerable. But by and large, the mixers were a waste. In time the word got back. When Gladys Knight & the Pips and Marvin Gaye said " I heard it through the grapevine," they was not kidding. The grapevine was real in our community. And the word spread through the grapevine that the brothers at Yale had it going on. We did. Before long, sisters started coming to the Yale campus, looking for us and the private parties we held.

Now Spook Weekend is to partying what the Super bowl is to the regular NFL season football game --- no comparison. Spook Weekend (which happened once a year) was like coming to shore from six months at sea. It was like coming home from that war, if only for a while. At Spook Weekend, a brother would grab even a ugly sister to dance. In fact, the ugly brothers did quite well on Spook Weekend. Having a great time - good clean fun and letting off steam from the Ivy League pressure cooker in which we all found ourselves, that is what Spook Weekend was really about. It enabled the first wave of black students, male and female, who were breaking ground in these prestigious white institutions, we didn't call them "predominantly White" back then, they was just plain "White." There was no predominant in it. We was predominantly missing. But for now as we were starting to come on to these campuses, often catching hell as we came, most of the time seemingly by ourselves, we were still largely thankful for the privilege and the opportunity.

The celebration was genuine. The spirit of partying and celebration was so strong, it was almost like Mardi Gras and Carnival all at the same time. Now we had our share of brothers and sisters from New Orleans and the Islands (the West Indies) so perhaps the Mardi Gras Carnival atmosphere arose quite naturally. In fact, this was not a party into the middle of the night, it was a party until the break of dawn. And I knows for a fact that the punch was likely to get spiked with some form of alcohol. Usually, it would get spiked with the kind where you could not really notice the taste. The science of partying was well developed and in full effect. And the music - now stop.

I remember that I hadn't long arrived on the scene, when "Function at the Junction" came on the box. I was not fully warmed up yet. I certainly hadn't sized up the place. But, when that record came on you'd think somebody had dropped a ton of money in the middle of the dance floor the way people was heading in that direction. It was almost like a stampede. People were throwing down (really partying) everywhere. You didn't have to head to the dance floor, the whole place became a dance floor. People were already screamin.' I certainly didn't want to be left out. I literally grabbed the first girl I saw. In fact, she may have grabbed me. Actually, we just made eye contact and started dancing toward each other like we was already in the midst of a great tango. When I got within reach, I extended my hand and she met it with equal vigor and we were as they say: "on it." Now, as far as I could tell in the dim light, she was not up to my usual standards. I know how that sounds, but that is the way young men think. Especially when they are out partying with their 'boys." 'Cause later on, you going hear 'bout it. So you had better be ready to handle the rap session after the party. Well I did give a damn about the rap session after the party, nor anybody's opinion either. I liked the way this Sister moved, she was poetry in motion, and she was "solid." She didn't have the body by Fisher, the deluxe version, but what she had she knew how to work it.

The relief one felt from just being with somebody who looked like you, who you could relate to, was good for the soul. It was a coping mechanism and strategy. Now don't get me wrong, many of our soul mates were white, and they fit in well, but they were a special breed unlike their sister and brethen who seem not to understand what we were experiencing. While we partied hardy, and while people came from all over the East Coast and the midwest to attend this great party, we literally rented every room in the Midtown Motor Inn on Chapel Street (cause there were so many of us, and these were still the days when if you had a woman in your room after curfew, she had better spend the night and sneak out in the morning, cause if you were caught with her in your room after hours, even if it was innocent, "your ass was grass."). The fact of the matter is that Spook Weekend lead the way to serious weekend conferences.

Function at the Junction, that song was our national anthem at the parties. When that record came on, no inhibition in the world could keep you off the dance floor. It was like you was possessed. Look, the way I am telling this story, you'd think I didn't have a shy bone in my body. Nothing could be further from the truth. But, when function at the junction came on, I found the courage. Talk about finding a way out of no way. Shoot! You see, asking a sister to dance, in the way a brother does it: is a lost art form. Back then, as a practitioner of the art, I was a beginner. South Dakota had not given me much experience with my own "sisters." I am sad to say. But I was a good observer and a quick study, especially when properly motivated. And the kid was motivated, ya hear me – MOTIVATED!

The straightforward approach, "may I have this dance? Or, would you like to dance?" That wasn't it. "Baby, you want dance?" was a popular approach. But I always had trouble calling women, any women, especially my beautiful Black sisters, "Baby." It didn't roll off my tongue right. Coming from my mouth, it sounded lame (vernacular - weak). It would be a dead giveaway: "where you from, South Dakota?" I might as well have worn a big sign on my chest: C-O-U-N-T-R-Y! All my "coolness" would evaporate; especially if the sister in question gave me the look; that up and down look: "Boy, are you crazy?" You sisters know the look. "If looks could kill," I bet they got that expression from our sisters. Hey it's possible. Maybe back in slavery times when the White slave master would take away your child, brother, or husband, you sisters would give the White man that look. It's possible. In any case, I wasn't trying to steal nothin,' I just wanted to dance.

I remember when I was in Law School, I told this beautiful, Sherri Belafonte, Jada Pinkett, Halle Berry looking sister. You know, high yellow fine. "Make you wanna Holla and throw up both your hands type fine." That tippy toe, top shelf, way up there kind of fine. Obviously, thinking about this sister, really brings back memories. She impressed me, ya hear. Well this sister, Sherry, was a New Yorker, and she was the "creme de la creme." New York sisters don't play. You had better come right when you speak to a New York sister, 'cause they have seen it all.' They don't impress easily. By the time I met Sherry, I had sized her up real good. I knew I would never have a chance going through the front door. That's where everybody else was lined up. I had to come at her mind. Let her see my intellectual acumen. Hey, I had a Yale education. And I had played mind games with the best of them.

"Sherry, here is the deal. I don't believe a man should mess with a woman he can't handle." What did you say? You heard me right. I don't believe a man should mess with a woman he can't handle? What do you mean by that? I know, I said handle but you heard control. I didn't say control and I didn't mean control. What I said is handle." By now she was laying those puppy dog eyes on me, but I wasn't going for it. "Look at this way. In her heart of hearts, every woman ultimately wants to have a real man in her life. Some one to share her life with, whether it be as a mate, or even as a lifelong friend. But, I'm talkin bout mate here. A man, not a boy. If a man is weak, a boy, then he will bring out the mother in his woman. She will mother him and love him, but down deep she will be unsatisfied, unfulfilled. She will inwardly long for a real man, and as such, she will be vulnerable to being hooked by one, should a real man come along. This means that she is so vulnerable, that her boy is vulnerable to losing her, and he knows it. He won't be able to hold her. He will always be looking over his and her shoulder. As such, their relationship is in jeopardy."

She was on the edge of her seat. I had her undivided attention, and I was loving it?every minute. "By the same token, if he is too much man, he will bring out the girl in her, and she will see in him as a father figure. Again, they both lose. She'll still want a man in her life she can deal with, and he'll want a woman. And she knows it. She'll always be looking over her shoulder and his. There's more, but I think you get the point. A man and woman must be in the relationship as man and woman, partners. If not, they won't make it, or at the very least something will be missing." I had her now, she was on me like "white on rice." She was intrigued. I was half way home. I had said it all without really coming out and saying, "I can handle you." She was ready to be handled, ya dig! She just didn't know it. I had finally given her the language to articulate what she was looking for. It was my duty, I owed to her. Surely, I jest. But, the girl was a project.

But back in the '60s, James Brown would wear us out with his music, but it would not stop there. Aerobics? James put the A, the E, the R, and the O into Aerobics. It would get so good to him, and to us as well, that he would start talking to ya. It would first begin while the "grove was really in the pocket" (kickin', on the money, just right). Then, as if one cue, he'd turn around and talk to the band. "Hey fellas?" "Yeah!" "I feel like doing my own thang." If you was dancing when James started to talkin' bout his own thang, you had better fasten' your seat belts, hold on to ya hats and wigs, and make sure you had your dancing shoes on, 'cause he was getting ready to do what Sly and Family Stone meant when they said: "I want to take you Higher." The grove would continue to cook, and James would continue to rap. "Hey Fellas? Can I do my own thang?" If ever there was a rhetorical question, here was one. No one on this planet was 'bout to deny James from doing his own thang. He would scream - eeyyya! That's all I can call it, but it was not really a scream. But James's vocabulary defies the narrative. He'd scream and break out in dance steps Sammy Davis, Junior would have envied, and he would simultaneously throw the microphone and yet call it back so quick that you'd think it was doing its own thang too. It was "showtime," so powerful that once you'd seen it, it would be indelibly lodged in your mind. Thereafter, to only hear James would be enough to recall the image of his performance back like a favorite movie. It was a life altering event, a defining moment.

Slow dancing was the "piece de resistance." How can I find the words. We slow danced back then. We held each other. I am talking about some real holding. We held each other so close, there was no daylight between the dancers. It was as though two were as one. Close was just the beginning. Movement was the accompaniment to closeness. Do I have to paint a picture? Let me put it to you straight. It was a "slow grind." That is what the slow dance was called. Brothers would be watching to see which sisters would 'slow grind.' Not every sister would. Dancing close was possible. Putting both arms around the lady was possible. But slow grinding was the objective. It was the closest thing to "gettin' some." Hey, I was still only 18.

I was so happy when the long loose fitting African dashiki shirt came out. It meant that after the slow grind you could walk away without being embarrassed. Up until the time of the dashiki, brothers would walk away with their hands in front of them, in a cool walk like they be really cool. The real deal was they be heading for cover. At the "house parties" they found the ultimate solution, they dimmed the lights. Dim ain't the word. With the blue and red lights, not to mention the black ultraviolet lights, it was closer to dark. This is before the coming of stobe lights. When you slowed the beat down, it was the music of Dells, and the "Queen of Soul" Aretha Franklin.

The Dells had one great hit as far as we were concerned - "Stay in my corner." This record was five minutes and some change. It was a long slow tune. The average 45 record, and that's what we played. The reel to reel, cassette deck and that "edsel" of the recording industry, the 8 track tape, were yet to come. The average 45 was only a single tune about 2 or 3 minutes long. Invariably, the last dance of the night, would always be, the Dells. And, you did not want to be caught slow on the move to get your favorite lady for the last dance. "If you slow, you blow."

By the end of the summer 1968, going into 1969, I "had it goin' on." I was a local celebrity. I was a radio personality. Our man "DJ Willie Wright" had made that possible with the great work he had done in New Haven. I was a lead singer in the "baddest" singing group in town, " Au Naturel," and I had one of the finest, I mean drop dead fine, beautiful women in the world as my lady. She was an island girl, M-A-N. You know the expression, "it's better in Jamaica." I am a believer. We were adventurous (but not exhibitionist) and sexually spontaneous. We put the spark and the spon in spontaneous. And, I had ladies in the wings waiting to take her place. But, I was cool. I was disciplined. Everyone just assumed with all I had going on, I must be dealing with fifty ladies at a time. But, I wasn't, not yet.

One day I was going through the food line at Ezra Stiles, my Yale Residential College. Ordinarily, my eyes and mind would be focused on the fine cuisine that had become customary at Yale. But on this day, I was distracted. I heard these sounds coming out of the kitchen, I almost dropped my plate. This brother, no more than a second cook at the time, was cookin'. And I don't just mean cooking food. He was cookin'. He was singing his butt off. " I know you want to leave me. But, I refuse to let you go. My mind and heart a pleading, but I Ain't too Proud to Beg. Please Darlin'. Please don't leave me girl, don't you go. If I have to beg and plead for your sympathy, I don't mind 'cause you mean that much to me, cause I Ain't too Proud to Beg." Now, if you know half a note about music, you know those are the words of the lead singer of the Temptations, Dave Ruffin, singing the hit - Ain't Too Proud To Beg. The brother was wearing the song out. He was on it.

I didn't even ask who he was. I went straight into the kitchen. I broke all protocol. I was not going to be stopped. And, I didn't care if his job was cleaning toilets. Singing like that, he was our new "Lead Singer." He had just auditioned, been hired, and he didn't know it yet. Singing like that, I knew he had it in his heart to sing. He would say yes. That's where I found Jessie Caraway, our lead singer.

The band came together like clockwork, and we were a hit almost from the beginning. Before long, we had celebrity status up and down the east coast. We played in every forum, but among my favorites was the college campuses. There we were in our element, especially at UConn (the University of Connecticut). I will never forget playing up there. When we would play, the way those negroes reacted, we knew they was starved for some 'serious throw down' party music. And we obliged them well. They wouldn't let us leave the stage. We would stop playing to take a break, and they would be partying still. "It's in the air, up on the roof, one hundred proof." They would get to chantin' and you swear we was working voodoo magic on them. We get them going and they'd send it back our way. Before long, we'd all be caught up in the spirit. I love UCONN. Even today.

But opening up for the Delfonics, playing with the Greats, and playing in venues throughout the country, including that time down south where these sisters literally had to be refrained. They was trying to pull us off the stage and rip our clothes off. Sisters mind you. I 'll never forget that gig. When it was over, we ran. You hear me, we ran out of there like a bat out of hell. We was in the wind before the last note was through. The band kept playing to give us enough time to get off the stage and make an exit. I don't know about this fame stuff. This is too much. But none of that even comes remotely close to what happened when we played this spook weekend gig at Yale.

My Jazz show was called 'Afro Blue," remnants of which still exist at Yale today. Afro Blue became a national prototype, it preceded the 'quiet storm and classic jazz formats. It made me a legend at Yale. Since I played trumpet and often harbored the desire to become a jazz musician myself, I didn't just play the music on my show, I gave it context. I explained what was going on with it. My explanations were not superficial, nor overwhelming, but lively and instructive. One night while I was on the air, I remember getting a call from an English teacher at a local High school, Hamden High, who had been listening quite attentively. His class was reading about jazz, and he invited me to come and give a guest lecture. I came, brought my music and my materials, explaining and illustrating the relationship between the artists, the evolution of the music on various instruments, and the historical context out of which the music arose. After all, the music was inseparable from the African American experience that gave birth to the music. This was the historical backdrop from which developed such jazz traditions as the one on trumpet moving from King Oliver to Louis Armstrong to Miles Davis to Freddie Hubbard. This was before there was a Wynton Marsalis who I would meet in 1980 when he was just a youngster "cutting his chops" (getting his experience and skills in order) traveling with Art Blakely and the Jazz Messengers. We covered the evolution of the sax from Coleman Hawkins to Charlie Byrd Parker to John Coltrane --piano from Art Tatum to Bud Powell & Thelonius Monk to McCoy Tyner. We got deep into it. I ended up staying for the whole semester teaching it as a course (to three different classes) which I entitled: "Jazz with an African American History Background." When I returned to Yale in 1982, Henry Louis Gates (my former classmate) then an Assistant Professor at Yale, now Chair of African American Studies at Harvard, asked me to come and lecture his class. This music and the show that it was my pleasure to do was far reaching. For when I was in Paris in summer of 1995, I met Europeans who had been graduate students at Yale during my Days at Yale. He was a Swede who had been a jazz bass player while going to Yale, and she was French, teaching French to Yale undergraduates by day, and working as a translator for the great French Poet Marxist Philosopher (whose name escapes me now) as her contribution to the revolution. Wait a minute. It just now occurs to me, that I had a real crush on my Yale French teacher. I wonder if this was the same lady?

I was working on my black belt, and I had just finished the summer working on Wall Street by Day, and partying in the Village and Brooklyn by night. I was a regular at the great jazz spot on the lower east side - "Slug's Place." Slug's was to sixties what midtown Manhattan's Minton's and the Harlem's Savoy had been to the 40s and 50s. Jazz was king and being transformed, and with it, the music world. The great ones- Miles, Parker, Coltrane, - just to name a few, were regulars too. Although, I just missed 'Trane (Coltrane).

After a time, I got tired of sitting in on Wall Street meetings, making money and just hanging out. I wanted to be productive. So I fashioned a plan. I got myself commissioned to put together a real plan that would indeed take advantage of bringing talented blacks to work on Wall Street, making it a meaningful experience for all involved? a real internship program. It afforded me the opportunity to travel and to examine Allied's entire national operation. I wrote them a plan they liked. By summer's end, they were so pleased, they offered me an additional $1,000 and asked me to return to Yale and implement the plan. When I graduated, and every summer until I did, I had a permanent job waiting for me if I wanted it.

By the 1980s, this kind of program would indeed exist in a more formal fashion. It would be called "Summer on the Street." (Wall Street). But in 1968, I had other fish to fry. Besides, this was the "establishment, " big time. And, I was a young revolutionary. I couldn't be working for no establishment. I was flattered, but I had to decline. I turned down the $1,000 and their wish that I implement the plan. Isn't it funny, the choices we make. Often as youth, we are called upon to make some of the most important decisions of our lives, when we are least prepared to make them.

Now this was the era when poverty was king. President Johnson was waging his war in Vietnam and his war on poverty, and he was losing both. The body count on both fronts was mounting. Yet, the money kept rolling in. Johnson had fashioned a new strategy. He called it the anti poverty agency and the model cities program. Because of Yale's presence in New Haven, and the Ford Foundation's interest in the matter as well, a joint venture, a collaboration if you will between, government (FED,STATE & City), the private sector (Ford Foundation), and education (Yale) was formed. The first of the country's antipoverty agency was formed in New Haven (CPI).

CPI was big stuff. It has over 300 employees, two thirds of them women (60% of them fine), and its budget had to be approaching $20,000,000. Frankly I don't recall the exact figure, I can't attest to the 20 mil, but I can attest to the 60%. At any rate, in 1960s dollars, it was a whale of lot of money (in the vernacular a "shit load"). To make it interesting, the CPI concept was one of having neighborhood government. It was a genuine attempt at grassroots governing. Each Neighborhood Corporation had sufficient funds to run neighborhood based programs tailored to its unique character. The executive directors were an assorted lot, many had come from the ranks of rebel rousers who gave the City a fit, petitioning on behalf of their communities. Some were even to be feared. Be that as it may, some folk felt that when these rebels got these prestigious jobs, they lost their fervor. It was a test of character and commitment. Like most tests, some passed and some failed.

The summer of '69 I worked as a program evaluator of four of the neighborhood corporations (Dwight, Dixwell, Newhallville, and the infamous Hill - which was like the Harlem and Watts of New Haven). This was a key job, because my evaluation would determine whether they would be funded again the next year.

When I started work, I never told the neighborhood folks I went to Yale. I had been in New Haven long enough to know that to tell them I was a Negro at Yale would be the kiss of death. I just told them I would be writing their grant for refunding. It was my job to learn from them, help them where I could to improve, and to be their advocate for refunding. How's that for turning that evaluator thing around. But I was sincere. At the time, I genuinely believed that the neighborhood programs and the CPI concept were rooted in the right motives and presented an opportunity that was worth pursuing. And I wanted it to work.

I evaluated the programs by enrolling in most of them. Before the summer was over I learned to sew, hop scotch, the latest dance, and acquired more skills and friends than I could have ever thought possible. By the time they found out I was a Yalie, it was too late. They already liked me. They had met me before they had a chance to see me through a label. Isn't that wonderful.

I worked in radio but became determined to find a way to own my own station. By the beginning of 1970 the opportunity presented itself. It all began when the word got out that the local TV station, Channel 8 (which was at that time WNHC TV 8) was on the auction block. As a part of the deal, WNHC 1340 AM which was one of the TV station's properties, was being sold as a part of the package. Capital Cities Broadcasting Company was going to purchase channel 8 and its radio station. The FCC required that they do something for the communities that would be affected. They held a town meeting in New Haven, where about 100 of us showed up to hear what they intended to do. Some stuffed shirt rattled off in his most sincere and humble voice what their plans were and how these plans would really be good for the community. It was looking like the old "okey dope" routine me. I stood. "I hear your plan, it sounds good enough. But, I think we'd like to see the written plan you are going to submit." You'd think I'd said something offensive 'bout his mama. Then, one shownuff soul brother, Sherman Adams, stood up. He had a humungous Afro that even Angela Davis would have envied. He was a good 6'3", without the Afro. He was from the H. Rapp Brown School of Articulation. He got your attention. When Sherman spoke this White Speaker was sweating bricks. When got through, the whole audience of 100 was saying, "yeah, where the hell is the plan - muther f...ker! The nerve of you coming in here not telling us about the written plan. That's why y'all catch so much grief all the time from us." The station manager said he would show us the plan but he'd like us to appoint or select two representatives to meet with him to discuss the matter further. The group selected me and Sherman.

With Sherman on the scene, they was happy to talk to me. He knew they was scared of him, so we used that to our advantage. He would speak when it was necessary to ruffle their feathers, and I would probe and move them along closer to our goal. It was the good cop, bad cop approach.

We didn't know it at the time, but Capital Cities Broadcasting's purchase of these properties was being contested by a prominent Citizens Communications (CC) lobbyists group in Washington, D. C. There was a lot at stake. I guess when Citizens heard about the ruckus we was causing up in Connecticut, they suggested representatives be appointed for each of the groups in other cities negotiating with Capital Cities (Cap Cities). Of course, Citizens was leading the way, but their strategy was that if we weren't pleased with the Cap Cities deal, then they would continue to press their suit and hold up the sale. Washington, D.C., here we come.

I don't know how it happened, but I ended up the leader of the six representatives when we got to Washington. Maybe it was because I was the only one both a community person and working in the business.

Not making much progress with us, they sent in this brother, Andy Jackson. Years later he would become a Capital Cities Broadcasting Vice President. As soon as Andy walked in, I said: "look, we know why you're here. We realize that we can't ultimately stop this sale, we can only make it costly and wreck havoc in the meantime. Our real goal is to own something. We'd like to buy at least one radio station. We know we can't do that now but we need money to help us get organized. It takes money. If you let us know how much money we can get out of these people, we will work with you. What can we get?" Andy did not even blink. He was cool. "Well, I think you can get a million dollars." Now in the sixties, that was a lot of money. And, we said fine. We had a deal, and sealed it with a handshake. With real people, their word means something.

We put together a sweet deal where Capital Cities would have programming time set aside each week for the community, and hire minority staff not just to focus on doing that program air time, but they would work in other mainstream parts of the station as well, all funded out of the $1,000,000. Furthermore, a watchdog broad based community panel would be set up. It became the prototype model for the integration of the air waves.

When we got back to Connecticut we formed the Connecticut Minority Communications Panel. Our purpose was to do the same thing that we had accomplished in Washington, DC for New Haven, to do it all over Connecticut. We succeeded at Channel 3 in Hartford, the State's capital. Many distinguished media professionals came from those days. It was a great achievement.

Friendships and these experiences would serve me well. Unbeknownst to any of us, the Black Panther trials of Black Panther Chair and founder Bobby Seale, National Panther leader Erica Huggins (whose husband New Havener John Huggins had been killed in a shoot out at UCLA where he was the captain of the Los Angeles Black Panther chapter), and local Panther, Warren Kimbro (who was well respected and loved in the New Haven); their trial was just around the corner. Because of my working in the community, coupled with my musical and radio celebrity status, I would be able to go places in the community that others could not go. I could reach people others could not reach. And, I had the their trust and confidence. All of this, in part made possible because of CPI.

Just before our graduation in mid May of 1970, the New Haven Panther Defense Committee in the wake of the Panther trials of Black Panther Chairman Bobby Seale, and Black Panthers Erica Huggins and Warren Kimbro (trials then occurring in New Haven that were being watched by the nation), put it on the line. "Yale University in New Haven, Connecticut?is one of the gold spots in the educational/cultural network of capitalist society. It serves as a training ground for the elite?On May 1,2, and 3, revolutionary and righteous people will be gathering in New Haven to begin a preliminary investigation of this whole case. The first defendant will be Yale University."

One hundred thousand people, including the Students for a Democratic Society (SDS), the Weatherman, and ordinary concerned citizens were descending upon the Yale campus for these Panther trials, and all the press was salivating to get the story, a story that would have indeed been a coup if one could get the Huey P. Newton interview.

By now, my show "The Community Speaks" (the forerunner to WYBC's Electric Drum) was the show in New Haven. We were the WY BC Soul Brothers, and as one who had worked in the local community, it was widely known that I was fair. I was more than fair, I was "down with the cause." I had already had many leaders of my day on the show. So, I was tailor made for Huey. On my show, he would have his day in court. A day, an opportunity that the federal judiciary and the establishment had not yet allowed.

I don't know how I got it but I interviewed the Black Panther Party Cofounder and Minister of Defense, Huey P. Newton, on my WYBC radio talk show. I was in the thick of it. I was up to my neck in history. Sometimes it felt like it was over my head. I was excited. I was fairly well informed as well. Although my specialty was psychology, I had already nearly completed the philosophy major at Yale, so I knew the Marxist and Hegelian line of thinking that supposedly underlie the Panther philosophy. I had already worked in the community, and I knew what grass roots meant. I knew the local Panthers personally. We had broken bread and shared the weed (marijuana). Even though I had declined their attempts to convert me, we had mutual respect. I had seen one of the most talented and intelligent sisters I knew, chose the Panther party over the Ivy League. I had seen someone whose family I knew, the Huggins, lose their son John (who had headed the Panthers in LA) in a political shoot out gone bad at UCLA. His wife, Erica, was now one of those incarcerated in New Haven. I was determined to get to know the real Huey P. Newton, and to give him an opportunity to get the real Panther story out.

My interview set the record straight. I should have felt extremely honored. I was about to have the most feared man in America, the Black Revolutionary's Revolutionary, the man on top of the FBI's enemy hit list - Huey P. Newton, the cofounder and minister of Defense for the Black Panther Party. My timing for the interview could not have been better. The Black Panther Party trials were occurring not just right here in New Haven, but almost on the Yale campus. The body count on the evening news for Black Panthers being killed in America was only surpassed by the body count of Americans killed in Vietnam. Fred Hampton's assassination raid provided further support to the Panther assertion that they were indeed political prisoners, not criminals.

By all accounts, this should have been a great day. My expectations were high. I was thoroughly prepared. Being a martial artist, I could fight. I had no fear. I was ready...whatever happened. But what occurred caught me by surprise. I did not see it coming.

When Huey arrived, he had his entourage in tow. I could not help but notice that some were ladies who would be considered "fine" in any setting. He looked just like his posters. He was manly, strong, good looking with the youthful face. As I recall, he had on the black leather jacket and beret that was the Black Panther Signature Dress. He may have had on a turtleneck as well. He was dressed for the occasion. It would have been good television.

Huey was pleasant enough, and I tossed him the kinds of questions a friendly interviewer would have passed. It was my intent to learn about the man, the party, and to give him the latitude that would enable him to lay out his case. But what I got was superficiality. What I got was dressing, but little substance. The commercial of the little old lady in the Wendy's commercial saying: "where's the beef?" comes to mind. Huey gave me rhetoric, and he gave me platitudes (more propaganda, than bullshit), perhaps enough for some, but I was disappointed. Sometimes we are better off not meeting our heroes.

Scroll and Key: Tales from the Inner Sanctum
"Set For Life"

By the spring of 1969, by any objective standard, I had arrived. I had made it. I was on the A list. I was part of the crème de la crème, the best of the best, not just in the Black community, but I was raising eyebrows of envy and admiration in the White elite community as well. Like most great moments, I may have missed it.

At the time, I do not think I truly realized and appreciated the achievement of being one of only 15 in the senior class at Yale to be "tapped" (personally selected) to join one of the two most prestigious societies at Yale - the Secret Society - Scroll and Key. However, as I was to learn, I was also only the second Black in the near two hundred year history of the society to be asked to join. This fact did not go unnoticed. For me this was a point of real sensitivity. So much so that the following year I would be instrumental in having four black students invited to the join Scroll and Key. If I had any personal impact upon the history of Scroll and Key, I hope it is this. I paved the way that others of my race and hue might have an opportunity to become "Scroll and Key."

Now I will be the first to acknowledge that opening up Scroll and Key to people of color was not solely my doing. I could count among the 15 of us in the "Collegium" (another way we described ourselves), many who shared my passion for seeing Scroll and Key open to people of excellence, character, and service, no matter their race or religion -- and before long, their gender. Within a decade of our graduation, one from our group, young Gary Trudeau (of Doonesbury fame) would lead the way to see women join our ranks. But in 1969, I would carry the banner for more racial inclusion.

The building that houses Scroll and Key is a remarkable tale in and of itself; almost as remarkable as the people who along the long corridor of Scroll & Key tradition comprise its membership. The senior societies as they are now called in the underground parlance of Yale tradition were historically referred to as "secret societies." This designation seems quite appropriate in that for generations what went on within the walls of the Society apparently remained there. The building itself has no windows. Like many of the other prestigious societies, this fact contributes to the buildings that house the societies being appropriately named: "tombs." We, its inhabitants, were called "Spooks." This was no Spook like in "Spook weekend" or Spook like in Negro (not to be confused with 'spade') or Spook like in Spy. No this was Spook like in "unseen power" - from realms unseen, but felt nonetheless. The connotation "tomb" was intended to imply veiled, secret order, eternal tradition, regal stature, and all the imagery that arises when one thinks of ancient Egypt. This regal connotation was not so far fetched. Besides the statue of its membership, Scroll and Key is located adjacent to Woodbridge Hall. Woodbridge Hall is where the office the President of Yale is located. Woodbridge Hall is Yale's White House.

Scroll and Key faces east upon College street and south upon Wall Street. Its back door faces the

President's office in Woodbridge hall. Power, both symbolic and practical, and on Wall Street no less. This Yale thing is deep (heavy, well thought out, intriguing, complex, you get the picture). Facing north the society sits adjacent to Woolsey hall, looking out upon its secret entrance where Woolsey Hall dignitaries enter. The place where Yale's most prestigious events are generally held. And that's just the outside of Scroll & Key.

Imagine when one enters. "Abandon All Hope Ye Who Enter Here." This was not Dante's inferno, far from it. Things often aren't as they appear. The outer door, like a steel upright trap door, when opened leads into a pitch black room no larger than an elevator. If you were so bold and ever so clever enough to get as far as this outer door when you peaked inside, you would see little, nothing that would entice you to go further. However, if your curiosity just wouldn't let you stop at the outer door, once you stepped inside - look out. 'Cause if you was even mildly claustrophobic, you would have already been back out the door, on the street, in the daylight so fast, panting, truly out of breathe, barely repeating the mantra – No Way! Or as they say in my neighborhood: "No Way, Jose! Not me, Cuz! Not the Kid! Not today, and you can take that to the bank." In a word, your journey- your great adventure would be OVER! I know, that's more than a word. So I lied, sometimes one word just ain't enough. But if you were bold enough, and could muster the courage to go inside this room and closed the door behind you, something that would be counter intuitive under the circumstances - in an instance -- that kind of eternal instance-- like falling through space -- the room would go pitch black?conjuring up in your mind the kind of foreboding mystery that Stephen King would love, replete with intrique that even Alfred Hitchcock would envy. But in that instance between fear and anticipation, even before you had enough time to think much less flee - in the blink of an eye, the little room would all of sudden light up. You would be temporarily blind, seeing stars. Before you could even recapture your vision, unbeknownst to you, an alarm, more like the alarm that one would attribute to a doorbell, is set off? Alerting those inside, some one approaches. The plot thickens.

Turning left as you enter this little room would be another even more imposing door. A door whose center consists of a giant combination lock. Like the combination one would find upon a vault, the kind of vault you might find in Fort Knox. If you knew the combination you could go on. If some one was inside you only need know the password. It would be asked of you in a language that no ordinary mortal would speak; Latin or Greek I suspect. You would not even know that you were being asked to provide the password. But if you passed this test, the door would open, and you would enter a magical realm, one that was like nothing I had ever experienced.

It was like a castle. On your left, a most elegant staircase made of a dark mahogany type, aged, vintage wood, leading up toward a realm beyond immediate view. On the right, a stately room where Port and Cherry were often consumed in great abundance in the most distinguished of company. While you stood in midst of this enormous vestibule with the high ceilings, with light flooding in from places unseen, with the staircase to your left and sitting room to your right, immediately in front of you lay the way to the Great Hall. The mythical Sherlock Holmes would have felt real here, really at home. One half expected to smell the aroma of his pipe. Imagination is a powerful thing --- more important than knowledge, so sayeth Albert Einstein. In this place, the imagination roamed freely, everything and anything was possible.

As is typical of "old money," I'm talking old...O - L - D!!! Scroll and Key emits quality without being pretentious. You could literally walk by it and not notice it was there. As I no doubt did for three of my four years at Yale. But once I became aware of Scroll and Key, I saw its influence every where. You know how when you buy a particular car, from then on, you seem to see that car everywhere you turn? It's not that there are now more cars of that type and make around, it's just that your awareness of such cars has been awakened. That's how Scroll and Key was for me. I saw its influence everywhere. Its reach was both pervasive and enormous, and it was impressive.

Being in Scroll and Key was like sitting around King Arthur's round table and being a knight of the realm. Scroll and Key was like a castle, and the table (in what I call the Great Room - the main room where we ate) was immense with a roundness that seemed like a perfect circle whose diameter approached 30 feet. This table steeped with so much tradition that it every nook and cranny lay a great tale to be told. This was the table where five Rockefellers had sat beginning with Godfrey in 1921, and James in '24; John in '28, Avery in '49, and James Jr. in 51. But even the Rockefellers could not out do the equally distinguished Auchinclosses. They put eleven around this table starting as early as 1879 with young

Hugh Dudley Auchincloss. And Hugh Dudley begat Hugh (1901) who begat Hugh, Jr. (1938) who begat Hugh the III (1972). That's not even to count Charles Crooke Auchincloss (1903) brother of Hugh (1901) and Charles Russell Auchincloss (also 1903) whose younger brother John Howland Auchincloss would come to Scroll & Key in 1908, along with two other Auchinclosses, James Coates and Gordon. And they ain't done yet. We mustn't forget Reginald La Grange Auchincloss (1913) and Richard Saltonstall Auchincloss (1932). Following their Scroll and Key lineage was akin to a journey of biblical proportions, like tracing Abraham's seed. This was a family of great lawyers, physicians, military leaders, and statesmen, whose contributions to America and the world were substantial.

But the Rockefellers were not to be outdone. In this year, 1969 - 1970, Avery Rockefeller, Jr. who had sat at this table in 1949, now sat at the helm as President of the Kingley Trust Association (K.T.A.) which was in effect the Board of Directors of the Society. Not enough was it to be President of KTA, he was a Governor of the New York Stock Exchange as well, a position he had held since 1964. The Rockefellers and the Auchinclosses - and that's just two families. All had sat here. Now here we sat as well, around this table, in enormous chairs bearing our names, chairs more like thrones than seats, partaking of a feast befitting King Arthur's knights, but a feast for far more than the body. If my first impressions of Yale were like entering Camelot, those initial impressions were now being confirmed. Three years after my arrival, I had reached the inner sanctum, I was a knight at King's Arthur's table. I was set, some say "set for life." As the great Black comedian extraordinaire Bill Cosby put it in his parody of Noah to God, R-I-G-H-T! Even with all of this, I was still a Black man in America.

Behind this table a great fireplace would blaze, and we would eat in courses that even the great sheiks of Arabia and ancient Baghdad would envy. Aesops' Arabian Nights didn't have nothing over these feasts. It almost goes without saying that the people who waited on us were Black. One, a distinguished gentleman, in the best tradition of class, service, and quiet wisdom, was Mr.George Musgrove. He was a remarkable man, and he had at least one remarkable son, George Jr. who would become a great civic leader in New Haven and later Baltimore. He was joined by a equally classy albeit elderly black woman, Ella Scantleberry. She did most of the cooking, and she could go (The woman could burn. She could cook, ya hear me!). Yet in her day time job she was the Treasurer of the City of New Haven. Can you imagine it? People of such statue serving food in Scroll & Key. I loved them dearly, and we enjoyed a special friendship. I think I made them proud. They certainly made me proud. But for my Tuskegee upbringing, I couldn't have even begun to understand why they would be working in such a place - in such a capacity.

They were typical of what had been the Negro's station in America all too long, waiting on and serving rich and powerful whites...waiting on the table - not being at the table. Now a change was in the wind, one of their own, was now at the table. I was determined that I would not be the last.

In this enormous room we were joined by a gallery of tables, scattered about like the positions on a clock, but clearly on the periphery. At this table would sit members of former Scroll & Key Collegiums, days long gone, but not forgotten. They were an impressive lot. Lindsey, Babbidge, Clark, Vance, just a few of the men who ran the country from pulpits, board rooms, ivy towers, or government shrines. As you know by now, they came from a long and impressive tradition of Scroll & Key men; men with names like Rockefeller, Auchincloss, and Vanderbilt -- going as far back as Eli Whitney who sat here 1869, a man after whom the New Haven School "Eli Whitney" was named. Eli was synonymous with Yale. And before him, Sprague in 1852 after whom the building across the street from the Society, Sprague Hall, was named. In the modern era, men like John Hay Whitney who sat here 1926, whose generous financial gifts to Yale in the thirties was responsible for building the first 10 residential colleges. Whitney was a special man of vision. His gift in the 1930s would be akin to the billion-dollar gift media mogul Ted Turner has given in the nineties to the United Nations. But more than a giver, Whitney was ahead of his time. When in 1970, while serving along with Vance on the Yale Board of Trustees, Whitney's words struck home. " In addition to business activity, I had been active in the production of movies, in the theater, in the publishing and in collection of art (before I became a Fellow)." They called the trustees Fellows. That term, Fellow, would emerge in a lot of places around Yale. I became a Faculty Fellow of Yale's Davenport College in 1983; even the women of Yale were called Fellows. Some words die hard. Yale as a place "For Men Only," primarily "Anglo Saxon White Men of Great Wealth and Proper Lineage," was the consistent mountain of tradition that faced minorities and women. Winston Churchill said it best: "I would rather be right than consistent." Being consistent with what had gone before, rather doing the right thing would have forever closed Yale's doors to people like me. But thankfully, then Yale President Kingman Brewster and Whitney as well, seemed bent on doing the right thing... long before it was fashionable. Said Whitney, "I established in 1945 a foundation which is concerned with improving educational opportunities for students from minority groups and with encouraging the teaching profession in the field of the Humanities." [Yale Banner - Documentary, p. 33]. Like President Truman who integrated the Armed Forces in 1945, Whitney was putting his money where his mouth was. He was a Scroll & Key man, who now sat around the Yale Corporation Board table, who had once sat where I was now. I was probably sitting here because of him. With men like Whitney on Yale's Board of Directors, I now better understand how Kingman Brewster could be such a courageous Yale President, bringing minorities and women into the Yale family. The list of Scroll and Key men like Whitney was like a Who's Who of America - past, present, and future. If Thomas Jefferson had gone to Yale, he would have been a man of Scroll & Key. He too, would have graced this table. But no matter how prominent, no matter how important, when it came to the affairs of Scroll and Key, and this table at which we sat, they were the past, we were the present, the right here and the right now. This was our day, not theirs - our shining hour. As Robin Williams reminded his students in "Dead Poet's Society," the great ones were gone, now just ashes and dust, and their mantra from their graves to us was: "seize the time." How appropriate, that was the mantra of the Black Panthers too: "Seize the Time! Power to the People." In time we would join them, as is the way of all flesh, but those of them who had not passed the way of dust, while they could join us, they could only sing along, follow our lead, respond to our direction, and reminiscence about when they sat around this big table, as we did now. Can you see it? How the very notion of power was being bred into us. Scroll & Key was working its magic upon us. And most of us did not even know it.

Our gatherings were no ordinary occasions. All would go according to an agenda, seemingly centuries old. We would sing a chorus that had echoed in these halls for longer than some States had been in the Union. I was Anselmo, following in a succession of over a hundred Anselmos before me. Yet, in this moment, I was the only Anselmo that mattered, as was true of each of us (in our respective roles). That first day at the table, I came to really understand what ceremony and tradition meant.

In the midst of all of this old foggy tradition, unlike our predecessors who followed the established order like loyal soldiers, we were a different lot. Hey, it was the sixties, and no tradition, even this one, was beyond evaluation. We had some changing to do.

To begin with, we ended the policy that only Scroll & Key men could enter. And on those rare occasions when someone extraordinary non member was allowed to enter, they had previously been relegated to the first floor, the outer realms at that, a segment that was only a fraction of what lie within this vast complex. We changed that too. We took whomever we wanted wherever we wanted, so long as we did not bring them to our meetings; so long as we showed mutual respect for one another. This we did with great ease. We really liked one another. We got along famously.

Just as we had transformed Yale, our class would begin the transformation of the Society as well, perhaps more than any group then or since then. It would be most immediately apparent the following year when more people of color would be asked to join our number. In my Collegium there were two people of color: yours truly as the only Black, and Ralph Rexach from Puerto Rico. The year that followed there were 4 blacks and 2 hispanics; 6 people of color out of 15, about 40% of the Collegium minority? What a concept. What an achievement! It was revolutionary. Until our year, for almost 150 years of Scroll & Key tradition, at an average of 15 members per year, there had only been two Blacks, myself in 1970, and Allard Austin, III in 1967. That's a whopping .0008% - the moral equivalent of zero. You mean we was statistically insignificant? Yes, we were. Even though we were real flesh and blood human beings, we wouldn't even show up on the radar screen. For all practical purposes, Allard and I did not exist. With our collegium, we had made a great start to change all that. We were "talking the talk, and walking the walk.

To its credit, Scroll & Key was not just about power and tradition. It was about scholarship and learning. At the end of our formal meetings around the big table, we would retire to our private chambers. In the beginning, we would change into the robes that Scroll & Key men had adorned from days of old. In time, we abandoned the robes, the outer symbolic tradition, but we did not abandon the inner more important tradition of scholarship and lively debate

that would take place in the realms of the secret chambers. Over the course of the year, each of us would be expected to present papers and be prepared to defend them as well. It was a type of preparation for the world that lay beyond the Society's door. Consistent with true Yale tradition, we were being prepared to lead. But, we were not the elite; we were the elite of the elite. Elitism never stops, it always continues to further differentiate and divide itself. Being at Yale and in this Society, taught me that.
The experience had truly, 'set me for life.'

11. Henry Louis Gates, Jr., Yale, '1973[51]--How To Join The Black Overclass

TWENTY-FIVE years ago, I left West Virginia for Yale University, to join the blackest class in the history of that ivy-draped institution. I drove up on my own, without my parents. They were never comfortable in that island of leaded glass and Gothic spires, although you might say they spent much of their lives making sure I arrived there. My father worked two jobs--loading trucks at a paper mill, plus a night shift as a janitor for the phone company--to keep us well fed and well clothed, and to pay the premiums on "college insurance policies," a thousand dollars when we reached eighteen. It never occurred to me that we might be poor until much later a sociologist told me so, pinpointing "the Gateses" in a mass of metallic-tasting demographics that left me numb with the neatness of it all.

I suppose that Yale represented both a betrayal and a fulfillment of their dreams. Blacks are wedded to narratives of ascent, to borrow a phrase from literary critic Robert Stepto, and we have made the compounded preposition "up from" our own: up from slavery, up from Piedmont, up from the Bronx, always up. But narratives of ascent, whether or not we like to admit it, are also narratives of alienation, of loss. Usually the ascent is experienced not as a gradual progression but as a leap, and for so many of

[51] Reprint from Henry Louis Gates, Jr and Cornel West, The Future of the Race, New York: Alfred A. Knopf, Inc., 1996.

my generation that leap was the one that took us from our black homes and neighborhoods into the white universities that had adopted newly vigorous programs of minority recruitment. It should be said that the adjustment was a two-way street: we were as strange to the institutions in which we found ourselves as those institutions were to us. In short, we were part of a grand social experiment--a blind date, of sorts. We weren't a tenth, of course; and whatever talent we had wasn't necessarily greater than our compeers who were passed over, or who opted out; but we were here. You might call us the crossover generation.

To speak in strictly chronological terms, we are among the late-boomers who now occupy the White House and the Congress--an age grade that includes Bill Clinton and Robert Reich and William Kristol. But the sense of generational affinity is intensified within the race: ours was the first generation to attend integrated schools in the wake of Brown v. Board; to have watched, as children, the dismantling of Jim Crow and to wonder where the process might end; to be given the chance, through affirmative action, to compete against white boys and girls; to enter and integrate the elite institutions just as the most expansive notions of radical democracy made an entrance.

I picked Yale almost out of a hat. After a year at a junior college near my home, a place where "nigger" was hung on me so many times that I thought it was my name, I decided to head north, armed with a scholarship and a first edition of Strunk and White's The Elements of Style.

By day--and it was still light when I first arrived in New Haven--the university is a tangible, mortar-and-stone manifestation of an Oxonian ideal of Gothic perfection. By night, the sense of enchantment increased: the mammoth structures, strangely out of keeping with the surrounding town, guarded their streets with bearded shadows made by the half-light of the lampposts. At Yale, battle hymns were Congregational, with delicate changes of key. The building that just bade to be the college cathedral turned out to be Sterling Library. Every feature of the place was alarming and exhilarating. Welcome to Never-Never Land, I told myself. This is your world, the world you've longed for and dreamed of. This was where the goods and entitlements of the American century were stored and distributed. It was the grown-up version of the world of Captain Midnight Decoders; the repository of all those box tops I used to ship off to Kellogg's in fair exchange for laser guns. If college was a warehouse for what we've modishly learned to call "cultural capital," the question wasn't how to get it but what to do with it.

Many of the black kids at Yale were the first in their families to attend college, and they congregated in the pre-med and pre-law tracks, searching for a secure place in the newly integrated arenas of the nation's elite. Others were scions of old "colored money." Most of us took at least one course in the new program in Afro-American Studies, probably in part out of a sense of team spirit, partly out of a yearning to tap our cultural unconscious. I took several such courses, and at least three times found myself assigned to read Du Bois's essay "The Talented Tenth." (Only Harold Cruse's The Crisis of the Negro Intellectual was assigned more often.) Du Bois's essay was read and critiqued, almost defensively, for its vanguardism; but its vision of the educated bourgeoisie as the truly revolutionary class--Marx stood on its head, you might say--exerted an unmistakable sway on us.

A PAIR OF ACES

AND THEN there was the talented tenth of the Talented Tenth: la crème de la crème brûlée. As far as I was concerned, they numbered exactly two: Glen DeChabert and Armstead Robinson. I first met them in the pages of the Yale Alumni Magazine the summer before I set foot on campus. In it was an article about a conference held at Yale on the prospective shape of Afro-American Studies in the academy--a conference, bringing together illustrious scholars and prominent activists, that had been orchestrated by these two Yale sophomores. (That conference, and the book that came out of it, would profoundly influence the institutionalization of the field; and indeed, the program in Afro-American Studies came to Yale the same year I did.) I studied their photographs. DeChabert seemed to have a cappuccino complexion, an aquiline nose, an impressive crown of hair, and a compellingly regal bearing: I was half convinced he was descended from African royalty. Robinson's customary attire was more in keeping with countercultural dishabille; he had wavy, unkempt hair in quantity and wore the black rectangular glasses that were then standard issue for young black activist-intellectuals.

Soon after my arrival, I attended my first meeting of the Black Student Alliance at Yale, at which Glen DeChabert-or DeCh, as he was called-presided in his capacity as "moderator." He was every bit as charismatic as I'd imagined, and I hung back like a supplicant. Besides, there was a lot to take in. I could only marvel when students complained that there weren't enough "brothers" on campus; looking around at the two hundred or so students in attendance, I felt as if I were in Africa, or Harlem, anyway. Outside of a few camp revival meetings in Moorefield, I'd never seen so many black people my age. I'd grown up in colored Piedmont; here I would truly learn how to be Black. If my arrival was a narrative of ascent, it was at the time one of immersion. Then it came up that they needed a new secretary. This was my cue. After the meeting, summoning my nerve, I pushed through a crowd of DeCh's admirers and volunteered my services. I felt anointed when he accepted. From then on, I took notes during meeting after meeting, participating through the sedulous act of recording. It's a role that I return to now with some trepidation, but I have no other way of explaining what is, in part, the story of my generation.

If DeChabert--with his impeccable attire and his lordly way with a cigarette--struck me as the perfect embodiment of black leadership, Armstead Robinson was an equally commanding picture of black intellection. Thin and ascetic in his unpressed dashiki and uncombed Afro, Robinson--Robby--was the first black "Scholar of the House," part of a competitive senior year program in which a major scholarly project was pursued instead of regular course work. Robby, we knew, would change the way we understood our past and our present, by dint of his extraordinary and well stocked mind. He was the son of a Memphis minister, and his verbal facility was displayed to equal advantage in the high-flown language of the humanities and in the revolutionary lingo of the streets. Once I gained his friendship, I'd go over to his room at Morse College and sit on the floor cross-legged as he typed away. "I won't bother you," I'd tell him. "I just want to watch you work." The truth is that I was starstruck: I'd never met a black scholar before, and in some almost mystical way I wanted to witness the act of creation, hoping that the magic would rub off.

They respected each other, Robby and DeCh did, each ceding the other his turf. I remember when a number of representatives of the SDS came to campus and we were supposed to hold a "meeting with the white boys." DeCh couldn't go, and asked me to attend in his place, to report back. "I just want to know one thing," he'd said when I caught up with him afterward, lighting up a cigarette impatiently. "Was Robby there?"

Best of all, DeChabert was a man with a plan. A very practical-sounding plan. What black America needed, he often said, was economic development, and the only way that was going to happen was if we did it ourselves. Economies grew: that was what they did. And we were a nation of millions, more populous than Canada. Black capitalism was the answer, and he was going to be its Johnny Appleseed, lending out start-up capital for black entrepreneurship and reinvesting the proceeds until the relative deprivation of black America was a distant memory--and until it truly was a force to be reckoned with. Of course, he did recognize there was a long way to go.

THE SORT of institutions through which elites sustain themselves always seemed to inhabit an arcadia of their own, and yet somehow, in my mind, they always loomed like the clanking, infernal machinery of Fritz Lang's Metropolis. I should say that Yale wasn't my first encounter with one. I was in tenth grade when Exeter came about; a friend at a church summer camp told me about the place. Going to Exeter, you understand, was not something people in Piedmont knew about, not the way people at Yale "know" about Exeter. What I knew was that it was a place with a big library which offered a lot of courses. And in the main, that's what it was for me. An interview with the young Jay Rockefeller, an easy entrance exam, and a full scholarship later, I said bye-bye to Piedmont and drove with my uncle to the New Hampshire woods. My parents said their good-byes in Piedmont, as if there were a boundary they preferred not to trespass.

As quickly as Exeter came into my life, however, Exeter left; or rather, I left Exeter. Sometime in my first semester, I "up and decided" that it was past time for me to go back home. Dean Kessler checked my records what seemed to be a hundred times-my test scores were perfect, I had straight As. There was no reason, he said. "Who gave you authority to leave?" he wanted to know. That's what settled it for me. I thought the knock on the door was just my classmate Joel Motley, whose room was next to mine. It was the dean, red-faced, angry, and a bit disappointed. I think he thought if he yelled at me, somehow I would cower my way back to French I-A. I gave up Exeter at that moment, staring blankly into his crimson, pockmarked face. "Think of our people,"

Joel, the soul of black insouciance, said that night. "Think of yourself. Where is Piedmont, anyway?" "I'll be back," I told him, and somehow knew I would, though I didn't mean Exeter exactly. That was the first airplane trip I ever took. I still don't know for sure why I felt I had to leave; I think that Piedmont was just too far to fall back into, so I decided not to have to fall at all. Homesick for Piedmont, I went back, and soon became homesick for Exeter.

But I stayed at Yale; DeChabert and Robinson were my polestars, and would keep me from ever getting lost. I stayed and I graduated, as a number of my friends did not, and I did so not as a matter of course but as a matter of will. I still remember that crucial first month, with daily sessions in the Linnonia and Brothers reading room, working out inorganic chemistry problems by the light of the low-wattage table lamps. I had convinced myself that at Yale I would be average; a C+ was what I was aiming for. Learning to speak out in class, always my forte before, now came slowly and painfully. But it was History 31 that made the difference, in Burrell Billingslea's discussion group. Never have I put so much work and expectation, fear and care, into the preparation of a five-page paper. Had the returned grade been a Pass, or just a High Pass, the tenor of my years at Yale would probably have been as gray as a New Haven winter. But there it was, in unforgettable bright red letters: "Honors. Nice Paper." Fifteen students--eight seniors, four juniors, and a handful of others--and one Honors. I remember deciding that very night to go to Africa the next year as a "Five-Year B.A.," and one day to be a Scholar of the House, just like Robby.

It soon became apparent, once the anxiety of "making it" was allayed, and once the sheer joy at being black (with about two hundred other black folks!) was tempered, that the fundamental challenge of my years at Yale would be whether or not to allow blackness to rob me of what I wistfully and portentously called "my humanity." This problem went beyond, I think, that peculiar brand of "Mau-Mauing" we so avidly practiced during the late 1960s. You see, as long as I identified the angst of youth with discovering and then shouting for all to hear just how the white man had subjugated the black man, then the matter of being a human being was not a problem at all. (Try it sometime.)

But it was only when you put aside the hulking specter of Bull Connors, arms folded before the passageway, that you would be made to confront all those inconvenient matters. So if you were no longer sure about who you were, it was awfully convenient to have a Bull Connors for distraction. Maybe that explained part of the strange spectacle we presented at Yale, preoccupying ourselves with the minute examination of the metaphysical nature of the "Pig." We wanted to dissect his brain, to explicate his soul, each of us determined at all costs to unlink the Great Chain of Being that had enslaved us since 1619. How better to serve our people, then, than as students at an elite institution? "Changing the system by knowing just what the system is"--that was our rationale, a rationale that was recited so rotely and smugly that the white kids stopped asking us the sort of questions that might prompt it--questions like whether we "felt guilty about just being here." That was the sort of question we would not even have answered in private, among ourselves behind closed doors or alone; we certainly would not have been frank with the white boys. So it was another device by which to mystify them, and mask our own fears.

Not everything was fantasy and posture; in 1970, certainly, the issues of the day were real enough. There was Bobby Seale in a New Haven prison, tried each day in a courthouse just a half-block from Calhoun College; there was Eldridge Cleaver, unjustly exiled in Algiers; there was John Huggins, whose mother would sometimes let our fines slide over at the Sterling Library, murdered by cultural nationalists out in L.A.; there were the atrocities of the Cambodian "sideshow." None of these issues was conjured up for the occasion; our growing conviction was that such were the evils against which only a moral elite of the young could prevail. Yet throughout all our strikes and protests and steering committees, I tried to shrug off a vague sense that had these things not been there, in the world, we would have invented them; or at least a sense that these things were doing double-duty for us. My grandfather was colored, my father is Negro, and I am black--so I wrote in my college application essay. Those appellations, of course, did not contain who I was, or even serve to limit who I thought I could be. Yet each successive generation of black folks living in this country has shared certain peculiar psychic and social concerns that come as regularly as dusk in a society where being black was from the start a restrictive covenant that one could run from or live with, but that one could not escape. It was always a fact of Negro life that one's membership could be taken for granted, could be assumed in much the same way one could assume that back home those Saturday sessions at Combie's barbershop would be rife with Combie's "boo-shit" and with the good-hearted lies that provoked it. As my understanding grew of just what all the post-1966 Black Power rhetoric meant, of just how ideology could come to bear upon personal, everyday relationships, I came to the painful realization that what "da revolution" implied, what that elusive vanguard was based on, was membership in a club so exclusive that, as one for whom the warmth of a village was sustenance, I couldn't begin to afford its ideological membership fee.

Not long after I arrived at Yale, some of the brothers who came from private schools in New Orleans held a "bag party." As a classmate explained it to me, a bag party was, a New Orleans custom wherein a brown paper bag was stuck on the door and anyone darker than it was denied entrance. That was one cultural legacy that would be put to rest in a hurry--we all made sure of that. But in a manner of speaking, it was replaced by an opposite test whereby those who were deemed "not black enough," ideologically, were to be shunned. I was not so sure this was an improvement.

The sixties bequeathed us new and inventive ways of talking about race, thus presenting us with a chimera called the "black community." And sometimes, to be sure, solidarity was conjured into existence--at least a provisional existence. In, 1970, a day before the legendary May Day rally in New Haven, I noticed two Black Panthers leaving my entryway at Calhoun "College," as the undergraduate dorms are known. Brimming with the spirit of brotherly bonding, I introduced myself to them. Panthers were glamorous creatures, after all--the shock troops of our beleaguered nation. I told them my name and, for their future reference, my room number. They looked at each other uneasily. I understood why a little later that evening, when they knocked on the door, bearing my yellow windbreaker, my copy of Bobby Seale's Seize the Time, and Karma, the Pharoah Sanders album--all items they had stolen from my room earlier. I hadn't noticed their absence, and I felt oddly touched by their return. I suppose I didn't know whether this was a parable of brotherhood or of the limits of brotherhood. It was not an uncommon quandary.

THE TALENTED TAR BABY

CERTAINLY it might have been nice to hear a few words about ambiguity and ambivalence when I first learned to be black, back when the blaxploitation flicks were first-run, and the draft boards were quite pleased to take college dropouts. The flrst time as tragedy; the second time as farce: for me, the first time wasn't tragedy, quite, but it was as much melodrama as comedy. Still, maybe there are limits even to the ludic. Sometimes the relentless ironicism of contemporary culture feels like a vaccination against earnestness, which is the sort of precaution you take when you've been--in a phrase of Baldwin's--betrayed by too much hoping.

Sometime in my sophomore year, I found myself fighting between becoming the individual I so longingly came to Yale to become and wanting within the deepest part of me to feel black and a vital part of the collective. But wasn't this a game we had played before, when we had baited the white boy? Always before we had won. The game came down to the matter of name. Ralph Ellison describes its workings as follows:

> Tar Baby, that enigmatic figure from Negro folklore, stands for the world. He leans, black and gleaming, against the wall of life utterly noncommittal under our scrutiny, our questioning, starkly unmoving before our naive attempts at intimidation. Then we touch him playfully and before we can say Sonny Liston! we find ourselves stuck. Our playful investigations become a labor, a fearful struggle, an agony. Slowly we perceive that our task is to learn the proper way of freeing ourselves to develop, in other words, technique.
>
> Sensing this, we give him our sharpest attention, we question him carefully, we struggle with more subtlety; while he, in his silent way, holds on, demanding that we perceive the necessity of calling him by his true name as the price of our freedom.

The idea is that we have always had to trick the white man into learning not to take appearances at face value, especially social roles or relationships so tradition-bound as to seem "human" or "natural" or universal.

I didn't know my college dean very well. It was his first year at Calhoun, as it was mine. I remember with some unease those first few months in the college when, walking as nonchalantly through the courtyard as I was able, I happened too frequently for accident (and frequently enough so that for years later I avoided that route) to cross paths with him. "How's it going," he'd invariably ask, his brow wrinkling with concern.

Do you find our courses difficult? Are you studying enough?" Until the first time he asked, perhaps well into the third week of school, I had pretty much forgotten that I was supposed to feel anxious; I had forgotten the sociological consequences of being black from Appalachia and "at Yale." But I'd try to smile and retort coolly the most relaxed "Yeah" I could manage. And yeah, I was studying every night, all night. ?When I visit today, those walkways reverberate with those "conversations" still.

Amid all the racial and political ferment, I'd decided I wanted to spend a year in Africa (yes, it was an attempt to flee, and maybe even to resolve some of the racial perplexities I'd been experiencing). I went to the dean's office and stated my case as cogently as I could. He smiled benignly, because he understood, then told me how impossible the whole thing was. I think I stopped listening once I heard his tone; for "yes" and "no" are secondary to tone, at least when you find yourself sitting across the desk from some white man whose wallet you're trying to persuade him to share. He wanted to know my name; and I, a Tar Baby, was an arrogant enough part of Yale by now to treasure secretly the knowledge that my college dean didn't know my name. "Hustler" was his first guess; to him, I'd venture, I'm still "hustler" to this day.

For me, it was a matter of getting my bearings. I learned to be black in a world where DeCh and Robby ruled--one infused with the banked outrage and the revolutionary temper of the times. Most of all, I counted myself lucky that I saw DeCh address the May Day rally in 1970, speaking out against the wrongs of Viet Nam and Cambodia, the abuses of the FBI and other nefarious government agencies. He was in his fullest glory that day, as he galvanized a crowd of a hundred thousand with his words and with his very presence. He sizzled; he smote. He was mesmerizing, artfully plaiting mordant humor with passion and uplift, defiance and courage and common sense: he was Malcolm X and Martin Luther King, Jr., in one. This was DeCh at full strength--a man, as I say, who could lead us into the promised land.

And then? People said he peaked at the May Day rally. Yale was where he'd excelled and Yale was where he would stay, for the longest time. It worried and depressed me that he wouldn't leave New Haven. Years went by, the rest of us dispersed, and he was still in New Haven, where he got a job working in the financial aid office. I think he had dreams--mad, emancipatory dreams--and he needed to wait for those dreams to die. He did leave, finally. One day, he decided to attend law school at the University of Pennsylvania; and he ended up working at the FCC, though he never seemed quite happy there. Whenever we met, over the years he'd still be chain-smoking his way through a pack and his eyes would sparkle as he repeated stories from the old days--especially the one about how I volunteered to be secretary of the BSAY. And I would smile, and nod, and remember, and sometimes get misty. I was the one he had deputized as his official stenographer, his Boswell. I had seen him at the height of his magnificence, and not only that, I had taken notes.

And sometimes he asked about Robby. Robby, who founded, funded, and ran, superbly, the Carter G. Woodson Institute at the University of Virginia. Robby, who became actively involved in alumni affairs and--it was one of the proudest moments of his life--was awarded the Yale Medal by President A. Bartlett Giamatti. That was one answer you could give to the question about Robby. But there was another answer, too. Robby, the most brilliant scholar of our set, completed his dissertation with difficulty; and then gave up the ghost. His book? The book, he'd explain, was really two books, he was coming to realize. At least two. He never published the book, though, or anything much at all. Something had more or less stilled his pen for the rest of his professional career. Instead of writing, it seemed, he put on weight.

DeCh died first, less than a year ago. A couple of weeks before, when I learned he was dying of lung cancer, I wrote him a long letter, trying to explain something of what he'd meant to me. Then, a month ago, Robby died: he'd been felled by a stroke, then a heart attack. The weight, the blood pressure, people said--the way middle-aged friends tick off the risk factors, anxious about their own mortality.

Some of the black students I knew at Yale dropped out, or pursued militancy to a point of no return, or went mad: these were still the early days of affirmative action, and this business of recruitment would be considerably refined in the years to come. Jerry was the first to die, stricken, as he was, in the middle of his junior year. Two rumors competed for his epitaph: "overdose," skeptics said; "hemorrhage," replied his friends. There was Tommy, gunned down by Gil Rochon--the tall Am. Stud. grad student from New Orleans who had freckles, a conical Afro, and a wife whom Tommy was sleeping with. There was Eddie Jackson, my roommate, who "broke down" not long after, in hot pursuit of his blackness; later he killed himself by plunging a butcher's knife into his heart.

It is also true that some of the black students I knew at Yale have gone on to serve in Congress, as big-city mayors, as presidents and vice presidents of major conglomerates. This is what members of the crossover generation are supposed to do: cross over. This is what the civil activists and social engineers who recruited us had in mind. It's how the trope of the "Talented Tenth" was to be retrieved and refashioned for modern times. And yet there's a sense in which DeChabert and Robinson represented more to me than any of the "success stories"; and their failures of fulfillment (the oldest college story of them all) grieved and rankled me as my own. I didn't go to their funerals: the truth is, I wasn't ready for them to be dead, either of them. We were supposed to storm the citadel together, to serve on the Yale Club board of directors together, to summer at Martha's Vineyard together, to grow old together. They would be on hand to explain to me the difference between selling out and buying in. Our kids were supposed to marry each other; to graduate from schools where we would give the commencement addresses. Ours was to be the generation with cultural accountability, and cultural security: the generation that would tell white folks that we would not be deterred--that, whether they knew it or not, we too were of the elite.

But then they had shown me that playing the name game with white folks was relatively easy. It was when we turned the game upon ourselves that the rules became much more subtle. It is a sticky business when two Tar Babies demand to know each other's names. For the names changed from moment to moment; as we discarded one--"the Talented Tenth," say--another would take its place. Scars heal slowly and only partially: Flesh be not proud. You might think of it as a cultural counterpart to the physiological response known as "hyperpigmentation": the medical fact that black skin responds to injury by getting even blacker. Of course, many of our injuries were self-inflicted.

And even as I was defending myself against those black fellows who had forgotten my name, I found myself struggling to keep white people (even at Yale) from changing my name, taking my name from me. "Black, scholarship boy, remarkable verbal potential for one in his demographic group; mediocre performance. C student." This sort of naming ritual, a self-fulfilling appellative prophecy, they fit interchangeably onto so many of those bright black kids I loved at Yale. So many of us who came to New Haven eager to fulfill that part of ourselves long repressed in ghetto schools and communities far too numerous to name saw our deepest dreams dashed and our deepest fears realized in that sociological naming ritual. If we weren't crushed in a dialectic over what was "black" and what was "blacker," then we were crushed by those bored administrators and jaded teachers who could not see the longing and the impatience to learn buried deep behind the particular mask that each of us chose to wear. Perhaps slipshod, perhaps not so holy, yet these were our masks, and the care and the concern and the struggle and joy that went into fashioning and wearing them was all that some of us ever had at Yale and all that some of us have, even now, left of college.

But I was fortunate; I loved the place. I loved the library and the seminars, I loved talking with the professors; I loved "peeping the hole card" in people's assumptions and turning their logic back upon themselves. I had more chip than shoulder, and through it all I demanded of every person with whom I chanced to interact that they earn the right to learn my name. More often than not, white folks stopped at "hustler." And I, like Tar Baby, would tell myself I had won. For years, I would listen for news and watch the mail for word of those I knew there, for news of those I loved and those I despised, of those I trusted and those I feared. Only sometimes do I feel guilty that I was among the lucky ones, and only sometimes do I ask myself why.

12. Charles Martin, Y'1974—Tentacles and Sting

Bio:

Charles Martin, B.A. '74, Ph. D.'88, is Associate Professor of Comparative Literature at Queens College/City University of New York and a photographer whose images are internationally exhibited and part of such museums and public collections as Brooklyn Union Gas, the Tokyo Metropolitan Museum of Photography library, the Museum of the City of New York, and the Center for Photography at Woodstock. His publications include the catalogue Home & Away and articles in journals such as Black Renaissance/Renaissance Noire, Genre, Studies in Latin American Popular Culture, and the Yale Journal of Criticism. The National Endowment has awarded him grants for the Humanities, the Research Foundation of the City University of New York, the Tinker Foundation, West Virginia University and Yale University.

For my father, the fraternal twins of college experience were Lincoln University and Yale. His half was Lincoln and mine was Yale. Just outside of Philadelphia, Lincoln, along with other colleges around the country such as Howard, Spelman and Fisk, had long been a powerful, productive magnet for black students more comfortable in an environment where their color marked them as the norm rather than as exceptions or excluded. Langston

Hughes was graduated from Lincoln after beginning at Columbia where, he wrote, he felt greatly alienated and less attracted to the Ivy walls than to surrounding Harlem and truck farming in Staten Island. Hughes did, however, take Lincoln to task by bringing to light that the college then employed almost no black professors, a policy he was surprised to find endorsed by a majority of students. Other Lincoln graduates include Kwame Nkrumah, Benjamin Azikiwe and the father of Paul Robeson.

All his life, many of my father's friends were classmates, and sons often followed fathers to Lincoln, as at Yale. For myself, it is mostly memories, not friends that have endured from my undergraduate days.

Lincoln graduates could be inordinately proud. I remember going with my father to a reunion of several classes where one man stood and spoke of the glories of his classmates. There was rousing applause and then a weak shouting squeaked out of an old man who used a cane and moved with careful effort forward to the podium where he asserted, when he got there, that he was the oldest alumnus present, that few of his classmates were still alive, but that as a barely remaining group they still could do better and with more grace and vigor anything that was possible for any class represented in the audience. He challenged the first man, or any others who dared, to meet his class in any way. He said his few living classmates stood ready! His outburst was followed by even more feverish applause from all assembled.

When I was about to go off to college in Fall 1970, Dad enjoyed draping his face in a long, dampened look at gatherings of his 1940s classmates from Lincoln and woefully noting that I was not enrolling in his alma mater. "Make him!" one outraged graduate said once. "I can't make him" my father lamented. "And now it's too late to apply. I'll just have to let him go where he got in. To Yale!" A bright mood rekindled at this punch line, and the Lincoln men joked that Yale wasn't offensive as an alternative. My father retold the story at every possible occasion. He liked the idea that I went there, and he liked it, again, when years later I returned for a Ph. D.

In some ways it was surprising that I went to Yale. I had gone through most of high school expecting to go to college, but without thinking about where. My parents were not much worried by such a future choice either. Their only concern was that my grades be good. I always liked school and worked at it, and study to me was fun. I don't know if Yale actively recruited my high school, but one day the guidance counselor, Mrs. Donnelly, told me that someone with my good grades ought to apply there. Yale's name did not stand out to me. I do not recall it from before. Princeton was close enough to the Philadelphia area--my hometown, Yeadon--to know about, and I knew one older boy who had gone there. I knew about Harvard, too, as another local boy had gone there. Along with Lincoln, I knew about the local schools such as, Swarthmore, Drexel, Villanova, Temple, and University of Pennsylvania. I told my parents what the guidance counselor had said, and they said Yale was fine. I believe I was the first person from Yeadon High School even to apply to Yale.

The decision to go was not automatic, even after the offer of admission. For a long time I wanted to go to Brown University whose reputation was "progressive," though it wasn't clear to me exactly what that might mean, and to my parents such an idea was irrelevant. Grading there was switched from the usual letter system to something else, but that is about all I remember of it. Maybe Brown went to Pass/Fail. Yale halfway followed suit and came up with a grading system of its own that left hierarchy intact, but minus one rung: Honors, High Pass, Pass and Fail were substituted for the usual letter grades, effectively eliminating only "D."

Because I was so interested in Brown, I made a visit there for a special weekend that showcased the campus to black students who had received offers of admission. The students were from many places, with a concentration from the eastern seaboard. Academic programs were advertised and described, and campus life was touted, but I don't recall the facilities such as libraries, dorms and dining halls nearly so well as the musical groups that played those evenings. (Years later I learned my way around Brown, academically, as I taught a year there in Afro-American Studies.) Isaac Hayes and the Cannonball Adderly Quintet performed, and I was a fan of both. The good time I had further inclined me towards Brown, but several of the school's students candidly appraised the weekend to have been a great few days, but a high rise from a usually more subdued and level plain. The place was nice, they said, but not as good as that weekend's atmosphere. I thought about that carefully and finally did listen to the many people, especially my parents, who were saying, that Brown was fine but not a rival to Yale in history, tradition or clout.

That visit was the only campus excursion that I made to help in choosing a college. I accepted Yale's offer of admission without making any inventory of the campus. I figured the school library would be good, that my room would have a bed in it, and that the dining hall would serve food not as good as my mother's. All proved true. I did, though, glance at the campus before moving in. Some high school friends and I drove to Cape Cod--a last outing of people who had gone to high school and graduated together. New Haven was on the way, so we stopped for a brief inspection of the place where a few weeks later I would start classes. I saw Beineke Plaza with its marble walled Rare Book Library and sunken sculpture pit, with freshman Commons--the freshman dining area-- behind. I found my room in Silliman College. An empty wine bottle was in a closet and layers of dust had accumulated all around. We found our way back to the car and drove on to the Cape.

Over my years at Yale, I came to think of the place as a tentacled creature. Yale is not a mother image. It is not soft and caressing. It does not nurse you at a breast. Yale is closer to a sea anemone, that poisonous animal that is beautiful at first glance to the little fishes, but which kills them when they approach its waving tentacles--unless they are clown fish, in which case the sea anemone protects them. In return, the clown fish lure other fishes to the anemone, which lunches on the catch. Once in a while the anemone makes a mistake, or is just in a bad mood, and it devours a clown fish too. I was originally attracted by Yale's waving tentacles of prestige, learning, the mythical name and a cache of snob cachet. In my first year at Yale, it was not entirely clear that I was immune to Yale's sting, though the selection process was supposed to have assured me that even though I might not have been the most handsome person on earth, nor the richest, nor the best athlete, I was fit to be a Yalie and, through four years of Yale I was guaranteed to be at least a clownfish.

Nevertheless, that first year was disconcerting. I became best of friends, by way of books, with Messrs. Sartre, Kierkegaard, Pope, Eliot and others. It also seemed that most whose acquaintance I did not make through a book I would hardly know at all. I had few friends and ate many of my first meals with my three roommates, one of whom was an outsize boor. He was convinced that College Board scores made the man and, since he was white, he thought probably he had outscored all of us on campus. He talked of scores all the time but without filling in his numbers. This annoyed me though I knew that he couldn't possibly have outscored me in everything. My combined general score was a little over 1370, and my best specialty test was a few points over 720. My dentist in Philadelphia, whose son was about to go to Williams College, always said with approval that I'd have gotten in anywhere--"even if you'd been white," as he put it. School, and my parents, moreso, had made me quite used to being in general at least an equal among the races.

I led my roommate along paths that were trickier than he surmised. After having many times replied only obliquely about test scores, one day I brought up the subject with him and added casually that scores weren't so important anyway. He was not so sure about that, but conceded that there might be some truth to it, that someone with low scores might do well at Yale, or if not there then in life. My roommate went on to announce his scores and waited for mine. The end of the '60s and the beginning of the '70s marked affirmative action, and there were white students on the prowl to worry those for whom the usually closed doors had been pried a little ajar. I had outscored my roommate in half of the tests. Inwardly, I gloated and smirked and my minuscule opinion of this roommate compressed even more. We didn't much talk about test scores after that, which further thinned our conversation. Other black students--of higher and lower scores, alike--approved of my scores and took them to mean that public high school had served some of us well. In high school, on the days we received report cards, our teachers usually wrote on the board the names of the students whose grades put them onto the Distinguished Honor Roll and the Honor Roll. I usually made the "distinguished," which pleased me and my parents, though none of us was obsessed with grades.

Those high school grades likely would have gotten me some kind of academic scholarship to college, but my father never had such a thought. At Lincoln he had run out of funds and been forced to halt his studies for a couple of years while he worked odd jobs to raise cash to meet college costs and reenter. He never stopped resenting that his parents had not been able to help pay for his schooling, and he carried as a badge of honor the obligation to pay for the education of his children. Once I graduated from college, he never gave me a penny, nor did I ask, but he paid for everything until then. My school costs were, in his mind, the ones that his parents should have managed for him.

In college, race took on new dimensions. It became, for some, less an effortless state and more an exerted territory. In my hometown, black families lived for the most part together in a few neighborhoods, while whites lived apart in theirs. (There were no other groups.) There were a few blocks of spillage where the residents were integrated. The elementary and high school, however, were integrated and race did not define hard lines of friendship though, the school day over, most kids returned to their neighborhoods and that was where most time was spent. On summer visits to my grandmother's home in Culpeper, Virginia, as soon as I was out of the bus station and onto her farm and those of my cousins, the only people I saw were black--and they were mostly family and neighboring farmers. My parents, Southerners both, hated racism, but they, themselves, were not racists though my mother, informally and unstated, held most whites suspect and more or less on probation pending proof of some merit.

But Yale was a marked change, with everyone no longer limited to studying together, but now actually living together. I made friends of all colors and from many places--black, white, brown and yellow Asians, Latinos. In this, I was not alone, but friendships according to color were of concern to some. There were kids who actively sought out other black kids, searching for critical mass in numbers without much regard for affinity. There were also students who, simply, wanted nothing to do with whites--and felt that was the way it should be for everyone. I remember a girl from Honduras who found herself pressured. At Yale she found that many expected her to distance herself from whites, even though she herself was of interracial parents. Such issues were new to her and without use for some others.

And there were white kids, who, though they had occasional black friends, felt comfortable only so long as the circle of friends was mainly white. There were also black kids who, so far as I could tell, had no black friends at all.

Many of Yale's students seemed concerned with impressing each other and the professors, but not with making friends. In most of my courses, we went into class and picked a seat without directing more than cursory greetings to anyone. After an hour or so in class it would be time to go. Most picked up their books and left, once again with few if any words to each other.

There was a good deal of work to do, and since there are never enough hours in a day, numbers of students extended their waking hours. Will power worked for some, others swallowed cups of coffee, and a few downed amphetamine tablets as though they were vitamins. Winter nights were cold. I typed quite a few papers freshman year huddled in sweaters, wrapped in blankets and wearing gloves because, in the seventies, the country weathered the "energy crisis": worry that the country's oil reserves would run out and that overseas sources, not controlled by the U.S., might slow or close. To conserve, according to public service and news announcements, cold weather thermostat temperatures were to have been kept down at sixty eight degrees. And that was during the daytime, I think. Yale did its part by turning off the heat at night. As many students made it a practice to study late at night, either in their rooms or in libraries that remained open, such as the ones in the colleges, this made for a somewhat frigid student body.

This was, as well, the time of the Viet Nam war and, in New Haven, the then recent trial of Black Panther Party leader Bobby Seale, whose situation had been underscored by the university's attention when its president, Kingman Brewster, publicly doubted, the year before, that Seale would get a fair trial. Another prominent campus figure was the college chaplain, William Sloane Coffin, a warm-hearted person who spoke of the need to mix belief, social concern and action. The school year before my arrival at Yale, the college's classes did not finish, as many students became interested and involved in the Black Panther trial, from discussing its issues to demonstrating. Such attention to New Haven issues was rare and some did not like it. There were Yalies whose relationship with the city of New Haven consisted of little more than occasionally shopping for an ivy league outfit or a dinner out. Some students, at the announcement that the semester's exams were suspended, simply left town. As one student speaker at the freshman conference put it, phalanxes of limousines and long cars arrived, picked up wealthy Yalies, and escorted them early to summer endeavors.

Yale anti-war demonstrators, especially those of my class, often seemed to me to embrace causes as temporary diversions. With festive yells, Yalies packed off to demonstrations, but often they kept one eye on their watches intent, like Norman Mailer at the Washington peace march which spawned the book Armies of the Night, to return to parties at the end of the day, celebrating in the name of the cause, chic and hip. Of course, some of the activists were dedicated, but they seemed outnumbered to me.

I was among the ranks of the uncommitted. Not because I had no beliefs, but because I found no believable way to express them. The antics of the committed students were hilarious to me, and I knew that my joining their ranks would simply make me ridiculous not to them but to myself. I was never much of a joiner, so I observed. Often, I found myself sitting on the outer circle of events, analyzing them with an eye not cold but distant, recording and categorizing. I noted the things that I did not want to be. I noted the things that I would avoid being. But there wasn't that much that I wanted to be.

Not surprisingly, the majority of the people around at Yale seemed to be preparing for professions. Some wanted to be doctors and lawyers. My parents thought that either profession would be fine for me, too, commanding respect and earning good salary. Lawyers are needed everywhere, my parents told me. For a while, I went along and thought I might be a lawyer one day. But there didn't seem to be any compelling reasons for doing any of those things. In spite of the enticements, I could generate no internal fires to drive me along those paths--respectable but without attraction for me.

It was easy at Yale to be insulated against the outside. A thirst for liquor could be quenched without leaving the dorms. (Liquor stores delivered door-to-door on campus, though the state drinking age, at 21, was set above the age of almost all of the students.) For dances, the "mixers" brought women from other schools onto the campus. And secret societies thrived, the most insular groups of all. All of that was changing a little in the 70s, nudged if not rocked by the radical events of the country. For black students, most of these activities were of little, if any, appeal.

Changes, such as they were, though, were seen as momentous, even upheavals. My class was the first that entered with women. A few years before, Yale began the transition from male to coed by admitting some women as transfers. The idea that a rising women's enrollment might cut down the number of entering men--since the entering classes could only be so large--moved the Yale Corporation in 1971, at the prodding of the alumni, to state it would never let the number of entering male Yalies drop below 1000, as this country--and maybe others as well--annually needed the benefit of 1000 new male leaders working for its advancement.

It was lonely away from home, its conveniences and old friends. Before college my visits away had been to two summer camps: Atwater, a black camp in East Brookfield, Massachusetts, farther away from home than Yale would be; and Onas, a Quaker camp on the Neshaminy Creek in Pennsylvania. Neighbors of mine went to Atwater, so a part of home was there with me, and Onas, the first time I went, was an easy transition as my stay was only two weeks. Now college was a real move, and my first extended experience without people I had known since kindergarten. At Yale, I didn't know anyone. The prep school kids had an advantage: they had friends from their schools. College was also the first time that most of my friends did not know one another. In fact, my college friends were separate pockets with little interchange.

One of my roommates and I, not much liking Yale, spent many nights considering alternative plans for the coming years. We thought of the leave of absence: go away for a while and see some world. Find out if it was as forbidding as Yale. But we couldn't decide when would be the best time to take off or where to go. A departure after freshman year would mean, whenever the return, facing three more years of the rut we now were in. We stayed.

The dining hall was another often desolate area. Whenever I entered it alone, I swept it for my few friends. If I didn't find one, I loaded my tray with food and headed for an empty table, preferably in a comer, and sat down to eat, silent, in the noisy dining hall. My college, Silliman, had tables for two by windows, and I liked them. Sometimes there would be two, even three people at one, but I remember one day seeing at the small table someone who had moved a chair to the side of the table so he faced the window, his back to the rest of the dining hall. He may have loved the view, whatever it was that day, but it was clear that he didn't want to be bothered.

Intimidation by the dining hall--or annoyance with it--was common and could be seen every day. I had a friend who most of the three years I knew him at school, would not enter the dining hall by himself. He either called friends on the telephone to come to lunch or he waited until his roommates were around, or he found someone in the courtyard to go in with. But he never went through the dining hall parade alone. There are other people who bring books to the dining hall, and then go directly to small, empty tables, where they will be free to read. A scrutiny of these people would have shown that they rarely turned the pages. They were not doing much reading, but without a book they would have been defenseless. Sometimes I would eat in other dining halls, just for change.

Still, the dining hall staff made an effort to make the place special. There were theme nights where the fare would be French, Hawaiian, southern, "health food" and so forth. There were also experiments with soy-burgers and other replacements for the typical. The staff generally was friendly. I remember an Irish woman, Mary, who always greeted diners with a smile. Michel, a French cook who, by the time I graduated, was director of all the university dining halls, would come to the French table that met weekly or so. Lina, from Nevis, especially liked me, and asked one day, "Where are you from? South Carolina?" I told her no, that I was from Pennsylvania. "All the same thing," she said with a smile. She found that very amusing. Why?, I never knew. She often would mention to me South Carolina (which is where my father was from).

After dinner, the main thing was study--to the library for books and to read and write there. My library of preference was Sterling. And if I remember, correctly, the Cross Campus library had not yet opened. That first year, the lawn across the street from Sterling was blocked by wood pickets and behind them was a construction site. We were told that Yale was building the Cross Campus to house the books typically most made use of by undergraduates and so relieve Sterling of the heaviest predictable use. Traditionalists did not want the lawn destroyed, so the Cross Campus was built below ground and then the lawn was replaced. Before I graduated, the Cross Campus was opened complete with the tunnel that connects it to Sterling. I always preferred Sterling, particularly the large Main Reading Room, but also some of the smaller rooms near its entrance, such as L & B. I liked roaming through Sterling's stacks whose books, though often dusty, seemed unlimited. One reason that I chose to return to graduate school at Yale was the opportunity again to have use of Sterling. As a grad student specializing in Portuguese, I often felt that a portion of Sterling's holdings were mine personally. Hardly anyone worked in

Portuguese, so the books often were untouched. When I pulled older editions off the shelves to flip through the pages, clouds of dust would rise.

Yale, the tentacled anemone, was attractive to me by the second semester of freshman year. I had gotten over homesickness and settled in to campus life, especially drawn to areas of expression. I took an art course, for which I drew, workmanlike. The professor gave general instruction, and his grad student teaching assistant was very kind and encouraging. She found in my drawings "childlike purity." She didn't have it in her to say I was lousy. I was and I knew it, so easel art was not long with me. Math was a let down, too. I placed into an advanced course, but did not understand anything the teacher said, a problem complicated by his bare command of English. I guess writing down the symbols was supposed to have been adequate.

I met with the professor a few times to tell him I could not get through the advanced calculus course. He insisted I could, though he never indicated how. He seemed to feel that no one understood anything, making me just another yet to see the answers. One day, he said, I would get the equations. Finally I convinced someone that was not going to happen, and by then it was late in the semester and the more basic course, that I switched into, still calculus, had covered more ground than I could recover. I stopped going to math altogether and, I don't know why, at the end of the term I checked the exam schedule and took the final. Of course I flunked. It was the only definite thing that happened to me in that class.

Another course I had trouble with for very different reasons was the prerequisite poetry course for the English major. I was not sure I would be a major, but I always liked to read and it made sense to take a course whose major I might want. (I did in fact major in English.) In high school I may not have always liked the reading I did for English, but in this freshman year class it drove me to hell--some of it via Milton's Paradise Lost. One of the class's bookmarks was a student who found a way to insert into any discussion of hell, heaven or in between--i.e. just about anytime--some references to Dante's Inferno, which he pronounced always as though he were in an Italian class. I found him as insufferable as the readings. Back then, I don't think I knew what was canon, but I would have liked to have melted it. Nor did I like my professor, a polite, mild mannered man whom I would have liked to fire to any of the hells we were reading about. But I guess I was worried that he, like Dante, might have had a Virgil to bring him back, so I never tried to put him away. Instead, I skipped class regularly and remember at least two occasions when I sent a paper to class, via roommate. I was absent but the papers were on time. And I did well, too.

In other literature classes, I was always told that I read too politically. This was before the recognition of what today would be called cultural studies. Back then it was heavily New Criticism, especially at Yale whose professors included Robert Penn Warren and William Wimsatt. The critical winds swept over English literature but soughed softly without rustling up much criticism of society. I would find in books issues of class and social position, only to be told that such items were not the significant subjects of the works at hand. It was possible, indeed standard, to read Faulkner without more than a perfunctory noting of race, and to read, say, King Lear as a story about unfaithful daughters without noting why they were so, or that the bastard of the play, Edmund, was a social outcast who understood that his only avenue of respect would have to be paved by himself and over his opponents who could only be met roughly.

I kept reading literature, but found little engaging in the English Department. Offerings of appeal to me in the rest of the humanities were sparse. At such times during the first year, I thought a good deal of taking time off, but I decided to stay and make the best of my predicament.

There were some academic bright spots. One was learning French. The language opened to me France, which I came to like for both Paris and the southern coast. Besides the land, there was the literature. French literature had some things that I enjoyed, from the existentialists that everyone was reading then--Camus and Sartre and committed littérature engagée--to the swashbuckling tales of Alexandre Dumas. But what especially drew me were such Francophone writers as Aimé Césaire from Martinique; Senghor and Birago Diop from West Africa; Frantz Fanon, the student of Césaire. The political writings of Fanon made immediate sense to me and fit much of the confrontation of black and white societies. Césaire made the same kind of sense, and I could lose myself, as well, in his poetry and theater, such as his play on King Christophe of Haiti.

But Diop's work had the most impact for me, his Tales and New Tales of the griot Amadou Koumba. These animal stories and accounts of ordinary squabbles, jealousies and resolutions in village life stood out for me because they showed, in foreign language set in foreign place, life and circumstances, relationships and people far more like those I knew at home and throughout all my life than the violent, pained and polemicized work of celebrated American writers such as Richard Wright or William Faulkner. Diop's stories, fables of everyday, made sense to me and, most important, they were not bitter, but happy and sad; not distraught, but successful or facing chicanerie and setbacks. French, out of the classroom, opened a world of literature to me whose characters not only suffered and cried, but rejoiced and laughed. And they did so where to be black was not to be questioned or put on trial. Years later, Diop before he died revealed that the stories were lifelike, but contrary to what was indicated, not all taken from a single griot. Amadou Koumba was a composite, which for me meant that even more people knew such stories, and so multiplied their worth.

Another language that was a spot of some light for me was Arabic. I began to learn it mostly as a break from the school's typically Western offerings. I had really wanted to learn a West African language, but none were offered. Arabic was as close as I got, but as it was not what I really wanted, I let it go after a couple of years. There were other courses that I liked, and more particularly, professors whose minds sparkled.

I liked the stories of Jorge Luis Borges, from Argentina, and an especially good course for me was a seminar on Latin American literature. The teacher, a Latin American man, was informal, widely read, easy going and served a bottle or two of red wine at our weekly classes. He thought we should be relaxed and learn literature in a salon environment. We read a novel or a book of stories just about weekly, and wrote about them, each student presenting a paper in every class. The work of Garcia Márquez, Cortázar, Juan Rulfo, Nicanor Parra, Pablo Neruda and others was introduced to me there, and I learned more about Borges. When I met, a few years later, a niece of Garcia Márquez who studied at Yale, we used to talk about the work of her uncle.

Another excellent course was my senior tutorial guided by Emir Rodriguez Monegal. I would read for a week and then meet him in his office and we would talk about the books. My reading was Latin American novelists--nearly all the writing Garcia Márquez had then done--the occasional book of short stories, and many of the novels of William Faulkner. The fictional locales of Macondo and Yoknapatawpha were regular places of visit for me, and I much preferred Macondo, where one could dream and float in the clouds. Yoknapatawpha was mired for me in nightmares and mud. My final examination was before Monegal and, from the English Department, Michael Cooke, who I had not had any real contact with since dropping, freshman year, a course of his on Romanticism because the questions he posed were, to me, incomprehensible. This second meeting was much better. I got the impression that the final exam was a good moment for Monegal. Though I was an English major, I wanted to work with someone in Latin American literature, and I think the English department had its doubts about the wisdom of one of its majors so directed. Monegal looked at the whole thing, I always thought, as an opportunity to show the marvels of his department and the writers whose work he loved, and some of which he had published.

Latin American writing was so fresh that I wanted to go to Cuernavaca, Mexico, after graduation, and enroll in one of the several crash courses offered there in Spanish language. I dropped plans to go when, just before graduation; I got a job as a newspaper reporter. It probably worked out for the better, as that first interest in Spanish transformed into a desire to learn Portuguese which, many years later, I did in graduate school, where I stayed and got a doctorate and began my acquaintance with Brazil. Now I know Brazil reasonably well, whereas my experience of Spanish has been limited to a few days in Madrid and stops in the Cuban-Chinese restaurants that were downstairs and around the comer from an apartment I had in New York at 101st Street and Broadway.

Norman Holmes Pearson, a professor of American Studies, was another professor whose course I liked. His course was another that required weekly papers in response to fiction that we were assigned to read. I used to get up early in the morning and knock out the papers on my typewriter. I liked the discipline of it. I had worked the summer before as an intern feature writer at the Philadelphia Bulletin, and had grown used to, even quickened, by deadlines. I was used to typing, anyway, since my mother, once a secretary, had taught me to type in high school. I delayed and delayed learning typing until one of my last years in high school and then, I don't know why, I suddenly wanted to type. My mother had me at the keyboard and practicing drills before I would have had a chance to think about it, and at Yale, as at the Bulletin, it paid off.

Meetings with Pearson in his office were always scheduled and on time. He told our class that if we were going to be more than five minutes late not to come, but to call and reschedule because after five minutes had gone by he knew he could shut his door and read at least twenty five minutes before someone else would come in.

Pearson was an old man, sometimes in need of a cane, who taught young literature. Some of the class' reading was Ishmael Reed, William Melvin Kelly, Toni Morrison, William Gass, John Updike, Saul Bellow, Erica Jong and Joyce Carol Oates. Out of class, Pearson and I talked about Tom Wolfe. The New Journalism was an increasingly noted trend and Wolfe drew further attention to the movement, both as a central organizer and participant, by collecting together into a book a disparate variety of articles whose primary connection was their different authors' striking use of openly subjective journalism. I did not know, until he told me, that Wolfe had gone to grad school in American Studies at Yale, been Pearson's student, and had to write two dissertations to qualify. I wanted to know how bad the first one had been.. It was brilliant, wonderful writing, Pearson said. But not academic. So he had Wolfe write another. Pearson often had a glint in his eye and an impish grin. He would say such things and then ask how my own papers were coming along.

Aside from literature courses, I took some courses in writing, and two that stood out were ones taught by Loudon Wainwright and William Zinsser. Both courses required weekly writing--elements of this essay began in Zinsser's class more than twenty years ago--and Zinsser's demand always was for clarity and simplicity. He was an advocate of the ideas of Strunk and White, and after Zinsser taught his course for several years its methods became his very popular book, On Writing Well. His class was enjoyable and he always encouraged us. He wrote a recommendation for me for the job I took as a reporter after graduation, but I never saw him again for twenty four years.

His collected papers were donated to New York University, and his students were tracked down and invited to attend. I sat at the front of the room before the beginning of the ceremony--the acceptance of the papers. From the back of the room I heard his voice which, unmistakable, I recognized immediately. I got up and walked to where he was and, when he paused in the conversation he was having, I said to him, "Hello, Bill Zinsser." He replied in turn, "Hello, Charles Martin." Some teachers forget everyone, and some forget very little. Then again, there probably were not a great number of black students who had gone through his class, so I might have been a stand for color alone.

There were some professors who hated Yale. I took a philosophy course with one who barely required attendance and probably wouldn't have cared whether or not we did the reading. I remember meeting him at the end of the semester, on the lawn of the Cross Campus. We talked and chatted and, at the end of forty minutes or so, he remarked that the conversation had a great deal to do with the paper topic that I had planned. He told me I had earned an A, and he looked with a sneer at the students talking and walking around the lawn. He said he was satisfied with my work, and that was the end of the course!

Unrelated to classes, I spent much of my college time listening to music and playing drums. In the marching band I watched the football games, though I stopped after freshman year, realizing at last--as I had not in high school--that the crowds came for the action on the field, not for the band. As I never liked football too much, I did not continue with the band. With the concert band I played in concerts around the campus and went on tour to England, Holland and Belgium. The high point for me was our bus trip through southern England where we visited Stonehenge, which then was not fenced off. You could walk up to the stone monoliths and stand among them. I played in a number of informal bands and, in sophomore year, helped start a band, Mainspring that stayed together the rest of my college days. We played mainly on campus, in common rooms, dining halls, and sometimes outside on the Old Campus. Our taste was formed by everything that we heard. We played original music, most of it written by Jamie Snead, and whatever else we liked which included the work of Miles Davis, Freddie Hubbard, Flora Purim, Yusef Lateef and Traffic. Most of us listened to a lot of Hendrix, Sly & the Family Stone, George Clinton and James Brown, but the band was basically a jazz group. The group's personnel varied over the years, but Jamie and I were always in the band. The band practiced in several places and eventually found a more or less permanent rehearsal space in one of the squash courts in Trumbull. No one played ball there, and we covered the walls with sound absorbing material. Eventually some other bands got wind of our space and moved in, too. At one point, there was equipment from three groups loaded into every bit of the space.

As a group, Mainspring was more about music than friendship. We did not spend time together collectively. We did not visit each other much. Some never visited at all. The piano player and I were friends. The guitar and saxophone players were friends. The bass player's friends were not in the band. Even so, we had dinner once a week in the same dining hall, though we usually did not all eat together. We might visit tables for a few minutes, but off the music stand, our interests varied: science, art, religious studies, writing, etc.

Along with playing drums in the band, I often played guitar in my room or in Silliman with some friends whose taste went from Buddy Guy and Junior Wells to Bob Dylan to Hendrix to Crosby, Stills and Nash. Again, we played in squash courts, but these were still used for squash. We'd go over and, if no one was there, we'd go in and play. The echo made it something like singing in a reverberation chamber. Guitar playing was not a strength of mine, but our audience for those informal jams was only us.

I was always impressed by items such as the squash courts, which were to me an example of the degree to which Yale furnished, physically, so much. Though Silliman was a rather ordinary looking place, the campus boasts architecture of many styles and periods, with towers, arches and courtyards replete with gargoyles, and the often plush interiors of the college's spacious common rooms, high ceilinged, wood-worked dining halls and hidden rooms with secret compartments.

The Payne-Whitney gym contains on the third floor the largest suspended swimming pool in the world and elsewhere is equipped, for example, with a wooden horse mounted on curved floor without comers so that a polo player could practice shots alone, with the ball always returning. The gym also includes set ups of oars in a sizable mock up scull built into a small pool of running water to simulate the force of actually rowing through a river's current. The crew team could practice indoors. I was aware of crew at Yale since, before coming to school, Yale requested information of the incoming students, ranging from interests and dislikes, to size and weight. Accordingly, the school suggested areas and activities that might be especially appropriate.

The athletic department notified me in the mail that though I was perhaps a little too tall, my light weight suggested that in sport I might be right to be a coxswain--the person who sits at the stem of a rowing scull and bellows "stroke" to the oarsmen to set the tempo. I'd often seen people rowing in practice and races for crew along the Schuylkill River in Philadelphia, but I'd never thought much about the sport. And there at the gym, the training apparatus beckoned. One thing, architecturally, that I did not like was the look of Davenport College, where the pillars and white arches called up for me images of old southern plantations and imaginings of slavery.

Yale's exaggerated sense of scale that begins with gargantuan and grows to mammoth is not confined to the architecture. The Yale Daily News, rag that it was, was "The Oldest College Daily." Similarly, the Yale Record, was billed as the "Oldest College Humor Magazine." The marching band was the "Oldest Precision Marching Band." Yale's football team won more games than any other football team in the history of the nation. And, hyperbole of hyperbole, there is the supposed grandeur of the slogan, "For God, for country and for Yale."

The trip to Yale opened the door for me, too, to travel, exploration on my own. After freshman year I spent the summer in France. I had studied French through high school without managing more than a bare acquaintance with the language and the first year at college I learned a little more. A good way to learn for real would be total immersion on location--a visit abroad. My parents were not wild about the idea, but they did not oppose it since I had an older brother who lived permanently in Italy. I only wanted to travel for the summer, not relocate, so they were not too much worried that I would be lost to them. My parents must have seen it as a continuation of the move away from home, a step that was not traumatic rupture, but due course. For my father, to be away from home was to move forward through a cycle. He was from South Carolina and had been away from home for college and before that, too. Once, one of his sisters went to the train station to catch a train somewhere, and he went along to see her off. At the station while they were waiting, a friend of my father approached and said he had a ticket to Philadelphia for a trip that he could not make. He asked if my father wanted it. My father said yes. The train to Philadelphia was leaving before his sister's train, and my father told her that now she, not he, was the one sending someone off. He asked some others at the station to tell his parents, and he departed. At least I let them know in advance.

To help me find out about flights abroad, there were newspapers, magazines and word of mouth, all providing lots of information. Icelandic Air was cheap. You went to Iceland and on to Luxembourg. Paris, my destination, was a train ride away, just a few hours. When I exited the airport in Luxembourg, I went to Paris where I spent only about a week before going to southern France and spent the balance of the summer, several weeks of it in a campground run by Catholic priests--who seemed to be about the only religious people on the grounds. From there I made a quick trip to Italy and back to southern France before returning in the Fall for sophomore year. The following years I visited other places I had never been to before. I went to Key West and drove across the country to California. I went back to Cape Cod. I'd been bitten by the travel bug.

At Yale I had my first experience of living in a city proper, though the campus was in many ways removed from surrounding New Haven. Some of the colleges were surrounded by empty moats, imposing walls stood in front of just about all of them, and large iron gates demarcated Yale's domain. Even so, the gates were usually open. The campus was a fortress, but not a locked one as it would come to be as crime and fear rose in New Haven over the years.

New Haven was small and manageable, and struck me rather as a sleepy town. The downtown greens, once walkways of great elms before the city was struck by Dutch Elm disease, were essentially sprawling lawns. I heard otherwise about New Haven from Willie Ruff, a French horn player and bassist who played both classical music and jazz. He had recorded with Miles Davis and was a professor in the School of Music. I got to know Willie while I was an undergraduate, and also would see him while I was a graduate student. He told me about the days when New Haven was alive with jazz. Almost any jazz musician, he said, who played in New York City would play in New Haven before or afterwards, so there had been great music in New Haven all the time. Willie was a good person to know, as well, because he was cheerful and ever in good spirits, one of the folks who it was nice to see around campus.

Photography was twice an affair for me at Yale--as an undergraduate and as a graduate student. As an undergraduate, I was introduced to the darkroom by an upperclassman who informally taught several interested people. I watched him go through some basics of darkroom chemistry, though the way this guy did things it was more like making soup--quite inexact. I developed film and printed pictures, but all of them are gone, which is just as well, as I did not make too many images of note.

I was more interested in taking pictures than in processing them, which still remains true. It was not until grad school that I seriously applied myself to the darkroom and to image making, but that second time around I was working mostly in the Art School. It was at Yale, in the Afro-American Cultural Center, that I did my first photo shows.

Senior year I had a pleasant job. I was a freshman counselor. The pay was something like free room and board. The job was to advise about sixteen or twenty freshmen students. Advisement consisted of looking over their schedules, making suggestions about courses of study, and generally fielding their questions about the place. As a senior, the freshman counselor also stood to show, if there were any doubts, that four years at the place were manageable. I got along well with most of my freshmen, and being their counselor was generally no more complicated than keeping the door to my room open. If any of them wanted to come in, they would. Not surprisingly, I was closest with the several who lived on my floor, as they could drop in on their way to and from their rooms. Getting down or up the stairs from the floor below was hardly insurmountable, but the distance was sufficient that I did know that group less well. I remained for them more a counselor, while for the nearer group the relationship was more informal and less dependent upon an organized meeting. I can't say that I did anything for my counselees but I can say that I don't think I did anything to ruin any of them.

In my last year at Yale, I applied for a job as a newspaper reporter. The summer before I had worked as an intern reporter at the Philadelphia Bulletin, and I'd liked it, and it seemed a reasonable way to write for a living. My first job after Yale was at the New London Day. I tied down the job well before I graduated so, unlike friends of mine who had no secure next step, I was not worried about what was to come.

I had time to think about the soon to be finished years at college. Despite the difficulties of adjustment and the falseness and pretentiousness of many around me, I liked Yale. I discovered that Yale was the anemone whose tentacles could sting, but that I was a clownfish of sorts, comfortable among them, but soon to be in search of another home--perhaps a less stinging one. As for my father, he continued to remark that Yale, after Lincoln, was not so bad. He put a blue bulldog Yale decal on his car.

13. Carlton Bush, H'1976—Bicentennial Blues

The Fillmore East had long closed, so New York would never be the kind of oasis I imagined Cambridge would be when I arrived in fall of 1972. Freshman year, outside our world, Nixon. and his cabal of droogs ran rampant through civil liberties and constitutional rights like Forbidden Planet's monsters of the Id. The prevailing political and social landscape remained venal and meretricious, prey to a spiritual pollution contaminated by indifference and benign neglect. But thanks to the vestiges of Lyndon Johnson and the Great Society, the primary concern of students was democracy, not the economy, and though the Vietnam war still thundered in Southeast Asia, in Cambridge, we worried about the quality of our lives and not necessarily the quantities associated with it. To some degree, freshman year among the majority students was tinged with nostalgia for Fifties' culture--cars, American graffiti, doo-wop and record labels. For students of any ethnicity, our eyes dared to poise on the future and what role we may play in its unfolding.

So Harvard, under nattily dressed President Bok, provided a utopia under construction, which, indirectly or perhaps intentionally, stimulated a permissive freedom for hothouse flower children, also under construction. This pedogenesis, nurtured with a steady atmosphere of jazz, cultured the Harvard student's DNA. Derek Bok, a former labor lawyer, known to be part of Nixon's "enemies list", had married the daughter of Gunnar Myrdal, one of the leading European theoretical social scientists concerned with race and America. So we were emboldened in our freedom by our proximity to someone who might have understood us. One day freshman year, Paul Ruffins, noticed Bok walking across the Freshman Quad and remarked, "oh, he must be a Harvard Student". Bok smoothly responded, "Why, do I look snotty and stuck up?" without breaking stride. No matter how much of Harvard was annoying, you had to appreciate their somewhat real awareness of the student community.

Humble, tasteful, patient, sharp, stylish--black Harvard undergraduates were none of these things in the 70's (and in truth, we thus provided an exact microcosm of society). We didn't have time. Everything was important with an equal urgency--like Chicago's Compass Theatre or Second City--we all wanted to make sure we made life "something wonderful right away" at sixty seconds a minute. But time caught up with most of us.

From the prophet Isiah: "...He has sent me to build up the brokenhearted, to proclaim liberty to the captives and the opening of prisons to them that are bound....

Q: Did the prophet mention me at all?

A: No.

We felt like Watergate-style journalists at that school: everyday we were going to grab the world's attention and expose hypocrisy, rectify injustice and be fabulously wealthy and happy. By the time I got there, the Afro-American Studies Department existed;

women lived in the freshman quad houses, I believe for the first time. There was a long prior history of women in the upper-class houses, so those artificial barriers had long been trampled. We really did not have battles with the school as a corporate culture; our enmity was reserved for Nixon, J. Edgar Hoover and those minions, fools and copperheads that would support them. From our collective analysis of history, we pretty much knew that there had never in the history of the world been a dictatorship so overpowering that it became impossible to fight. But we also knew never to assume that the public was behind us, because if they said they were, we were going to need field binoculars to find them. But, in my time, Harvard never demanded our silence nor denied our right to grow. So we lulled ourselves to contentment, happy to educate each other and ourselves in the hopes that eventually we'd align ourselves in a manner consistent with running the machinery of the world. And, de minimis, we educated ourselves to the peak of capacity. As any reader of Melville can tell you, the waters they are very beautiful, yes; but there are monsters underneath.

Now, we were conscientious enough to sidestep as many of these monsters as possible. And we had various sutras to pass on so that others might avoid them too. But some of these sutras, were so hilarious that propriety forbids me from repeating any of them now. Of course, there are certain lessons of history that a survivor is duty bound to teach, and so, dear reader, read on. But keep in mind that life often had its mythic aspects to it. And in the ancient Greek myths, some heroes and heroines went on great adventures in search of fortune and fame and some, indeed, perhaps as a function of youth as much as courage, went to fight monsters. The seventies were a lot like that.

"...because it was fun. You'll never know how much fun it was...."

- Hunter S. Thompson, journalist, explaining to an NYU audience why old people talk about the sixties so much.

We existed as an ensemble of band leaders, some quiet, some playing crazy people's music. We lived in a college town, in the heyday of Northeast college towns with friends, and parties everywhere, with brothers and sisters at Wellesley, Boston University, Amherst, Northeastern, Mount Holyoke, Boston College, everywhere. I didn't know any black people at M.I.T. Time and space held no barriers to entry in our self-proclaimed kingdom. None of us were vassals. The difference between generations then and now remains our advantage, not of protests, but of "teach-ins"--those indisputably long episodes where the superannuated cognoscenti would always try to pass on the ineluctably valuable essentials of history or perspective that the casual observer might unavoidably overlook. The seventies etched a framework of teach-ins in a nation of teach-ins heldover from the sixties. Harvard raised a black intelligensia post-'68 and pre-Baake as diverse a melange geographically as one could then muster, all fiercely gifted, all fiercely opinionated about just about everything, all quietly articulate. Even I did not find it unusual to audit entire courses when I didn't feel the need to get a grade, nor to try a diversity of sports (crew, fencing, archery, judo) simultaneously without eventually joining a team. I still have memories of rowing the Charles River in an eight man shell at six(?) in the morning while snowflakes are falling and enjoying every minute of it. Of course I would run along the banks of the Charles in my sweats through Cambridge-Somerville and I did get stopped by police. I had run far. He asked if I was from the neighborhood. I said yes I'm from the neighborhood and flashed my ID. He said oh, Harvard student, well actually this isn't your neighborhood, your neighborhood's over there (he waved beyond me). I started laughing. He said lemme tell you why I asked--I interrupted him and laughed harder. I guess, in hindsight, I never took sports seriously after that. And actually I haven't thought of that episode in over eighteen years and did not think anything of it at the time, but obviously it was a portent.

Harvard had fraternities but didn't have them (they were called "eating clubs') and had teams but did not have them (teams of individual members, if you will). We just stuck together--to respect our predilections and diversity, to comprehend that everybody adds value even if they should add it far away, to understand our mutual goal--school in Boston-Cambridge was a good place to start but a bad place to stop. We played our individual hands, we moved along our respective or mutual paths and we communicated face-to-face.

That halcyon bucolic nightmare (think: Edward Munch's "The Scream") seemed the natural progression of the previous decade from global issues to personal issues (like the ancient Greeks--start at the universal, move to the specific) highlighted by issues of personal liberation and growth and concern for the environment. Tom Wolfe classified it the "Me" decade, although traveling through it we had no name or personal road maps; after the death of J. Edgar Hoover (at which conscientious people actually inwardly danced), we were in uncharted territory--our goal was beyond the visible darkness inevitably looming ahead and, if we were truly in gilded cages, we knew. Nina Simone once gave her definition of freedom as "no fear". So God writes this story, we just lived it.

With the seventies came the waning days of "AFRO" the organization if not "Afro" the hairdo and the waxing days of disco dancing. We had divas, termagants, normal people, ophidians, primates, troubadours, sylphs, ladies men and gentlemen. No roos, no marsupials, but pretty much everything else, and all of us danced. I come from the generation that danced all the time. The drug culture passed us by completely without touching us. We must have been overworked. I remember a lot of bid whist (a card game) being played. I played a lot of chess, hoping to look more like Steve McQueen than Bobby Fischer. One of my later roommates was squash champion and, when playing him, I never won a game and I'm not even sure I ever won a single point. Another roommate was a former wrestler and I distinctly remember being twisted like a pretzel (there's no point in denying it). I went to school and worked a forty hour week or more on campus. That's another story, though. My favorite job was senior year, maybe eight hours a week, in the official Map room, cataloging maps of the world with a nice man from the History Department (a professor). It was only the very beginning of freshman year when I didn't work, even in the summers, so I have no knowledge of the leisure time of the scholarly life associated with my time there. For me, it was an institution. It was hardly a hardscrabble existence. I didn't live in a favela, I had time enough to engage in the solipsism of my colleagues. I always read the alternative weekly The Boston Phoenix and its rival, The Real Paper. I had the Village Voice flown in by mail. I had missed the campus riots and the street people's riots but I arrived to guest-star protests at screenings of "BIRTH OF A NATION", inadvertently earning the momentary (or not) obloquy of the handful of black young conservatives lashing themselves to the government department. All in all, time well spent.

During my pre-admission Harvard interview, discussing the relative merits of novels versus "movies", I argued for the novel as the higher ambition because it represented the greater challenge to achieve successfully. Like most Harvard students, I always tried the more difficult (if not most difficult) option. Harvard students love to make definitive statements. Sometimes the hardest thing for people to give up is their mystery.

The memories of music that stir my mind most reverberate the voices of Marvin Gaye and Stevie Wonder. Over time, we developed neural systems and pathways burnished with specific sets of specialized spatial relationships between the intuitive and creative hemispheres enabling us to interpret social relationships, to understand the natural and urban environments, to grasp physical laws of possibility and probability, to speak to each other. For the early stages of development, read Piaget. For everything else, understand music. The higher reaches of applied mathematics parallel the quantum subtleties of music and the attendant complex simplicities of reaching beyond the popular. At Harvard, music was our air, our water, the manna for our minds. We championed the merits of Coltrane and electric Miles, Lee Morgan or Weather Report, Santana or Mahavishnu. But as the quadrivium remained intellectual, the crooners taught us how to talk with advantage in negotiating the mystery of women who were always two or three steps smarter than we were at our peak. If you did not receive political commentary from DOONESBURY, you paid obeisance to the Funkadelics. If you did not understand art history, you must understand Billie Holliday. At a moment's notice, Muddy Waters, sweatin' happily, wailed history at Paul's Mall; we'd fall over each other watching New Birth at the Sugar Shack; I'd hit the late show of George Benson and his protege Earl Klugh at the Jazz Workshop and figure out how I'd get home after the Metro shut down at Midnight. We'd see Kool and the Gang at their peak of melding jazz and rhythm and blues like it was a tutorial. The president of Rahsaan Roland Kirk's Vibration Society lived in Boston and Phil Sampson took me to see his more than five thousand albums. Most importantly, music survived as our cultural touchstone. We could increasingly marvel at the growth and emotional progression of an artist with each successive release and use it as a mirror or personal chart for comparison testing to our own growth and progress. Sometimes, like church, like the African drum, that linkage with our culture (our ancestry and our future) kept us afloat in the sea of struggle. Ours was an intellectual war, the daily battle: Would you lose your soul and give in, would slavery be voluntary? Would you lead your people and be targeted to die like Martin or Malcolm or Fred

Hampton or George Jackson? Could you be the one? Do you know the difference between the Persuaders, and the Persuasions? We were walking against the tide and the moon was high and perhaps drawing to its last quarter. The current was growing stronger. We prayed to God that we needed to know how to swim. We prayed in our time, and God answered in His time. Sometimes, the answer was music.

And the debate over Smokey Robinson or Eddie Kendricks was relevant in the age of the Flintstones. You always talked through all the music anyway so your mind had to operate on several levels simultaneously, which was always part of the fun. There were no preference falsifications, no self-censorship, and also no personal computers, no Internet, certainly no Internet research capabilities. A world of manual typewriters, electric (not selectric) typewriters, white-out, liquid paper, corrasable bond paper (which always ended up smudged and blurry as if you typed with mud and soot), those horrible little correctype rectangles which never helped for lines of mistakes. Almost inconceivable, like something out of Dickens. There were times you would forget a word or two letters in the middle of a line and you would rephrase that section just so you could retype it "in the space available, only because THAT was less work than retyping the whole line or section. Since I could not even type, it took me all night, on the average, just to type an eight-page paper, sometimes for the next day. For four years, I might as well have had a stone slab with a hammer and chisel to strike letters on it.

It was not all a life of lachrymose paucity and truncated digits. I hold the splendid daylight in my hands, inwardly grateful...My freshman year, I discovered Godard in a Kennedy Institute of Politics seminar on Film and Political Ideology with Joel Haycock who screened "LETTER TO JANE" (the answer to his own contemporaneous "TOUT VA BIEN" with Jane Fonda) and "LE GAI SAVOIR" ("THE JOY OF KNOWING")--a filmic interpretation/homage to Jean Jacques Rousseau's EMILE, itself a French political tract on Education. Heady stuff for a freshman in 1972, especially the post -screening discussions with lively upper-class and graduate students who would reference Voltaire and Flaubert at the drop of a hat. I loved the freedom implicit in the content of the films and the avant-garde style of Godard's method. I freely admit I don't know what the hell they were talking about in the post screening discussions and they graciously did not mind me hanging out with them a bit. I quietly nodded affirmatively as if knowingly week after week. They probably thought I was a mute, but I assure you mutes are more intelligent. The process did engender a love of film as a serious endeavor and political philosophy as an academic discipline. I formally listed my major as Government and Philosophy and then tried vainly to avoid as many of those courses as I could. I prided myself on passing the language requirement by testing well before college. (And, of course, post-law school I ended up traveling to France on business almost yearly, torturing the natives and French-speaking peoples of the world for almost the next twenty years with my inept and clumsy memories of two years of high-school French. Lucky them. You wonder why they seem to hate Americans. Thank you. Thank you. I'll take my bows now.) I did actually learn quite a bit, but I won't bore you with that now. Remember, this is before video, before consumer VCRs. Yes, there was television, but we only watched it with the volume muted while we played records and studied. Boston TV was a test pattern. We subscribed to the Black Harvard Ethos--Do something while you're doing something else. Focus on everything.

Essay Question: If you could change one thing about the world, what would it be and why? Cite references.

Ah, distinctly I remember, that first year, a crisp September, walking outside the boundaries of the University in Harvard Square seeing large photo dazibao positioning opposition to the Gulf Oil Company in the freedom fight for what would later become Angola. One poster had a large photo of smiling army men (Portuguese mercenaries in a happy platoon posing, smiling, smoking cigars in a tight group) The words above the photo read something like, "we have told you we oppose the Gulf Oil Company in their fight in Africa. This is the reason why..." And then I looked harder at the B&W photograph. The group was happy, smiling, and in the center of the group, one of the men is cheerily holding a freshly decapitated African man's head.

Freshman year, I also took some non-credit seminars on the politics of Africa with representatives of ZANU and the ANC (also at the Kennedy Institute of Politics). I (presumably with the rest of Massachusetts) was shocked election night '72 that McGovern did not become the president-elect. (I was too young to vote then but I resolved to do my little part to help people understand each other) After working with a pro-bono Philip Brooks House group rehabbing Boston South End houses and apartment units for low-income housing my first summer, certain dynamics became inescapable about Massachusetts, Boston and the sixties. It was over. Boston became intractable over busig, students traveling with Harvard Professors did get pelted with rocks I lived in Mather House my subsequent years. One of those Harvard river houses chosen mainly by what we then called black students, so far removed from the other buildings on campus it was called Roxbury (a Black Boston neighborhood) by our white colleagues. There lived Mr. and Mrs. Frederick Von Stade, eminence grise and Master of the House and, eons before, a Harvard student himself. Skiddy used to tell how, in his day, he would ride the frozen Charles river in his ice boat. I spent my second summer campaigning for New York State Assemblymen and State Senators who actually worked for the public good. I remember when Baake first filed his lawsuit alleging reverse discrimination. Administrators talked to us in hushed tones that what disturbed them most was that B'nai Brith had filed an amicus brief in support of Baake's claim. Whatever alliance with the majority we seemed to have had, we didn't seem to have it any more. This is a theme that would repeat itself like a tape loop.

My final summer I lived in Porter Square, where the residents seemed to have a parade down my block every Sunday morning as early as they could. Late that summer, a black couple was harassed for vacationing at Carson Beach (a beach in Boston), The Boston Black community, outraged at the very undisguised racism, decided to hold a march to the beach (a "beach-in", if you will) the very next week, to "open" it. Two friends, Valerie and Silk, and I decided to survey the scene earlier than the march itself, more to get a sneak preview than to assault the battlewarks as a vanguard. Well, we got there. Beach was crowded. More, not a soul of color in sight. We walked; Valerie, at Harvard for the summer in a pre-med school science program, went swimming. I posed at the beach, casually, nonchalantly. An elderly man came oh five feet away from us, staring, spitting into the sand. Charming. We looked for sight of Valerie in the surf but she wasn't immediately visible. We casually asked each other, hmmm, where's Valerie? A cute little Beaver Cleaver tyke (okay maybe young Spanky) ambled quickly up to us. "We drowned her", he giggled. Then he repeated it. OKAY, we rushed down and got Valerie (who was unharmed and hadn't even been troubled). Okay, Valerie, we got your stuff, we're leaving, the vibes don't connect in an extremely positive and uplifting manner. Cool. We left, decided to surrey over to Boston Common (Paul Revere, all that) for a day in the park. While frolicking, we ran to the top of a hill. Well below us the entire militia of Boston law enforcement lay arrayed in waiting--cavalry, riot police. so many vehicles there could have been tanks there, maybe, maybe not. Maybe not tanks, but clearly a big army nonetheless. My my my, I pondered. These folks are not on our side. Later that day, the black community arrived peacefully, met with sticks and stones and plenty of names that, while not bone-breaking, were let us say less than spiritual in nature. Separating the two groups were the police, facing the black beachers and protecting the other folks-you know --the stone throwers. One police horse trampled and at least partially injured one Sista. Years later (last fall, actually), I met a black Boston native who, well, boosters the image of the town. It's too cold, I tell him, and it ain't that friendly (one of the advantages of a Harvard education is that you can use Black English where applicable and people do not immediately assume that you have a disability). Oh, he says, that's just bad press; that busing thing in the seventies, that wasn't that bad. Wait,I was there in the seventies I said. No, bad press, he smiles. I was at Carson Beach, I say. Oh, Carson Beach....well, then you know. Yeah, I say, I know.

That's the thing about Harvard. There are not too many dirty little secrets I don't know.

But that was my personal experience at Harvard. Like they say about cars, your mileage may vary (and I hope to God it does). I'm sure everyone there has their personal triumphs and their personal demons. We would all share in each other's triumphs and gloriously. I do not think that any person there was ever jealous of any one else for one second of their lives. And for the other stuff, well, there was always someone you could talk to and bond with for the rest of your lives for that one brief or long necessary moment. That was the sharing process. That was then and I hope still is now. It's nice to think that some traditions of our extended black family survive there. I know it was a lotta work and a whole lot of laughs.

One friend there was a poet and he used to characterize the black experience for our time thusly (I believe he said he read it somewhere else. We were all very well-read):

The first generation feels like strangers.
The second generation feels like guests.
The third generation feels at home.

We deemed ourselves to be the second generation. For all I know, it may have been a very long one but I think it falls in that post-'68 pre-Baake era (the Supreme Court's Baake decision was the initial tolling of the bell of the attack on diversity admissions and Affirmative Action). The first generation, as I surmise from an Alain Locke Symposium elegantly presented by Lewis Jones wherein I first heard the absolutely brilliant Albert Murray) was a long time ago. But if we were guests, we certainly treated ourselves to the best services, we never accepted any second-class status and we certainly were well behaved guests. Tony Jenkins went to Europe to play professional Basketball and then returned to the States and became a great lawyer in Detroit. Danny Jiggets went on to play football with the Chicago Bears. Athlete James Brown became color commentator for CBS Sports, Fox Broadcasting, Real Sports with Bryant Gumbel, other stuff. June Cross became a brilliant producer and filmmaker with PBS. Dr. Walter Royal, M.D. became a pioneer in medical research to combat the acquired immune deficiency syndrome. Most of us became lawyers, judges, surgeons, doctors, professors, law professors, theology professors and essayists, journalists and authors, research scientists, educators, artists, writers, computer designers (way ahead of their time), union organizers, labor union officials, activists, wives, husbands, fathers, mothers, musicians,, administrators, corporate executives and CEOs. A lot, if not most, went to some form of graduate or professional school. All in all, a good lot. And all, at the same time, unique for a time in history. For a bit of time, a bit of history opened up like a sieve and as many of us as could rushed through and tried to keep the seam wider. Then it drifted back closed again.

And for a NorthEastern West Indian-American prepschooler who sniffed his nose at anything below Pennsylvania, it was enough to open my senses vividly awake. As a Result of my time at Harvard, I love the South and anyone from it, from the hills of North Carolina to the big cities or hidden dust bowls of Texas. I love Virginia, Arkansas, Kentucky and most definitely one incredible lady from Baltimore, Maryland (whom I even met thanks to a college buddy, strangely enough). Peace to the memory of B.D. Boogie Down Holmes and the red dirt of Virginia under which he blossoms still. California Kenny Greene, Curtis, Wimbles, G. Otis, Luscious, Charlotte, T. Pierre and McGoo, peace baby friends. Victory sign to the Chocolate Cities, and to Wendy, Bob, Carla and Norma. Homage and Tribute to my ancestors.

And a special thank you to Mather House Senior Tutor John Harwell. But that really is another story.

Oh yeah, of course, I write this all now in hindsight, a spontaneous overflow of emotion recollected in tranquility. At that time, I thought everyone there was crazed.

14. Monique Burns, H '1977—Beyond the Black Table

During my freshman year at Harvard, I was assigned to live at Currier House. A 20-minute walk from Harvard Square—the student epicenter of Cambridge, Massachusetts—Currier House was isolated from the lively freshman dorms in Harvard Yard and from the equally lively Student Union, where most freshmen took their meals together.

If Currier House was physically isolated, its dining room was even more isolating for me. It boasted an institution known as the "Black table"— where many of the house's dozen or so Black students ate meals together, by choice, seated apart from their fellow white and Asian classmates.

I sat at the Black table only a few times during my early months at Currier House. Though I'd grown up in Brooklyn's all-Black Bedford-Stuyvesant section, I'd also spent four years as a scholarship student at a mostly white prep school in Massachusetts. Of 250 girls, there were only seven Blacks, so naturally we socialized with other white students. At Harvard, there were many white former prep-school classmates, since nearly a third of Concord Academy's 70-member senior class was accepted to the college in those days. In Currier House, as elsewhere at Harvard, most students were white, and two white students on my floor—a fellow Brooklynite and a fellow "writer"—become fast friends based on shared interests and experiences.

Sitting at the Black table on a regular basis would have isolated me from my white prep-school friends as well as the new white friends I'd made. I simply refused to do that.

Moreover, though I'd grown up in an all-Black neighborhood, my family experience had actually been multicultural. Both my mother and father had had close, warm relationships with their Black, Native American and white relatives. Like most people of color in the United States, I had been brought up to accept the "One Drop Rule," a set of laws and social conventions instituted during slavery, which stated that having one Black ancestor made one Black. But I also had been brought up to acknowledge and appreciate my white and Indian ancestors.

My deeply personal reasons for not becoming a "regular" at the Black table boiled down to friends and family. Even more importantly, I saw no philosophical reason for the Black Table's existence. The year was 1973. After the clamorous days of the Sixties, Civil Rights was no longer front-page news, and many college students, both Black and white, had cut their hair and gone "mainstream." After college, I would become part of the conservative, career-minded wave of young urban professionals known as "Yuppies," or, sometimes, if Black, "Buppies." To my mind, students attended college for the specific purpose of preparing themselves to function in America's larger professional world. That larger world contained many different kinds of people—the majority of whom were white. Besides having had a history of positive social interaction with whites, I thought it made sense to be open to friendships with all students, including whites, some of whom would later become my business colleagues.

My decision not to sit at the Black table on a regular basis did not sit well with its regulars. On several occasions, one of them took me aside and asked why I wouldn't sit there. My answer was simple: I had planned to eat with some friends of mine who were white and therefore could not sit at the Black table. The response was often a disgruntled shrug and sometimes rolled eyes. In retrospect, I wish I had clearly spelled out all my reasons—personal, social and professional—for not choosing to be a Black table regular. I also wish I had asked why the regulars felt that it was so important for me to sit there, too. We might have learned something from each other. We all might have changed our perspectives.

The other reason I avoided the Black table was that I felt it was, at base, hypocritical. While I had actually grown up in a Black neighborhood, in a working-class family, many of the Black table's regulars were pampered scions of educated, upper-middle-class Blacks, professors, lawyers and the like, and had grown up in classy white suburbs like Scarsdale, New York, where they attended mostly white schools. I had grown up in the heart of what many consider the "Black experience"—that is, the ghetto—where I'd seen drug addiction, violence, and unspeakable poverty and hopelessness. Despite my privileged academic existence, I did not need to sit at a special table to understand that many Blacks were suffering throughout the land.

As "members" of the Black table applied subtle pressure on me to conform—from occasional questioning to ignoring me to whispering comments when I passed in the halls—I reacted by refusing to sit there at all. It has always struck me as strange that minority group members who suffer pressure and even harassment to conform to the wishes of the majority group should seek to pressure members of their own group to conform to their wishes. I felt that my individualism and my individual rights were being infringed upon.

Moreover, I saw the Black table chiefly as a social, rather than a political, institution. I did not see how it could affect real change for Black people in America and, thus, I had little respect for its existence. One of its regulars, a handsome fellow with an Hispanic surname, affected a Che Guevara-style beret, but I saw no effort on that group's part to radically impact the lives of Black folks. How many members of the Black table found time to tutor poor Black kids in Boston's Roxbury section? A few, perhaps, but not many. What percentage of monies collected at dances sponsored by the Black table's regulars were sent to Black people in the nation's ghettoes? None that I ever heard of. Beyond its social function, there seemed to be no larger purpose to the Black table.

I was not the only Black freshman at Currier House to have similar feelings about the Black table. Indeed, many of the men and women who avoided the table came from socioeconomic backgrounds similar to mine. Poor or working-class, they had a genuine need to get beyond the upper-middle-class rhetoric of the Black table and concentrate on learning the academic and social skills they would need to succeed in the larger white professional world. There would be no doctor or lawyer father, with money and professional contacts, to help ease their rise up the ladder. Simply put, they, like me, had to concentrate on “making it”—or risk ending up back at square one.

Like many minority-group members, I had been reminded countless times, by family members and teachers, that because I enjoyed certain privileges, I had a responsibility to help less fortunate Blacks. It was a corollary of the 19th-century white philanthropic dictum: “To whom much is given, much is expected.”

Since I was not a political activist or agitator, by nature, I’d decided that the best way for me to help “the cause” was through my work as a writer. By venturing into the overwhelmingly white professional world, I would be helping smooth the way for future generations just as earlier Black professionals had done. By becoming successful, I would have the financial means to support worthwhile Black causes. By writing articles that spoke to Black issues and concerns, I could help educate Blacks and also help communicate our concerns to the larger world.

I had begun to move toward these lofty future goals, in small but deliberate ways, ever since prep school. On summers off, I returned to Bed-Stuy and wrote articles for a short-lived local newspaper called The Ebony Eagle; I worked as assistant to the host of a local Black radio show; I wrote an article or two for The Amsterdam News, America’s largest Black weekly newspaper. I spoke with kids from the neighborhood, as well as family members, about the importance of getting a good education and venturing out into the larger world.

Needless to say, because the Black table at Harvard’s Currier House was primarily a social institution, my refusal to sit there left me socially isolated from the community of color. Indeed, the Black Table's regulars included some of the most desirable Black men in my freshman class—handsome men whose intelligence I respected and whose post-college careers in medicine, law and other fields I would admire in later years. As I did not sit at the Black table, I rarely heard about dances or other informal get-togethers, unless I happened to see them posted on a bulletin board.

Throughout my college years, most of the men I dated would be white—or the occasional Black man who felt, as I did, that there was a larger world out there and that it was okay, even desirable, to associate with non-Blacks. One of these men, who later became a journalist and a lawyer, I met while "comping" for a spot on The Harvard Crimson, the college newspaper. One day while tapping away on a typewriter in the "city room," I looked up to see him and his best friend, a white man, hovering over me, grinning. Thus began an enjoyable, if not permanent, relationship.

In the years since graduating from Harvard, I've tried to maintain the lofty goals of my youth: to enjoy some level of success in the outside world, while contributing in positive ways to the lives of my people. Immediately after graduation, in an attempt to get closer to my Black roots, I went to work as an associate editor at Essence magazine, known as "the magazine for today's Black woman," turning down what many journalists would consider a more prestigious entry-level job at the New York Times. For several years, I volunteered to head up the New York-based alumnae association for a Better Chance, a non-profit organization that placed poor minority students in prep schools across the country. For several years, I was a trustee at my prep school, which was deeply committed to bringing about "diversity" through increased minority enrollment. As a full-time magazine editor, and now as a freelance editor and writer, I've made it a point to contribute to Black magazines as well as white ones—regardless of differences in pay scales.

Some months ago, I received a solicitation letter from a Black student group at Harvard. After reading the letter several times, I concluded that the group had no larger purpose than socializing, and that my contribution would be used for little more than funding dances and parties. So, I crumpled up the letter, and my check went unwritten.

Today, as I look back more than 25 years to my freshman days at Harvard, I find that my thoughts about the Black table at Currier House have changed. Although I've never questioned my personal reasons for not sitting at the Black table, I now question my understanding of the Black table's larger role. My thoughts have moved from the philosophical realm of college days to the practical. With first-hand experience of the difficulties Black professionals face in establishing long-term mentor relationships and support networks within the larger white professional world, I recognize the importance of establishing long-term support networks in college. Indeed, the very existence of a Black table points to a very real need for Black students at mostly white universities to develop such networks. Rather than seeing the Black table as a threat to my individuality and freedom of choice, as I once did, I now recognize that the Black table was an attempt—albeit a heavy-handed and isolationist one—to bring Black students together.

Black students at mostly white institutions need networks that not only provide support during college days—but beyond. White students often have built-in long-term networks through their families and through the communities where they grow up and vacation. Unlike Black students at mostly white universities, students who attend mostly Black schools seem, through the force of sheer numbers, to be in a better position to develop wider circles of lifelong support among Black friends and future business contacts.

I can never become a regular at that Black table—nor would I want to, even now—but the next time I receive a solicitation from Harvard's Black student group, it's very likely that I will make a donation. Ultimately, I still believe that Black people who work in the larger professional world—which is overwhelmingly white—must actively develop both professional and social ties with whites. Refusing to socialize with white peers, out of fear or prejudice, can cut us off from valuable professional and social experiences.

Yet, I also believe that there is a real need, both socially and professionally, for Black students at mostly white universities to develop long-term networks of friends and future business associates—to develop their own versions of the "old boy's network." Just as many Black professionals are socialized to support their communities in one way or another, I believe Black alumnae of mostly white universities must actively support Black student groups at their alma maters. While the initial raison d'être for these groups might be social, it's clear to me now that larger and more valuable purposes can unfold over time.

15. Robin Walker, Y'1984--My Yale Experience

"Robin, you're going to miss out on your 'Yale experience' if you have to work all of the time."

I clearly remember my freshman roommate telling me that as I raced off from my classes straight to the New Haven Register for my Friday and Saturday shifts as an editorial assistant. Although she meant well and was honestly concerned about my unusual work schedule, I realized that she could not understand that without my part-time job, I would not have a "Yale Experience" to enjoy. Unlike most of my new classmates, I did not receive a monthly stipend from my parents or have weekly care packages delivered by my grandparents, and I most certainly did not have a trust fund to look forward to upon graduation. So if I wanted money in my pockets, I knew I'd better take my "Yale Experience" to work.

As I walked up the stairs of Wright Hall for the first time in the fall of 1980, I had no idea what lay in store for me behind those ivy-covered walls. I knew that my status as an African-American honors student from a local high school (who had graduated a year early at the top of my class) had earned me the designation as a Yale Sterling Scholar. I wasn't exactly sure what that scholarship signified but I knew that it provided much needed money for tuition. I think I was the only minority recipient that year but

I don't remember if I ever thought of my Sterling Scholarship as Affirmative Action. I did know that neither my parents nor I could have afforded to pay Yale's $22,000 annual tuition over four years. Since my partial scholarship did not cover all of my tuition or provide for books and spending money, my part-time job gave me the wherewithal I needed to hang out with my friends at Naple's Pizza or buy that new sweater or dress that my roommates already had.

My first year as an English/Theater major at Yale was an eye-opening experience on so many levels. Even though I technically always knew it, I began to fully understand during that first semester that everyone was categorized not only by their race and cultural background, but more importantly by their economic class. Growing up as a "middle-class Black" who lived in predominantly white neighborhoods and who was generally only one of a few Black kids in school, I was accustomed to being the lone minority in most academic and social situations.

Before I went to Yale, I had always felt rather privileged. In fact, I knew that I had probably been exposed to more diverse people, places and things than the average young person had been whether they were black, white, rich or poor. My middle-class parents were very popular during their youth and community-oriented in their later years, with friends and colleagues of all colors, cultures, religions and walks of life. Visitors were constantly streaming in and out of the house, from multicultural coworkers to militant Black Panthers to proud Vietnam veterans and draft dodgers to affluent Anglo-Saxon neighbors. My father's climb up the ministerial ranks of the church also brought many colorful characters to our home, pious church members and officials as well as distraught people in need ("Daddy's strays" as my mother called the latter when she wasn't in the mood for company). Throughout my childhood and later into adulthood, my parents' associates shared their stories and gifts with me in uniquely personal ways (even "Daddy's strays" much to mothers chagrin), and I felt privileged because of those experiences.

Somehow "middle-class" was now a derogatory term used by my new college acquaintances who were rich or wealthy at best and upper middle-class at least. Suddenly being upper middle-class was the very least one should be, and that my parents, and therefore I, had hit below this magical economic baton - that, on top of simply being "Black." However, if I had been exposed to real money like my wealthier Black classmates whose parents owned Fortune 500 businesses or were national leaders, my freshman year transition surely would have been a lot easier.

In contrast by African-American standards, my salesman-by-day, minister-by-night father and my registered nurse mother were "upper middle class." But by the financial standards that were now being applied by my moneyed colleagues, I had barely passed the middle-class line. Until then, I thought my biggest challenge at Yale would be learning how to deal with professors, classes and grades. It suddenly hit me that my major problem, at least in the eyes of my white counterparts, was the lack of at substantial bank account and portfolio.

During my early days at Yale, I was so busy trying to fit in with my white colleagues that I almost missed the events geared strictly for "black folks." I soon discovered many activities for minority students, particularly at the Afro-American Cultural Center (a.k.a. "The House" as it was affectionately called) and the Black Church at Yale. I must admit I only went to The House for church and special occasions because I was usually too busy between classes and work to hang out there as much as others did. Because I was raised in the Greater New Haven area, my Yale years were fuller than recent transplants simply because of the family, friends and professionals that I knew long before and after I became a "Townie," a distinction only a few freshmen had.

One of the best cultural resources that I found at Yale was its radio station, WYBC. It was there that I began my career as a news announcer and it is also where I got to know some of the most interesting people of color, a few students but mostly New Havenites. The blacks at 'YBC were dynamic, outrageous, intelligent, outspoken and always ready to party. Cliff Webb, Martin Fortes, Jazzy, Debbie Reynolds, Melodie Thigpen, Dawn Slade and Karen Harris were just some of the townspeople who wanted to get into the radio business and used WYBC to gain hands-on experience and an unofficial "Yale degree in radio."

At 'YBC, these townspeople infused me with a sense of black pride combined with a love of Yale that only local blacks who were not enrolled at the university could feel. Even though they never admitted it, these folks felt more strongly about the importance of WYBC and Yale than most well-to-do Ivy Leaguers. They were captivated by what Yale symbolized, by what they could learn and do at that radio station, in a way that captured my imagination more than my erudite classmates sometimes did. All were a part of the "Yale Experience" even though they did not matriculate. I intrigued them because I was one of a few blacks who actually went to school there and was from the New Haven area.

I sometimes felt that they were more into being a "Yalie" than I was. Yet because of my student status, they also stayed on my case. I remember Karen Harris, who was WYBC's program director, asking me what role I wanted to play at the station. I said I was just trying to get on-air experience so that I could get a real job in radio. She seemed shocked and appalled that I didn't consider WYBC to be that place. I wanted to tell her that 'YBC was just kid's stuff and that what most attracted me each week were the cute guys who were smitten by me (mature black men who I didn't see in my classes). I knew if I told her that that she would look at me with a worse look on her face than she already had. Even though Karen thought I didn't get it, I realized that everything that I was learning at WYBC would become the springboard for my career launch into the media.

After almost a year at 'YBC, I took my on-air reel and shopped it around and got my first offer from the second largest radio station in Connecticut. I left my editorial assistant job at The Register and started working at WELI Radio doing afternoon and evening reporting. I was on top of the world. Freshman year was about to end and I had my first real job as a broadcaster and a couple of suitors. My friends at WYBC were happy, though taken aback by my good fortune, and my classmates at Yale started to think, "Hey, Robin really does have an interesting work life." However, even I did not know that my work at WELI would expose me to news and community leaders, personalities and politicians who would shape my college years and beyond.

With my new job in radio and newfound confidence, I felt that I was ready to move off campus in my sophomore year. I found a charming little apartment on Chapel Street that I could actually afford right behind the Afro-Am House. I had my first college party at my apartment and my fellow Yalies began to be impressed by this middle-class black girl from New Haven who was starting to live like she was upper middle-class on a part-time salary. It was then that they started to appreciate my juggling act with classes and work.

For me, one of the most frustrating aspects of black life at Yale was the low number of black male students. Black women outnumbered black men, and many guys dated only white women, were gay or simply not my type. Because of that, I felt that my love life at Yale suffered more than my friends' who had gone to black colleges. When I visited a high school buddy who attended Morehouse, I was amazed by the sheer number of black guys just walking around the campus, not to mention the parties. Those Morehouse parties were nothing like Yale's keg parties or soirees at Morey's. There was an unspoken passion about how the Morehouse students entertained themselves that I did not feel in my predominantly white social settings at Yale.

Although my intellect was being satisfied at Yale, I felt like I was missing out socially as a black woman. I wanted to meet eligible black men regularly like the ones I had been exposed to at Morehouse. That was one of the few regrets that I had about attending Yale. I longed for the kind of social interaction and experience that comes from attending an all-Black college. I remember thinking I got more attention from black men in one weekend at Morehouse than I had during my first month at Yale. A lot of white guys had asked me out and I dated a few of them to the dissatisfaction of my family and friends, but I still wanted a black boyfriend.

Upon my return to campus in my junior year, I was pleasantly surprised to find that the new dean assigned to Davenport College was a handsome, refined African-American man who had taught and traveled around the world, spoke six languages and was one of the best conversationalists I had ever met. Dean Donald Billingsly would have a tremendous impact on my life at Yale, eventually taking me under his wing as an uncle of sorts. I would tell Dean Don (who always had the most cultured and interesting foreign and local visitors) that I needed to meet more black men and every time he had a male visitor of color, he would introduce them to me. It was shortly after these gatherings that I began to look at some of the Black professors with more than academics on my mind.

Dwight Andrews, Willie Ruff and Henry Louis "Skip" Gates would become my quintessential African-American professors at Yale. Each were pioneers in their respective fields. Gates had made a name for himself in the literary world and Andrews and Ruff personified everything that made music, specifically jazz, a celebration of African-American life. Not to mention the fact that Dwight was also the pastor of the Black Church at Yale and directed musical productions at the Yale Repertory Theater and that Willie also actively performed jazz around the world with the Mitchell/Ruff duo. I also deeply admired Professor Charles Davis and Yale Repertory

Theater director Lloyd Richards whose work would also have a peripheral impact on my love of the theater. However I did not get a chance to know either gentleman well.

The professors that I met in the African-American Studies department would change the way that I would read, hear and think about black literature, art and music from that moment forward. In my opinion, African-American history had not been studied seriously in my high school other than slave epics and other black tomes. Of course I had heard of and read traditional black authors like W.E.B. DuBois and Frederick Douglas as well as contemporary authors like James Baldwin, Alice Walker and Toni Morrison. But it was in Skip Gates' class that I began to truly appreciate the cadence of their words, their lives and their contribution to black life through art. Gloria Naylor, who would later become a literary force in her own right with "The Women of Brewster Place," served as Gates' teaching assistant. Through this course, I quickly learned how important early black writers like Phyllis Wheatley and Zora Neale Hurston were to our heritage, and I also developed a cultural affinity with contemporary Hispanic authors, especially Gabriel Garcia Marquez. With his engaging classroom style, Gates made me seriously study and consider the issue of race and literature differently - a talent that he would share with the world as one of America's leading scholars on the subject and later as chairman of Harvard's African-American Studies department.

I respected Gates' intellect and style but there was something very special and magnetic about Dwight Andrews and Willie Ruff -- they literally mesmerized me. Although I had very little musical talent, I was determined to take Dwight's jazz class which was one of the most popular music courses at Yale. After the first few weeks, I realized that I either didn't care to learn about jazz syncopation or that I was more interested in watching Dwight talk than studying his weekly assignment. I remember noting the last drop date for his course and thinking I only had a few more classes to just stare at him in amazement. I was shocked when long after I had filled out my drop course slip, Dwight said "Robin, you're going to have to work harder if you're going to pass my class." I meekly told him that I had dropped his class weeks before and was much too ashamed to admit missing my weekly staring sessions.

At least I felt confident enough to converse with Dwight regularly in class or at church. With Willie Ruff, I barely managed the courage to introduce myself after one of his concerts in the hope of getting to know him better. It took another year or so of seeing him walk to and from class before I tried to speak with him again. He was so full of ideas and projects, he was going to Rome to record how the melodies from his French Horn affected the acoustics in the great chapels or he had just returned from Africa where he had played music with the Pygmies. He was always busy with the most interesting cultural activities. Unlike Dwight (who I was only mildly infatuated with), Ruff could make me study jazz syncopation or whatever he was working on.

However later that semester, I would get a chance to know Dwight better socially. His house was like a black fraternity and one of my favorite Yale guys lived there. Vinnie Peterson, a fellow lover of literature and budding gourmet, would become one of my oldest and dearest Yale friends. Ian Straker, a divinity school student who was Dwight's best friend, lived there as well as a funny guy named David Alan Grier (a drama student whose face and name I remembered only when I saw him on "in Living Color" years later). Dwight had the most soulful parties at Yale, a close second to those passionate Morehouse parties. It was at Dwight's house that I, though still a lowly undergraduate, began to forge real friendships with black upperclassmen and graduate students.

By this time, I had developed a wonderful posse of black male friends, not romantic partners but brothers who would become an important part of my Yale network. Vinnie Peterson, Chuck Martin, Leslie Crain and Tom DeFranz were my African-American running buddies and I also made friends with several African students. One of the sweetest foreign guys was Kofi, a medical student from Ghana, who exposed me to African culture with traditional ethnic foods and stories about our mutual heritage. Kofi and Dean Don's African friends planted important cultural seeds with their stories of Africa and my link to the motherland and her people. I would only begin to fully appreciate and explore those cultural links many years later.

Kofi would prepare African dishes for me in an apartment he shared with two drama students named Charles "Roc" Dutton and Angela Bassett. I remember hanging out with Roc one night, listening to him quote Shakespeare on one of the rocks in my dormitory courtyard with a passion that I had never seen before in a black man, and thinking "this boy is consumed by acting." I knew then that Roc was destined for theatrical success. In classes or through various friends at Yale, I met many aspiring actors who would grace America's stages and movie screens with their amazing talent. People like Dutton, Bassett, Grier, Jodie Foster, Danny Glover, Courtney Vance, Jennifer Beals and others who have gone on to become Hollywood and Broadway stars.

All of the people that I met during my four years at Yale - undergraduates and graduate students, townspeople, professors, visiting scholars, university officials and workers impacted my cultural life significantly and I will always be grateful to them. In small and large ways, their words, actions and love for their field of study or interest made me think, act and respond differently as a scholar and a person.

As a black woman, I know that my "Yale Experience" was critically different from my white colleagues' due to my racial and economic background. However, I would never have had such an incredibly diverse undergraduate experience had it not been for my middle-class work ethic and clear understanding and appreciation of how my race affected my four years at one of the most prestigious educational institutions in the world.

In looking back at it all in a 15-year old mirror, my freshman roommate may have been right about missing out on some things. After all, I was never recruited by one of Yale's secret societies, which remains a major disappointment. And I will certainly admit how desperately I miss not having trust fund disbursements now (I fear I may never get over missing that). Despite those missed opportunities, I'm still glad I put my "Yale Experience" to work then and now.

16.Brotherman--By David Thomas, Y 1987

Brotherman, Brotherman where for art thou brotherman?

Where were you my brother when I needed you?
Where are you my brother now that I need you?
Let's let bygones be bygones
And look forward to a brand new day

No more talk about selling out
And who sold whom out
Lest you should hear me shout

No more rehashing the past
And all its painful scars

I forgive you my brother.
I love you my brother.
Don't you know the only way
we can stand is together.

Yesterday they pitted you against me
But today it's clear, now I can see
That you are my strength, and you are my life
You are me and I am you

So, what do you say my friend
Are we brothers or are we not?
You think that we can give it a shot

I stand here awaiting your earnest reply
Don't leave me hanging, and don't say goodbye
For you've got to know the reason why

I'm your brother in arms and yours alone
The one, the only, Brotherman

17. Farah Griffin, H'1985[52]-- On Hair and Harvard

Farah Jasmine Griffin was born in Philadelphia on 23 February 1963, and prepared for college at the Baldwin School for Girls in Bryn Mawr, Pennsylvania. As an undergraduate she was a reporter for the Harvard Crimson and was also active in several black organizations. She received her degree in 1985 with honors in History and Literature. Following a period as research associate for Judge A. Leon Higginbotham Jr. in Philadelphia, she embarked on a Ph.D. program in American Studies at Yale in the fall of 1986. She received a fellowship from the American Association of University Women to complete a dissertation on migration and urbanization in African-American culture and obtained her doctorate in 1992.

On Hair and Harvard

Upon entering Holworthy 22 in the fall of 1981, I wandered into the bathroom and confronted a big, old, white urinal. This building was not erected with me in mind, I thought. So, after three weeks of daily confrontations with that contraption and all that it came to represent for me, I left one institution of education and acculturation--Harvard, in search of another--an old-fashioned black hairshop.

[52] Reprint from Blacks at Harvard, New York:New York University Press, 1993.

I found Lucielle's in the not yet gentrified South End. Wherever I've traveled in this country, I've been able to find places like this', where funk, jazz, rhythm and blues or gospel emanate from well-equipped sound systems, or old radios, and where next door there's a fried chicken joint, on the corner a Chinese take-out place, and across the street a bar. Lucielle's was no different, but it was special because it was my first. After three weeks at Harvard it felt good to hear the heartfelt laughter and melodic voices of black women. The place reminded me of my grandmother's kitchen and that was criterion enough for me. Lucielle was a small honey-brown woman of about sixty years or so who coddled me, called me baby and fussed over "all that thick, beautiful hair on your head, Child!"

Poor, black and female, I sought out black beauticians in search of my sanity for the next four years: men and women, young, old, gay, straight, conservative, radical, even a few evangelists featured in this motley crew that reaffirmed my value as a thinking, feeling, and growing young woman. Through hours of press and curls (no chemicals, thank you), cuts, trims, and braids I sat and prepared for another two weeks of Harvard. We would talk about politics, sex, relationships and God. After one of these sessions I always returned to Cambridge feeling relaxed and renewed.

If hairshops were places where I established my equilibrium, Harvard was the place where it was again shattered. For me this was both a triumph and a tragedy. Harvard was a sea of contradictions. On the one hand, I sat in a lecture given by a noted historian who painted a portrait of the Old South, sentimental and full of little "playful pickaninnies" (those were his words); on the other hand, I came to know and love "my professor" Nathan Huggins, who taught me to begin taking myself seriously as an intellectual and to be committed to establishing African-American subject matter as material worthy of scholarly inquiry.

In the journal entries I kept for my History and Literature sophomore tutorial I found myself engaged in a written debate with one of my tutors. In response to my frustration over the dearth of black authors on his syllabus, he wrote that he was forced by time to limit his selection to major American authors. "Henry James, my dear, is major because people like you have made him so," I thought. When I asked this same tutor if I could write my paper on Du Bois' The Souls of Black Folk, he said no because he had never read Du Bois.

In contrast, I also met an exciting recently arrived professor who brought such energy, enthusiasm and dedication to his teaching of African-American literature that he inspired me to want to stimulate a group of students the way he stimulated me. He made me want to teach, to write and he and Professor Huggins encouraged me to pursue graduate study. Their confidence in my intellectual abilities sustained me in much the same way as did those Thursday afternoons in hairshops.

At Harvard, a reader of my senior thesis complained of my failure to place Frances Harper, a 19th-century black novelist, poet, essayist and political activist, in the context of larger white women's movements. In fact, I thought the thesis was problematic because I spent so much time placing Harper in this context that I neglected to deal with her in the depth she so well deserved. Our differing perceptions of the weakness of the essay reflected our different understandings of Harper's significance as a historical figure.

Between 1981 and 1985, the deconstructionist literary critic Barbara Johnson was the only Harvard professor doing work on black women. However, through the various lectures, dinners and master's teas sponsored by the Afro-American Studies Department, Radcliffe, and interested individuals, I met Toni Morrison, Alice Walker, and Paule Marshall. At Radcliffe, where the Black Women's Oral History Project was underway, I came into contact with scholars of the newly emerging field of Black Women's Studies: Valerie Smith, Deborah McDowell and Linda Perkins were all fellows at the Bunting Institute during my years in Cambridge. During a lecture give by Perkins at the end of my freshman year I first learned of those dynamic 19th-century black women and it was then that I decided to write my thesis on Frances Harper.

The culmination of this avenue of my intellectual curiosity was the conception and organization of the first Radcliffe Conference on the Study of Black Women in American History. With Janet Bixby, a political white feminist, I dreamt, lobbied and helped to bring into fruition a two-day conference that drew on scholars from the entire country. Our greatest resource was past and present Bunting Institute fellows. Here were the models for whom I had been searching. They weren't visible at Harvard, so with financial assistance from Radcliffe, Education for Action, the Harvard Foundation for Race Relations, and the Radcliffe Union of Students, and with the support of my mentors, Professors Huggins and Sollors, and Radcliffe's Dean Phillipa Bovet, Janet and I imported them.

In short, the contradictions of Harvard taught me "to make a way out of no way." That was one of the most valuable lessons I learned during my four years in and around Beantown. It was reiterated in black hairshops in Roxbury, Mattapan, Dorchester, Medford and the now gentrified South End. The second most valuable lesson was taught me by five sister/roommates. We were as different as could be in demeanor, opinion and economic status. Some of our common threads were our blackness, our femaleness and Harvard. We were six spoiled little divas who had always been the stars in somebody's world, suddenly thrown together and forming what would become possibly the most important relationship of our lives. For eighteen years we had been the "Only." Suddenly, we were forced to recognize that there is no "only"; there are always more smart, talented, black girls out there. We also grew to understand that there was no threat in our newly discovered numbers, just strength and to some extent a certain degree of power.

These two lessons of my Harvard years prepared me in unexpected ways to meet a world full of contradictions where equilibriums are always on the brink of destruction. Now I simply paraphrase Aaron Copland's "New York": If I made it there (in Cambridge) I'll make it anywhere--provided, of course, I find a little music-filled black hairshop. (1988)

18. Denise Byrd, Y'1988

In the foggy recesses of my memory, my relationship with Yale began when I was eight or so, maybe before. Every now and then, my father, an avid jazz fan, would load my sister and I into his Buick and we would take a Sunday ride to New Haven. He was hoping to catch a free concert on the green and we were hoping to get fresh ice cream before the concert and not on the way back home.

The drive to New Haven was always a wonderful prelude to fresh ice cream. The road connecting Waterbury, the former brass capital of the world, to New Haven, the present home of Steve's Ice Cream, was nothing short of a tease with its dairy farms and large clear state reservoir. As we would drive down Dixwell Avenue (?), Yale would grow in the distance swallowing up everything familiar--everything like Waterbury, everything like New Haven, everything like us in our Buick--until there was only just Yale campus. I always looked up as we drove past those fortresses of higher education. Even though I lived only thirty minutes away, Yale was a place as rare and distant to me as the Buckingham Palace. The Fortress of Yale, I believed, was a place where the rich and famous went to school. My family was not rich or famous.

Years later when I ended up in a boarding school, primarily for the rich, those Ivy covered towers slowly began to diminish in size and fierceness. Perhaps I could pass through one of those tall arches on my way somewhere. As a Dean's List minority student in an elite boarding school, I quickly learned that I would not have to take the same painstaking path to landing in an Ivy League as my nervous peers. Basically, I didn't have to apply to elite, hard-to-get-into universities. They applied to me. Uneasy with the notion that life was going to change and that I was actually going to college, I'd sit mute across from the Director of Student Placement as he rattled off the latest offer. "Yale was out of the question", I told him. "My mother would bring me chicken soup", I explained. After spending my entire adolescence in a secluded boarding school, I wanted out, out of proximity to my family, out of Connecticut. I wanted something new. Yale was definitely not on my future radar screen.

Attracted to the idea of a creative curriculum, I chose Brown, got in early, and looked forward to life in Providence. I was cozy, happy, on my way out of Connecticut, when I promised my mother that I would at least apply to Harvard and Yale. I was leaving her. I had to give her that much satisfaction. I signed the papers, put them in the mail, went shopping for interview clothes, and looked forward to a free trip to Boston without any supervision. I didn't even think about the Yale interview. But, I still remember it. In fact, it epitomized my ensuing years at Yale, safe, but slightly off somehow.

My alumni interviewer showed up in a corduroy jacket, looking slightly disheveled and as if he was as uncomfortable in the stuffy Dean's office as I. He immediately suggested we take a walk. That was my Yale interview--a stroll through the wooded paths of Choate. We just talked. I remember no questions. I just remember the tattered elbows on his cord jacket and the briskness of his pace. He intrigued me. After four years at Choate, I had begun to associate all elite institutions with stuffiness, protocol, you know, blue jackets with crests on them. This guy from Yale was no blue jacket.

Two weeks later he sent me a note and a copy of the pages from the handbook outlining the theater department. We never spoke again. But, now I was interested. What could be the harm in taking the bus ride over for the accepted students' weekend? I could look inside. Take a peek. A weekend at Yale couldn't possibly be as bad as my Harvard experience whereat I awoke in the middle of the night and took the first train back to Wallingford. Boston, a city where blacks are expected to move over for whites on the sidewalk, frightened me. After my short but powerful experience in that scary, too-white, too-uptight city, I figured that maybe I should stick with what I know.

In the tradition of well-worn corduroy, Yalies proved to be laid back and black--a combination that had been sorely missing in my life. It had been a while since I had been outside of my little coterie of black pals at Choate. At a grand total of thirty (out of a thousand students), we didn't necessarily love each other; but, we admitted to needing each other, like family. And like any other family carved out of circumstances, our similarities often did not extend beyond that one bond. Yet, here I was sitting on the floor with an ex-Choatie and her friend, eating Kasha, discussing Baldwin, and the pros and cons of Ivy Leagues in general. I had a feeling that in the Fortress of Yale I could actually pick and choose my black friends. Perhaps here I could reach that ideal state our surrogate Mom at Choate had told me about--the state of social identity in which you didn't feel like you have to change your clothes to be around your friends.

Having become a bit of a hippy in boarding school, I often found my new self not fitting in when I arrived home to hang out with my "real friends". And, so, I longed for the day when I would not have to change my clothes to be around my pals. Later that night, standing in the House in the company of more Blacks than I had been around in years, something clicked. I felt at home--and properly dressed.

I don't know if it was the kasha or the party at the House, or the cute guys; but I left that weekend knowing that I belonged at Yale. Maybe I could put my mother on a schedule. Maybe on the weekends I could meet my father for ice cream. Maybe doing the "right thing" and still feeling normal and alive was possible. In the Fortress of Yale, I felt I could finally have both elitism and comfort. I was wrong.

I should have known life would not be normal when they placed me in a suite with three other "creative people". Perhaps here I should mention that I went to boarding school on an art scholarship. At fourteen, "When I Grew Up", I wanted to be Ruby Dee or Lorraine Hansberry. At Yale, in the company of my "creative roommates", I spent my freshman year not cramming and hitting the books all night but, instead, creating songs with my roommate on Biology so that we would not fail. On the weekends, while most freshmen sweated away in overheated dorm basements getting to know each other, we were out in New Haven nightclubs pretending to be foreigners because it was a good acting exercise. The only time I pulled an all-nighter was to learn a hard bit in Tennessee Williams or Eugene O'Neil. Somehow I wasn't fitting in.

The realization that my life at Yale was definitely not going to be like my classmates' sunk in at a critical moment in my sophomore year. When I did not get into a popular seminar on Intellectual History, I went to see the prominent Professor in hopes of begging for admission. I will never forget the humiliation I felt as he explained that when he asked for a creative interpretation of his essay questions, he did not expect me to write fictional monologues. I cried right there. I was way off course and didn't even know it. After that meeting, I resigned myself to being different. I better find out what I was doing there or I'd find myself constantly in tears. Shut out. Wrong. Not quite what Yale was about. And once I accepted that I was not an academic, I found my Yale.

Elitism became something new, something fresh. I started a weekly poker league and kept my apartment open to anyone who wanted to scribble in the tattered notebook on the table. More of my friends were graduate students than not. And more of my time was spent writing than reading. Somehow those tall buildings provided safety for me. I could just doodle and scribble down words that no one would ever read because hey, this was Yale. I let my hair grow wild, a la Don King, and started spending time at the theater in the House, which became one of the few places on campus in which I felt at home. There I met August Wilson, Lloyd Richards, Dennis Scott and a group of actors studying in the drama school and slumming in the House. They taught me what I was hungry to learn.

At one point, the high point of my days was running into August on his way from a coffee shop with a million characters still fresh in his brain. He would rattle off lines in funny voices and I would know that I was next to greatness. This was the place where Theater had lived and breathed and died and resuscitated itself. It was okay to be an Ivy Leaguer because I was living in the footsteps of greatness. Giants. Pulitzer Prize Winners. It was okay to want to be Ruby Dee or Lorraine Hansberry when I grew up. When other students looked at me funny in my father's old worn leather coat, (which he inevitably threw out while I was studying in London), I could look back at them like you don't know what you're missing. You don't know what Yale is about. You don't know that this place is really all about theater. I'm not different. You are.

In the mid-eighties, there was no better place to be black and involved with theater in America. Such crossbreed needs a very special place to feel at home. At Yale, I did for fleeting moments experience some beautiful minutes.

19. Susan Marie Jenkins, Y'1989--A Part of the Yale Tradition

In Preparation

Being 17 years old in 1985 meant that my world consisted primarily of high school classes, parties, volunteer work, trying to evade some of my parents' rules and working to get into college. As I attended an all girls public school, my daily life was a blend of what some might consider public school chaos (public transportation, girls from disparate backgrounds, and overworked teachers) and the inherent feminism of an all-female environment. What I mean by the latter is that with out boys there was a sense of the rightness that girls would be the star athletes and class officers, win academic and leadership honors, run extra-curricular clubs as well as being the class clowns, discipline problems, and trouble-makers. I am not sure at the time that my classmates, or I, realized the benefit we were getting from this school and how it would affect our lives. For me, I think it played an integral part in my going to Yale and I am convinced that it was critical to my graduating with honors four years later.

Let me digress a bit before explaining what Yale eventually meant to me. Although my world in the spring of 1985 revolved around a small set of core goals and activities, the rest of the world was dealing with things like the anti-apartheid movement, the middle of the "Regan-Era", AIDS, and the popularization of something called "black urban culture". Being African-American in the United

States, I think I may have been more aware of some of these phenomena than were my eventual Yale classmates. My up bringing, similar to many others at that time, meant that I had developed a dual identity and an ability to travel in many circles. I saw the racism faced daily by African Americans as well as the individual and community strength we possessed. From an early private school education and other efforts of my parents, I was familiar with the "dominant" culture and from the rest of my life I was comfortable with my "minority" status. These are the worlds that collided when I arrived at Yale.

Even though I came from a middle-class background, from parents with college degrees, and with an expectation of going to college myself, I don't think any of us thought seriously about my going to the Ivy League. While there was no reason to think I couldn't achieve in that environment, it simply wasn't the norm. From my high school of approximately 1,200 only one or two girls went to the Ivy League each year. Among my friends I think only one had her heart set on one of these schools. Even though my school was a public magnet school the counselors routinely advised White/European American girls to go to Penn State and Black/African American girls to go to Temple University. There was no precedent for an expectation that I would go to Yale. That is until I received a letter, based on my PSAT scores, from the Yale admissions office inviting me to apply.

Now this got me thinking. There was no guarantee of acceptance or success, but the invitation was enough to broaden my horizons. I had always assumed that I would go to college. I had the grades and background that would have made it a surprise if

I had not attended. The press is always full of stories of the first African American to go to college from this or that family, but among my friends, classmates, and neighbors college was actually the norm. Many of us had parents with post-graduate degrees. Although my father grew up in a racially segregated Washington DC, walking past "White" schools to attend the one for "Colored", three of the four children in his family went to Howard University. I am not saying that it was easy for them, and it is true that my parents were of the firsts in their families to go to college and in my mother's case onto a Masters degree in education. Nevertheless, among the middle class African Americans of my world, it was practically common for us to go onto college. However, that said, I still hadn't thought that I would go to an Ivy League college.

I want to say that there was little racial discrimination at Yale and that I faced very little hostility or unfair treatment based on my race, gender, background (or some combination of these.) But, I cannot say that with confidence because I cannot have full insight into the Yale experiences of members of the majority. I didn't feel that I had it particularly hard, but I cannot say that they did not have it easier. At the very least they did not bring an entire society's doubts about their academic ability or right to a Yale education with them to campus. They, as a group, did not have to overcome nagging fears about whether they belonged or would succeed. On the individual level, I am sure that we all brought uncertainty about whether we could do the work. But, in my experience, African Americans and other students of color also brought many group level external doubts. There were messages from majority group members that we were there only based on affirmative action, that we were not suited to the environment, and that we would be lucky to just survive (no mention of flourishing!) There were also pressures from within our own communities and families suggesting that our success was also their success. Even without the racism present in every other facet of society, which did find its way into Yale as well, we brought additional baggage to school that had to be dealt with in order to succeed.

Mostly, though, I brought the joy I saw on my parent's faces, especially my father's, when I told them that I had gotten into Yale. As soon as they knew I wanted to apply they also knew that they had to figure out some financial magic if I did get in; because if I got in there was no question of my attending. We all knew that to face life in America I needed as much credibility as I could get--and a Yale education certainly provides that. If I had to be twice as good to get half as much, as the saying goes, I knew that a Yale education was a good start. However, before the worry of how to pay arrived, their faces were radiant with pride at this achievement. For those first few moments and days we were all excited and proud. Then the reality of the whole thing started. I continued to go to other college open-houses and even went to the prospective student weekend at Yale with an open mind. The more people I talked to the more obvious it became that I would be throwing away a huge chance if I chose to go somewhere else. My parents, on the other hand, came to me a few days after my acceptance and many difficult financial discussions amongst themselves to tell me that I could go and that they would pay my entire way so that I wouldn't have extra worries.

Given that, any fears about the academic work and leaving home had to be put aside. I knew that if they were willing to sacrifice to foot the bill I absolutely had to go and better do well. Given this understanding of the situation I was determined to get over any concerns I might have.

Upon Arrival

I put on that brave face until my parents left campus after getting me settled in, and then I got scared. I didn't know anyone and wasn't sure what was expected of me. Luckily, as I had walked around campus with my family I ran into some others from the Yale minority recruitment weekend I attended the previous spring. We exchanged phone and room numbers. That evening I called around to see what the plan for dinner was and from that point had a built in set of friends. We did what White/European American people always complain about: we (a group of 10 black students and one Chinese-American who had grown up in Detroit) went everywhere together. White/European American friends told me later that they felt we were so lucky to have built in friends. But it wasn't luck. We knew how hostile the majority group could be, and how unusual we were to our classmates. Plus, we all had things in common by being black-identified in America. Even though we were from different parts of the country we had common musical, television, cultural, and family lives. Many of us shared common values and to quote the advice from one parent was to say something we had all been told at one time or another. This set of friends guided me into college and gave me comfort. Over our first year we started to drift apart and develop separate interests and other friends, but as far as easing me into college life, they could not have been more valuable.

Looking back at it now, I can see that while at Yale we dealt with our baggage. All of us in different ways, but we did what we had to to gain from Yale and to contribute mightily. There were opportunities available that I don't think I would have gotten anywhere else. Personally, I was a member of the Fencing team, the Yale Hunger Action Project, active in the Yale women's center, did several independent study projects, worked in the Yale archives, and made friends with a wide variety of people. Among the other African Americans, I had a friend who went on to compete in the Pan-American games in fencing, another who did research in Guyana on Fullbright scholarship, and another who went on to some political prominence in the Republican Party. These are not things everyone can do especially within the African American community. Being at Yale not only helped qualify us for these challenges it positioned us to have these kinds of opportunities.

While I was learning and broadening both my skill set and my mind, I was also changing some minds about African-American people. I met people from groups I had no familiarity with and whom, it was quite obvious, had had little to no contact with African-Americans. Through Yale, I made friends who were openly gay and bisexual, who were millionaires, who were from places like Haiti, Spain and Japan, who were from every region of the US, who had never had a television, who had attended some of the most prestigious prep schools in the country, and who had come from some of the worse neighborhoods imaginable. For me, Yale was a safe place to explore difference, to figure out who I was, to try on different hats, and to grow up. The student body was so diverse people brought their own norms and the requirement that first year students live on campus forced us learn to accommodate each other and, in some cases, appreciate dissimilar life styles. Even though I met many of my African American classmates as soon as I arrived and started hanging with them, I was forced (much to my benefit) to meet other people through my initial roommate assignment, extra-curricular activities, and classroom interactions.

Of course I attended Yale for the academics, but anyone can describe the classes, guest speakers, cultural outlets, and campus. The things that have stuck with me and shaped my life are the intangibles. This is not to downplay the value of the academic training I received. Through several independent study courses I learned the fundamentals of social research that I built on in graduate school and that I use professionally today. The math and science courses that I took while I was still pre-med helped focus my mind. To this day, I can quote facts learned in a Latin American fiction course and theories from a course on the life and times of Freud. Yet, larger than any of the individual facts is that my success at Yale increased my intellectual curiosity and desire to continue learning, as well as giving me the confidence to move forward with my dreams. At some point I realized that I was at least as smart and talented as my classmates and that if I could make it at Yale I had more than a fighting chance of making it anywhere else.

Conclusion

While I did not have the class and experiential barriers described by the subject of A Hope in the Unseen[53] my memories resonate with the cultural barriers described. I had the same doubts. I brought the same misperceptions about what my classmates would be like. And, in the end, I found the same comfort and success in my Ivy League experiences. Every day was not easy, but in total I would not trade the experience for anything. To this day, some of my best memories are early mornings in Payne-Whitney, looking out of my dorm window at cross-campus, studying in the Sterling reading room, and late night slices at Broadway Pizza.

Another way to look at it is that I am a statistic. Not the ones we so frequently see on the evening news or are led to fear by political campaign managers, but the ones described in Bowen and Bok's book The Shape of the River. [54] I am one of those people admitted to Yale based on affirmative action and diversity goals. I am also one of those people to graduate from Yale with honors, receive a National Science Foundation scholarship based on academic performance, and earn a Ph.D. in psychology from the University of Michigan in four years. My memories of Yale are very similar to those reported

---

[53] *Suskind, R. (1998). A Hope in the Unseen: An American Odyssey from the Inner City to the Ivy League*. Broadway Books: New York.

[54] Bowen, W. G. & Bok, D. (1998). The Shape of the River: Long-Term Consequences of Considering Race in College and University Admissions. Princeton University Press, Princeton: New Jersey.

by former students interviewed for their book. As did their respondents, I did not feel overmatched and that I would have been happier if I had had not had the opportunity and attended a school with more “evenly matched peers”. I was very satisfied with my education, I would make the same choice if I had it to do over, and I am confident that the skills and abilities that I developed as an undergraduate have had a strong and positive impact on my current success and well being.

As a statistic, rather than a case study, I have met more than a few people who can claim similar achievements. There is nothing miraculous or unreachable about us or about how we prospered at Yale and made it a better place for our presence. There is no secret formula or magic ritual that got us to where we are today or through where we’ve been. We are some of the everyday people who are a part of Yale’s history and tradition.

20. Erica S. Turnipseed, Y'1993--My first semester as a woman

On Friday, September 1, 1989 I became a woman. The change was unceremonious but immediate and complete. The day that I moved into Wright Hall on Yale's Old Campus was my first day of full-fledged 'womanity'.

Ironically, I had attended the Pre-Registration Orientation Program (PROP) and Freshperson Conference (with the theme "Life, the University and Everything"), but amidst my multi-tiered formal preparation into the world of Yale, no one had bothered to mention the change in status I was now experiencing. And compounding my new womanhood was my black womanhood, a phenomenon in itself fraught with peculiarities.

My first year plunged me into a troubled sea of Donald Kagan,[55] multiculturalism, and political correctness that I had only read about up until that point. The campus was awash with flyers announcing panel discussions, round tables, teach-ins and speak-outs on the issues of the day. Considering myself open-minded, I took it all in with grace. However, my interior world of roommates and friends and men ??(n?e boys) presented greater challenges.

---

55 Donald Kagan was dean of Yale College from 19-to 1992 (?) and a proponent of a core curriculum grounded in Western Civilization.

With no sisters to my credit (I have two brothers) I found living amongst fellow woman novel and occasionally difficult. The women who peopled my closest physical circle--my suite--were two very different white women and an Asian woman. Together, we represented affluent southern Florida, central New Jersey, small-town Connecticut, and Brooklyn, New York. While our school year together proved that Yale's system of matching up complementary personalities was mostly successful, I was not to know this truth for a while yet.

As one of my roommates--naked and lotioning herself from head-to-foot after a midday shower--talked to me incessantly on our first day as roommates, I wondered if I'd ever get accustomed to knowing so much about the habits of my non-relations. Despite the fact that she punctuated every second sentence with my name, I struggled not to look at her because of my 'unenlightened' sense of decorum that told me not to look at the innocently exposed crotch of another, even if she is your roommate. And so I didn't all year.

Seeking to find my feet in my new environment, I tossed about the campus that first weekend with classmates whose fragile friendships were the anchors of my new existence. Fortuitously, I found myself with what I thought were prospects of a boyfriend. When this very attractive southern 'gentleman' gave me his high school football ring to loop through my necklace, I was beside myself with joy and, at 2:00am on a Sunday morning, I floated up the Wright Hall stairs to my doom room. My roommates were already clad in nightwear and trading stories about their own escapades of the first weekend. My conquest however, had another level of seriousness. We considered the meaning of my ugly pendant that I wore with pride, and surmised that my 'beau' was a man of few words but great passion and therefore liked to express himself symbolically. Sunday afternoon was met by freshmen littered about the grass of Old Campus. I joined my PROP friends where they sat and immediately became the focal point. (Well, the ring caused all the stir.) And so I had the pleasure of recounting the simple romance of the night before. When they learned that I returned to my dorm room alone and hadn't so much as kissed my admirer goodnight, their prophetic silence forecasted an unpleasant outcome. The most worldly of the bunch informed me that I had blown it.

"Erica, he was looking for you to sleep with him. Or something?! Why'd you think he gave you the ring?"

"Because he likes me and he didn't know how else to say it." I defended my honor.

"And he'd still like you now if you had slept with him!"

Dumbfounded, I was unable to resist the humiliation of being marched to his dorm room by this same woman so that we could get further clarification.

His roommate came to the door. Securing our names and whom we wished to see, he closed the door completely to relay the message. Returning after a few minutes, he pushed the door ajar and told me that my fickle beau wanted the ring back. As I listened to his words echo in my brain, I peered past him to see 'my man' scrunched into a lounge chair, his eyes trained on the TV screen in front of him.

I responded to his roommate, "If he wants it back, he will need to come to my room to retrieve it himself." I smiled a smile that would become a fixture of my nascent womanhood and left. My accomplice was shocked but satisfied. I watched her as her thoughts scurried about her head and she assessed who had been the victor. I didn't show my hurt or disappointment at this rejection or my own naivete. Instead, I remained composed and wore my annoyance as a badge of honor. We returned to our assemblage of fellow new women and I stood quietly as my sidekick recounted the story. Satisfied that I sounded not too pitiable, I allowed them to bandy about the mantras of righteous women who can't take doggish men.

My first year continued to offer life lessons in bite sized pieces. I found that my mouth was always full. Could it be that I was really so na?ve that I could expect men, or women, so new to this terrain, not to challenge my own womanhood at every turn? But 18 was the oldest I had ever been in my whole life and I presumed that anyone older than that had wisdom, maturity and perspective. The members of Women of Color seemed to have more collective wisdom and experience than all of their ages combined. Andrea and I, the only freshwomen in the group, listened as juniors and seniors spun out cautionary tales, and cried tears of frustration and anger. We listened to stories of men who were not ready for the fabulous women there were and women who felt challenged by their greatness. Women discussed their forays into bisexuality, their coming out experiences and their reclaimed celibacy. They talked about remaining whole and affirming themselves and each other. After many of those meetings, Andrea and I would debrief, each of us caught up in the intensity of the varied experiences of "of color" womanhood.

Whereas my roommates and I were negotiating our individual identities in a collective space and Women of Color affirmed our many layers of identity, my women's a cappella singing group-The New Blue-sought to define our collective identity for each individual woman in the group. My singing group was a baptism by fire into the cult of white womanhood. Yes, of nearly 20 members, our group was among the more ethnically diverse singing groups on campus and boasted one Asian and three black women. However, we all integrated our racial and ethnic identities into our womanhood in radically different ways. And our singing group identity, like that of Yale in general, created a common denominator that was distinctly white and upper-middle class in that it took for granted the products of race and class privilege.

This truth was not lost on my black brethren and sistren, some of whom openly questioned my blackness when I first joined The New Blue. Tap night--the night I learned I had been chosen by the singing group--had been exhilarating (complete with a kiss and some dirty dancing with my momentary love). But the day that followed threatened my removal from the 'blackhood'. We were freshmen, and our loyalty to the inner black circle was fierce and unsophisticated. As I joined the lunchtime crowd at the black table in Commons that fateful day, the accusations of betrayal were etched into the body language and actions of my cohorts. Some ended their meals prematurely while others relocated to the hastily-formed black table beside me. Sensing the harbinger of trouble, Curtis, my ethnic counselor, sat with me. As he congratulated me for being tapped by The New Blue--then the best and oldest women's singing group on campus--he knew that this was the source of my problem. In the succeeding days, Curtis quickly did some damage control. Emphasizing to all who would listen how wonderful my membership to The New Blue was for "us," he tapped into my classmates' collective memory of the pride felt by their family and friends who reveled in their own matriculation at Yale. I continued to act normal, and together we overcame the suspicion of my wavering blackness and I was restored to the 'blackhood' with elevated standing.

Despite the apparent solidarity of the 'blackhood', we nevertheless suffered our own brand of differential treatment. Black women on campus, and particularly first-years, often reacted to each other based upon how they ranked in the collective assessment of black men. That is, the most sought-after women (who usually fell into a particular aesthetic) built their primary friendships amongst themselves. Those of us who found ourselves outside of that group (I was among that number) had more free reign, but we all reacted to the system the men had established. Though some of this antagonism dissipated during our tenure as undergraduates, its freshness in our first year created a stronghold that most of us could only fight within instead of against.

Perhaps my own way of bucking the system was to choose 'Renaissance men' for my affections. I reasoned that, because these men (a junior and a senior in particular) were actors and singers, they constructed their social realities beyond the 'blackhood'. They were universal beings, and therefore free of the scrutiny of the blackometer. But in casting my heart into the ring, I joined the throngs of white women who also sought to know their treasures. I also learned that my Renaissance men had largely opted out of the black thing in all things romantic. My status as a black first year who was not a member of the campus select won me no points with my 20-year-old tantalizers.

As the semester wore on and I cleared hurdles of woman-worldliness and black authenticity, I felt suddenly wise beyond my years. But while my cohort of friends and my Brooklyn hometown affiliation paid for my forty acres and a mule amidst the righteous blackhood (after my initial fumble), my womanhood was more uncharted. The savvy implicit in the appellation of woman was a constant challenge. The tacit game-playing in so many social interactions eluded me. The New Blue's beliefs about religion and feminism and body image ill-fitted my reality. And my membership in Women of Color allied me with women who many black women viewed as the [self] ostracized, the jaded, the bitter and the white-identified (because it was housed in the so-called 'white Women's Center').

But amidst the difficulties of defining my black 'womanity', or perhaps because of them, I was blessed to recognize the true friendship of a very remarkable woman who was to become the sista-friend I had never had before. It was a night whose coldness bit into our cheeks and crept into the spaces between our layers of clothing with the hope of finding exposed flesh. Tanya and I had gone to see a movie that night. Standing amidst snow on the crisscrossing stone walkways of Old Campus where our paths diverged to our dorms on opposite ends of the green, we talked for nearly an hour about everything our minds could think to discuss. There, in the space of two football fields, we were all by ourselves exploring the world through our words. Whereas our collective black womanhood may have initially drawn us to each other, the earnestness of our friendship nurtured a sista-friend closeness based upon mutual admiration and enjoyment.

Now, ten years after my first foray into womanhood, I am humbled and awed by far I've come and what I have yet to experience. Embracing my 'womanity', I marvel at the many ways my friends and I revise our notions of our own womanhood. And Tanya continues to be one of the sweetest parts of that journey.

Editor Bio

Born in Washington DC I, Jesse Algeron Rhines, graduated from Coolidge High School then attended Yale University's Summer High School and Transitional Year Program after failing the 12th grade. I worked as first janitor then photography instructor as I earned a BA at DC based Antioch College-BHP (Center for the Study of Basic Human Problems) in 1974. I completed an MA in African American Studies at Yale in 1983 after teaching English with the YMCA in Asia and leading students in Mali, French West Africa with Operation Crossroads, Inc., in 1980. While at Yale I worked as an IBM Systems Engineer before earning a Film Production Certificate at NYU. I earned a Political Science MA at UCLA in 1986 and a UC Berkeley PhD in Ethnic Studies in 1993. I was Assistant Professor of Political Economy in the African American Studies Department at Rutgers University-Newark when Rutgers University Press published my dissertation, BLACK FILM/WHITE MONEY, in 1996 and it won a Gustavus Mayer Human Rights Award in 1997. Since denial of tenure in 2003, I have been disabled with hip replacements, heart disease and cancer, which combined strongly encouraged my return to the warmer, flatter terrain of Los Angeles, CA. I taught English near Madrid, Spain with Vaughantown in 2006 and in La Rioja, Spain with Auxiliares Norteamericanos de Conversación in November 2010. I'm still single and have no kids.

November 11, 2010, Historic Gas Lofts, Los Angeles

www.ingramcontent.com/pod-product-compliance
Lightning Source LLC
Chambersburg PA
CBHW061337280526
45784CB00001B/48
* 9 7 8 1 4 6 3 5 0 4 4 1 0 *